'*Caro Feely has written a careening memoir in* Saving Our Skins. *So impassioned that it could inspire you to drop all security, move to the backwaters of France, and bet your life, all for the love of making wine.*'   Alice Feiring, author of *Naked Wine*

'*Should be required reading for anyone who loves wine! Even a teetotaller will drink up every page of* Saving Our Skins, *for the fascinating behind-the-scenes of organic farming. Making good wine is truly a labour of love and respect for the earth – often, we learn, at the expense of the wine farmer. Caro takes us along in her grape-stained pocket to experience the picking, the pressing, and the profit questioning: can her family afford to continue making natural wine? We quickly turn the pages, eager to find out – and we can't help but root for Caro et compagnie as they creatively keep on top of things, namely a precious heap of grapes!*'

Kristin Espinasse, author of *French Essais, Blossoming in Provence* and *Words in a French Life*

'*In* Saving Our Skins, *Caro's courage and determination leaps off every page, redefining what it means to be brave when you're at the mercy of the weather, uncertain cashflow and endless, often puzzling, French bureaucracy. Caro has produced a beautifully written sequel which in turn seduced and terrified me about the prospect of owning an organic vineyard in rural France. I thoroughly enjoyed the urgency of her writing – I needed a rather large glass of wine when I'd finished. Bravo Caro.*'

Samantha Brick

'Caro Feely understands that winemaking is an art, a science and a business. *Saving Our Skins entertains and informs as it tells the story of her family's struggle to make a living making organic and biodynamic wine in the south of France. Required reading for wine lovers everywhere and anyone dreaming a vineyard dream.'*
Mike Veseth, author of *Wine Wars* and *Extreme Wine* and editor of *The Wine Economist*

Praise for *Grape Expectations*:

'Captivating reading for anyone with dreams of living in rural France.' Destination France

'I was moved and delighted by this book, which has vast and useful amounts to say about wine and the passion of wine-making, about France and the great adventure of family life, and above all about the trials and challenges that build a marriage... splendid book.'
Martin Walker, bestselling author of the *Bruno, Chief of Police* series

'Really liked Caro's book; it's not the usual fall in love with France story, it's warts and all – including horrific accidents! Definitely the best – and most realistic – tome coming from the 'A Year in Provence' genre.' Joe Duffy, Irish radio personality

'bright, passionate, inspiring, informative and absolutely delicious' Breadcrumb Reads blog

'Filled with vivid descriptions of delicious wines, great food... a story of passion, dedication, and love'
Bookalicious Travel Addict blog

Saving Our Skins

Building a Vineyard Dream in France

CARO FEELY

summersdale

SAVING OUR SKINS

Summersdale Publishers Ltd
46 West Street
Chichester
West Sussex
PO19 1RP
UK

www.summersdale.com

Printed and bound by CPI Group (UK) Ltd, Croydon, CR0 4YY

ISBN: 978-1-84953-609-7

Substantial discounts on bulk quantities of Summersdale books are available to corporations, professional associations and other organisations. For details contact Nicky Douglas by telephone: +44 (0) 1243 756902, fax: +44 (0) 1243 786300 or email: nicky@summersdale.com.

Author's note

This is a true story. However, for privacy, certain characters have fictitious names and sometimes the order of events has been changed a little to suit the pace of the book. All speech is based on memory and aims to capture the gist of what was said at the time and the sense of the character speaking.

About the author

Caro Feely is a wife, mother, daughter, wine educator and tour guide, organic farmer, and speaker on wine and ecology. She lives in Saussignac in the Dordogne on the farm where this book is set.

'*Now this is a story of nature, of love, of family, of not giving up. A call to arms for the earth, for the vines, the flowers and the trees, for us.*'

Contents

Part One – Root..11

Chapter 1: Diamonds of Destruction...................13

Chapter 2: Gifts and Grace...............................21

Chapter 3: *Ploucs*, or Country Bumpkins............29

Chapter 4: Grape Skin Magic............................40

Chapter 5: Inhaling Grapes...............................46

Chapter 6: *Vendanges!*...................................54

Chapter 7: Animal Activists and *Amoureuses*........74

Part Two – Leaf...95

Chapter 8: A Seed is Sown................................97

Chapter 9: Roller Coaster.................................111

Chapter 10: The Last of the Summer Wine............120

Chapter 11: Wine-tasting Boot Camp..................130

Chapter 12: Snowed-in in Alsace and Burgundy.....136

Chapter 13: A Taste of California.......................155

Chapter 14: The American Dream......................167

Chapter 15: Fire!..176

Part Three – Flower...185

Chapter 16: The Gestation.......................................187

Chapter 17: Saint-Émilion Stories...........................199

Chapter 18: The Imperfect Day.................................207

Chapter 19: Volunteers and Red Tape.......................214

Chapter 20: One Hundred Guests.............................226

Chapter 21: *Noël aux Chandelles*..............................236

Part Four – Fruit...241

Chapter 22: Rose Hips and Risk...............................243

Chapter 23: Killer Chemicals....................................249

Chapter 24: Wine Adventure....................................257

Chapter 25: A Shocking Death..................................270

Chapter 26: *Chasse au Trésor* Périgord-style.............276

Chapter 27: Gold for Green.......................................284

What Can You Do to Ensure a Healthy Future?.................297

Acknowledgements..300

Part One

Root

In biodynamics we talk of a root day when the earth forces are powerful. It is a good time for a seed to take root, for root-related activities like hoeing around the base of the vine, and for us humans to feel rooted.

Root days occur when the moon is in the earth constellations Capricorn, Taurus and Virgo. It is easy to confuse these astronomic constellations, a reality visible in the sky, with the star signs of astrology that use the same names. They are different.

We found that the earthy elements in our wines were reinforced on root days; the forest floor, the truffle. It was a better day to open an aged red wine than a young fruity one.

The impeded stream is the one that sings.
Wendell Berry

Chapter 1
Diamonds of Destruction

The vineyard was dressed in shimmering diamonds; delicate buds perfectly highlighted with bling. From the window the vines looked like emerald clusters trellised on silver cords. It was silent, almost as if it had snowed: even the birds were in shock.

Seán and I walked from the eighteenth-century stone farmhouse to the first vineyard a few metres away, our footsteps crunching ominously. Up close, the buds were like fairies dressed in pink and lime cotton wool, then wrapped with silver spun sugar. My stomach cramped with fear.

We had been in the vineyard business long enough to know that the glitter came at a high price. On a winter's day it was beautiful; on a spring day after 'bud burst' it was devastating, fatal to the young shoots. Friends often spoke of a late spring frost fifteen years before that had destroyed ninety per cent of the region's harvest. My mind scrambled to the implications as I gazed at the scene.

Since moving to France three years previously our lives had been on a roller coaster. Renovating our property, converting the vineyard to organic agriculture and making our own wines were at times terrifying. Fear of the unknown, two farm accidents in our first year and constant financial worry had not put us off. We found our new life strangely fulfilling, though I often wished for a stable job with some certainty. Seán, the love of my life, and I worked all hours and we were still far from finding equilibrium.

We exchanged a glance. The anxiety in his eyes made my stomach churn.

The valley below was all blossoms and bright green, the odd strip of icy white showing on farm roads and ploughed fields. A ribbon of blue, the Dordogne, wound its way from Bordeaux to Bergerac in the middle distance. I drank in the beauty, wondering how much of the vibrant lime foliage would be left the following day once the frost had taken its toll.

Down the hill it was worse: we estimated more than half was lost. Seán tried to calm my panic but I knew he was worried. From the tall, long-haired, clean-shaven journalist I had met fifteen years before he had transformed into a rugged farmer, still sporting long hair but with the winter beard necessary to protect his face from the harsh conditions in which he pruned the vines. It was a hard slog through the three coldest months of the year but one of the tasks he enjoyed; an opportunity to be calm and quiet, to listen to the vines and the land with no interference except the rhythmic snip of his secateurs.

We had had our confidence shaken by the massive life change we had made – city professionals to farmers. At times I felt we were astronauts going through g-force into outer space rather than merely changing country, job and language. This latest setback was another chip in our security.

I told myself there was no point in worrying about things we couldn't control. We just had to get on and deal with it. We walked back up to the house, the frost crunching menacingly.

Seán reached into a filing box on the mantelpiece in the kitchen, then sat down heavily at the pine dining table worn with years of use. This was his makeshift office, the place where he kept track of mountains of paperwork related to vineyard and wine, overlooked as he worked by two paintings, a still life of fruit and flowers by my grandmother and one of sunflowers by me. He made observation notes in his vineyard file, detailing the estimations we had made. He looked resigned and tired. I plodded to my office to work on the quarterly accounts. A few minutes later I heard the kitchen door close then saw him trudge past my office window, down to the vineyard where he was finishing the tying down, the last step in the pruning process.

Our method of pruning was the Guyot system, the most widespread pruning and trellising system in Aquitaine, where one or two canes are tied onto the bottom wire of the trellis. In other regions different pruning and trellising methods are used depending on the climate. I needed to stop thinking about climate; it reminded me of frost. I turned to the accounts. Usually I avoided office work like the plague, but now it offered an escape from what was outside.

By the afternoon it was so hot it was difficult to believe there had been frost. The silver was gone, leaving a browning as if the buds had been burnt. As I kneaded a batch of dough, my thoughts were consumed by where we might be by the end of the year. Bread-making was part of my 'become the self-sufficient wife my husband dreams of' programme. I didn't expect to enjoy it but I did. There was something meditative and therapeutic about the process.

Throwing and kneading – somewhat more aggressively than necessary – I reminded myself that it was not the situation we were in that mattered, but how we handled it. I was repeating that rather frequently. After ten minutes the dough was perfect, like plastic clay, and I was serene. We were healthy, we had an admittedly leaky roof over our heads and food on the table. We would find a way out of this new hole.

A couple of hours and many invoices later, the sound of tyres on the limestone outside announced the arrival of our daughters with Sonia, our neighbour, who took the afternoon school run. I waved and opened the door for the girls then whisked the bread out of the oven, poured elderflower cordial in recycled glass yoghurt pots and sliced into the bread. A delicious yeasty smell wafted through the air as I spread a layer of home-grown fig jam onto the slices.

We were into 'reduce, reuse and recycle' mode, gratefully dependent on gifts from friends and donations and hand-me-downs for our daughters' gear. I had put off buying new shoes for them for ages, hoping some would miraculously appear, but they both needed shoes badly now.

I had learned to offer food immediately they got home; otherwise things went downhill fast. Ellie at three and a half could play the tough guy. Her pretty blonde curls and glasses were misleading. She would stare and say '*donne-moi des bonbons!*' (give me sweets!) – with 'or you'll regret it' implied. Seán assured me she was sensitive inside.

Sophia at five was already a sophisticated young lady rather than a little girl. Following a bumpy start after we arrived with her not speaking French, on my recent visit to school her new teacher had exclaimed: 'I knew Sophia was born in Dublin but I thought her parents were French! Her French is better than most of the class.'

My accent was still so bad it was clear there was no French family involved. I felt very proud of her.

As the girls chatted about their day and ate wedges of bread, another car turned up our road and parked outside the tasting room. I reminded Sophia to do her homework when she had finished her *goûter*, her afternoon snack, asked Ellie to draw a picture, and walked out into the glorious afternoon sun, across the courtyard to the tasting room.

Ashley and Rob Lamb stepped out of a smart 4x4 and we exchanged kisses *à la française*. They had discovered our wines the previous year and were back in the region for a quick visit. Ashley's mother and father breezed in with them, dressed in stylish linen, he as dark-tanned as a Sicilian and wearing a striking Havana hat.

We chatted as I fetched the samples from the stockroom, exchanging ideas of places to visit in the area: les Jardins de Marqueyssac, Renaissance-style gardens offering majestic views of the Dordogne; the market at Issigeac; the Château de Beynac where Richard the Lionheart lived for many years.

As they settled into the rickety garden furniture that sufficed for our furnishings, I poured taster samples of our latest sauvignon blanc vintage. We sipped. I swirled the wine around my mouth, enjoying the acidity and flavour, then spat into the *crachoir,* the spittoon, always set out on the table for myself and the driver. At the beginning of our adventure I had splashed myself liberally with wine and had to wear dark colours to tasting events. Now my white shirt was clear.

The wine was like diving into the sea: refreshing, mineral and zesty, like licking elderflower and gooseberry cordial straight off our fossil rock. The vineyard was on a limestone outcrop, a compressed seabed packed with million-year-old sea fossils. It seemed like decades since our first vintage release and a wine buyer's comment of 'thin, Italian style', although it was only two years. I was still sensitive to comments about our wines but now I had more confidence in them. I poured them with pride. It was a good feeling.

'I love your wines,' said Ashley. 'I never used to drink sauvignon blanc or sémillon. It's less than a year since we found you and I can't drink anything else. Others don't taste clean like yours. I never get a headache from your wines.'

I made a pretend grab for a microphone to record her comments. From the start we chose organic farming, something we felt strongly about, a motivation that went deeper than earning our daily crust; but we still needed to eat. After three years of organic conversion it was starting to pay off in the quality of the wines but we still had moments of doubt – not about organic, but about the economic viability of organic in the modern economy where most consumers chose on price and didn't really know what organic or chemical agriculture was or why they should bother.

'People at work can't believe we drink your wine during the week with no bad effects,' said Rob. 'We opened our last bottle of La Source red a few days ago. Delicious.'

I poured the new vintage La Source into their glasses. After taking a deep draught Ashley's father lifted his tanned hand.

'Please leave me with this wine for the afternoon,' he purred from under his Havana hat. 'A shady terrace, a cigar and I could contemplate life for hours.'

I felt like kissing them. It was the sort of encouragement I needed to lift me away from the worry about frost and our precarious future. We had good wines; it was no guarantee of making a living, but it was necessary to get back some of the confidence lost in our massive life change.

'What's the Irish connection?' he asked pointing to *The Irish Times* on the shelf.

'We lived in Ireland for eight years before coming to France,' I said. 'We were both born in South Africa, hence the accent, but we have Irish roots.'

I explained how Seán and I had dreamed of wine-farming for a decade before we had the opportunity and a moment of madness to leap in and buy our farm. We had roots deep in wine. His grandparents grew vines near Stellenbosch in South Africa's Western Cape after moving from Ireland in their youth – one of many Catholic–Protestant unions of the era that fled. Seán was bitten by the bug of winegrowing at an early age, helping them with work such as harvest as a schoolboy. My grandmother descended from the Frenches, a tribe that moved from Normandy to Galway to import wine in the 1300s. The Frenches were noted as significant wine traders in Bordeaux and Ireland in the golden era of the 1800s.

'So you know the Irish mafia?' he said, his eyes twinkling.

'Of course,' I said. I wasn't totally joking. We had rented an apartment in Dublin in the same block as a notorious drug lord; fortunately, the only time we saw him was the day of his arrest.

The Lambs were flying back the following day so they bought two bottles for the evening and promised to return with their car in summer to carry out the annual stocking of their cellar.

'I have a small gift for your two girls,' said Mr Havana holding out two five-euro notes. 'Tell them it's from the Irish mafia.' He winked.

Tears of gratitude pricked my eyes. His graceful gesture meant so much; but more than that, their comments had buoyed me up at a time when I was questioning our new lives, just as we had a year before when we almost sold the farm due to financial pressure. The frost had pushed my thoughts back down that road. I waved goodbye and ran inside to tell the girls. For years the only shopping I had done was for winery equipment and supplies. We piled into the car to go shoe shopping, Sophia and Ellie delighted by their good fortune.

Chapter 2
Gifts and Grace

Notwithstanding the low volume we could expect from the frosted vintage, we still had wine stock from the previous two years. Wine was a buyer's market. No one was knocking on our door and the revenue we needed to keep the vineyard wouldn't be met by the odd tasting-room purchase. We needed serious trade sales but they took a year or more to cultivate. I had a few in the pipeline but it was a slow game. I was worried. One of these contacts was Jon, the wine buyer of a quirky online retailer in the USA. He loved the samples, the information about our organic practices and the tiny appellation of Saussignac, and requested the latest stock levels of two wines so he could profile them to his customer base. I sent them – then heard nothing.

Saussignac, our commune appellation, had one of the highest percentages of organic winegrowers of all the appellations, wine areas, in France. When we bought our farm we had no idea, but most of our neighbouring vineyards were or soon became organic, a boon since it meant less residual agricultural chemicals – herbicides, pesticides and systemic fungicides – from spray drift and run-off on our borders.

We sent Jon a new label for the merlot featuring a sensitive crystallisation image. Sensitive crystallisation is a process for creating an image and profile of a product that goes beyond its chemical analysis. A solution of copper chloride, or copper salts, is added to the product – in this case wine, but it can be anything – and the solution is left to dry in a glass Petri dish in a controlled laboratory with no external sounds, smells or other influences for twenty-four hours. With a healthy, good-quality product the copper chloride crystallises into a beautiful shape, creating an individual thumbprint like a snowflake. Many samples of the same product are taken to ensure the profile is accurate.

The new label clinched the deal and Jon profiled the merlot and the Saussignac dessert wine in his daily email. I was nervous, sure that the description of sensitive crystallisation would not come across well in a short missive. We would seem like insane tree-huggers. I had required a two-day course to be convinced. On the course we analysed sensitive crystallisation of a natural vitamin compared to a chemically produced vitamin; city water compared to rain water compared to water from a limestone source where the rock had filtered the water clean; and an organic wine compared to one farmed with chemicals. In the case of the chemical vitamin, it was blank with a few black dots, whereas the natural vitamin was a crystal of beauty. The well-water image was stunning, the city water deformed with black holes. The organic wines created symmetrical crystals, whereas the chemically farmed wines created a Frankenstein version with many centres and black holes.

Jon's emails to his customers were compelling. I had signed up for his mailing list and his descriptions made me want to buy everything he profiled. Luckily, we couldn't, since he didn't ship to Europe. When his confirmed order based on sales from the email arrived, a mix of relief and fear flooded through me. We did a panicked count. The merlot was fine but we couldn't fulfil the Saussignac order by a few cases.

'Why did you give them the wrong stock numbers?' asked Seán, exasperated.

'I didn't give the wrong stock level. I gave the right one but that was a few months ago and we've kept selling the wine in the meantime,' I said.

Seán dredged bottles from every corner of the property, the tasting-room fridge, the display cabinet – which we usually didn't sell, but this was an emergency – and all the wines we had put aside for our wine library. With every last bottle, including one without a label – don't tell Jon – we just made the numbers.

As the panic subsided I felt rather proud, as if we were a *grand cru classé*, reduced to buying our wines back because they had become so sought after. Seán's sister in Kent had bought about ten cases on their last visit: we would buy some back from them.

But day-to-day we were far from *grand cru classé*. We were just scraping by. We had developed the 'Wine Cottage' for rent and a small operation selling our wines direct to clients online and in the tasting room. Together they provided a core income to meet a major part of the day-to-day costs of the vineyard. To have a long-term going concern that would allow for a little shoe shopping and the reinvestment required for a farm like ours, we had to go further. Living from hand to mouth, even to follow our dream, made no sense. One of our ideas for reaching this equilibrium was to offer educational visits. We hoped they would sell wine and bring in extra income.

It seemed to be working. My first double booking was a Dublin couple and a Yorkshire couple, the latter foolishly cultivating the dream of moving to France to buy a vineyard and start a new life with two young daughters. I was sure I could cure them of that.

They arrived at 2 p.m. for an afternoon course on French wine appreciation, *appellations d'origine contrôlée* (AOC) and the elusive term *terroir*. I quickly applied lipstick – normally my lips went *au naturel* but for classes I needed the professional look – and went out to greet them. The hours flew, with humour flashing around the tiny room that served as our tasting room and fledgling wine school. The visits reminded me why we had come here in the first place: our passion for wine.

Since early on in our adventure I realised that living the isolated life of a farmer's wife in rural France was not for me. As a city professional I had worked with teams, run workshops for high-powered executives and interacted intensively with people during my working days. Landing in rural Dordogne as a full-time mom and farmer's wife had been an extreme culture shock. The rising tide of tourism and direct sales provided interaction with people and an opportunity to share what we had learned about organic farming, both of which were fulfilling and necessary for my sanity.

The Dubliners gave us gifts of Barry's Tea and bought cases of wine, then made their way onto Saint-Émilion for their next stop, while Dave and Amanda Moore, the Yorkshire couple, stayed for a cup of tea to meet Seán and hear more about what it was *really* like wine-farming in France. They were tall, fit and good-looking. Dave was a builder and all-round handyman, ideal for what they were setting out to do, unlike us. Seán had been a financial writer and I an IT strategy consultant. Little wonder it had been tough and Seán now had a short finger after an argument with a dangerous piece of machinery.

We took a walk in the vineyard so they could see the flowering, a key moment in the vineyard cycle. As farmers we were soldered to the seasons, feeling them intimately, flowing with them. The risk of frost was gone and the trellising was filled with green foliage, the vines reaching skywards, their graceful canes and spiralling tendrils dancing in the breeze.

Each tiny, delicate, cream flower in the right conditions would become a grape. We had to get up really close to see the caps, some of which had fallen off to reveal the stamens, the male parts, five in a circle around the stigma, the female part, doing their darndest to drop pollen onto her, essential to fertilise the eggs that would become the seeds around which the fruit would form. The vines were erotic, the field filled with their summer excitement. It was also a time of angst for us since flowering was a key determinant of the quantity of harvest. If we had wet, damp weather the caps wouldn't fall off and the fertilisation would fail, devastating our yields.

There was so much to talk about we invited Dave and Amanda to stay for dinner. They laughed at our no-holds-barred descriptions of the previous three years and we laughed at theirs of the properties they had seen. I offered seconds of the rice and dhal lentils, one of my regular 'fast food' dinner solutions.

'Don't mind if I do!' said Dave in his thick Yorkshire accent as he lifted his smart shirt to expose a T-shirt underneath that proudly announced 'Mr Greedy'. We all laughed as I heaped his plate with seconds. He was remarkably lean for his appetite.

'He's Mr Greedy and I'm Mrs Picky,' said Amanda. 'I'm vegetarian and allergic to lactose and gluten. So no cheese or bread for me. My God, what's the point of moving to France?

Oh yes, I remember, for the wine!' Amanda lifted her glass, took a sip and nodded approval. 'Definitely worth it for the wine.'

Later Dave emailed to say they had found a property fifteen minutes north of Saint-Émilion with 'three hectares of vines and a few buildings that are a wreck and full of poo'. Although we had only just met, I felt like I was on the roller coaster with them. I was disappointed their potential vineyard was a good hour away. We got on so well I had hoped they could settle closer.

A few days later as I set our places at the old pine table for lunch, I looked up and caught the view of the Château de Saussignac through the kitchen window, perfectly framed behind the mass of red roses that formed the entrance to our potager, where I had been collecting hardy salads minutes before. Seán's boots resonated on the footpath outside then I heard him scrape mud off on the bootscraper. He entered and handed me a fistful of wild garlic, a spring onion like alium from one hand, and red purslane, with crunchy red stems and succulent green leaves, from the other, both collected in the vineyard on his way up. We sat down to eat.

I opened the post as we ate and found yet another invoice that needed to be paid: 'I can't take this feeling of angst every time I open an envelope,' I said to Seán. 'We have to get ourselves to the next level or we have to get out.'

'We have to plant the old peach field to vines,' said Seán. 'I know planting vineyards is very long term, but to make the farm viable we have to have more vines.'

'Then you'll need a new tractor and that will mean another major investment,' I said.

The authorities had decided that higher density – more vines planted per acre – meant higher quality, and were forcing growers to comply. To fit more vines on a given surface meant the rows had to be closer together. Less space between the rows meant we needed a new tractor because our old tractor was too wide. Legislating density sounded mad to the winegrowers from America and Australia who booked visits with us that year. Frustrating as it was, though, we had to get on and work with it. It was a classic case of agricultural bureaucracy.

'But with a new tractor I'll be far more efficient. It will halve my time on the tractor and I will do a better job. I'll be able to do two things at once. It will make far better use of my time,' said Seán.

'What do you mean?' I said.

'The hydraulic power means I will be able to do shoot removal and mowing at the same time, rather than making two passages. We'll save on fuel and have less soil compaction.'

Seán really wanted that new tractor. He knew that saving on fuel was a great way to convince me: I loved any savings, but fuel even more, since it saved our bank balance and the planet at the same time. When we had met in Joburg, Seán and his friend Mike Murphy had a comic strip stuck on the pinboard in their shared house: it was of two old men in rocking chairs, one reading an invoice, glasses balanced on the end of his nose and saying, 'Let's celebrate, the last payment on our student loans is due next week.' I laughed but actually the idea scared me so I gave Seán a 'Savings 101' course. Despite being a financial journalist, he still had a massive student loan and was paying off the minimum even when he had a bonus or cash to spare. Within a year he had paid the entire loan off. He loved to tell the story; he couldn't believe how quickly he did it through a few less beers and a change of attitude.

'Not only that, you won't have to do shoot removal by hand anymore,' said Seán, knowing that would clinch the deal if the savings didn't.

As organic farmers, shoot removal, taking off the suckers that come out of the base of the vine, taking valuable sap and energy away from the main plant, has to be done manually or mechanically rather than chemically. Doing this work by hand involved a very long steep hike interrupted at metre intervals by a deep squat – 25,000 of them, to be precise. It wasn't a solution for our size of vineyard. We had to have that tractor.

'But how can we afford it?' I said.

'The money from the sale to Jon is enough for the first down payment,' said Seán.

'But then what?' I asked. 'We have no visibility for the payments into the future.'

'I know,' said Seán. 'But we have to have faith. If we want to stay in this business we have to make this investment. Otherwise we might as well just give up.'

Getting the vineyard rights alone had taken a minor miracle, so we couldn't stop now. Our ability to meet the ongoing payments and stay in the vineyard game would depend on many things, including how bad the effect of the frost turned out to be. We decided to make the leap.

Chapter 3
Ploucs, or Country Bumpkins

I set off for Saussignac, following the serpentine route that swept up to the village alongside our vineyards, feeling delicious, free and wild. Seán had given me a pass for the *Randonnée Nocturne*, a night walk organised by our local village *syndicat*. I ran, skipped and twirled intermittently from sheer joy, the warm air like a caress on my skin and the landscape filling my eyes and soul. It was my first night out alone in more than three years.

A journalist had described Saussignac as a 'quintessential charming French village' and it lived up to the description that evening. The massive stone chateau built in 1591 that formed the central feature of the village was bathed in sunlight; my friend Laurence's roses, a riot of scarlet in the front garden of the chateau, threw clouds of perfume into the air. Opposite, on the main square, a crowd chatted in front of the Lion d'Or restaurant. I spotted a few people I knew and caught up on news, and then we were off, two guides in fluorescent jackets setting the pace at the front and two more bringing up the rear.

From Saussignac village we crossed the ridge to the west above the Dordogne valley, the sunset highlighting the contours of the vineyards, creating an impressionist palette of greens and yellows that followed the hillside off the Saussignac plateau. Below us the patchwork of vines, plum orchards, forests and old stone buildings was tantalisingly flecked with gold by the setting sun.

Very quickly, even those who didn't know each other were chatting as we walked. There was something different, exciting, almost dangerous about a night walk. Monique, one of the guides, pulled in alongside me and struck up a conversation about what we were doing in our vineyard. She heard we were not only organic but biodynamic. Word got around fast in a small place.

Fully expecting the blank look I often received, I launched into my explanation: 'For me, biodynamics is three things: thinking of the whole farm as a living thing, working with the calendar of the earth's position in relation to the moon and cosmos, and homeopathic-like preparations or treatments for the soil and plant.'

I glanced at Monique to see that she was with me. Behind her was a vineyard that looked like a desert. We were passing between that on one side, the herbicide-treated soil baked hard like concrete, and a certified organic vineyard on the other, lime-green growth between the rows and soft-worked soil under the vines. The difference was glaring. It reminded me to add that to go biodynamic you had to first be certified organic. It is impossible to work this way without good farming fundamentals already in place.

'Man has used the sun, moon and stars to guide his agricultural activity for millennia, knowing that the moon and planets and constellations affect life on earth. Before wristwatches, we told the time via the sun, moon and stars, and we were accordingly more connected to these bodies. They determine much of what takes place on earth, but many of us have lost touch with them and with nature itself, living in a world of concrete and light pollution, thus finding these ideas hard to swallow.' We turned onto the high vineyard path running towards Razac as the sun dropped below the horizon, darkening the landscape. Seeing Monique nodding, I continued.

'The moon moves the oceans; it has a major influence on water, so the moon's phases influence the way plants grow, through the different levels of moisture in the environment and in the plant. The moon affects wine as well. Racking our wines – taking the clear wine off the sediment – on a descending moon rather than an ascending moon reduces the need for additives like fining agents to clear the wine later on. It is the moon's gravitational force at work.'

'How do you know if it is ascending or descending?' she asked.

'If you don't have a lunar calendar you can mark the position of the moon in chalk on the window at a specific time one evening then again at the same time the following evening. If the chalk mark is higher the second night it is ascending; if it is lower it is descending.'

'*Tiens!*' said Monique, meaning 'How intriguing!' She seemed interested and comfortable with everything I was saying. Learning about the fundamentals and seeing the results had convinced my own sceptical city-dweller heart about biodynamics. But often, especially on hearing about biodynamics for the first time, it isn't easy to swallow. A few months before, I had been in Dublin for a marketing trip, staying with best friends Barry and Aideen O'Brien. They had been a lifeline for me when I moved from South Africa to Ireland at the start of the Celtic Tiger boom, and when we lived in Dublin they were like family to us. Aideen was my saviour when Sophia, our firstborn, arrived with her oesophagus attached to her lung pipe instead of her stomach; she coached me through the first tough weeks, helping me to breastfeed in the exceptional conditions, accelerating Sophia's recovery and my ability to cope. A business coach for a large tech multinational by day and a life coach by night, she still offered me regular wisdom on motherhood, relationships and business.

That evening Barry's parents were over for dinner. Barry's mother Mary and her husband Seán had been subjected to warehousing ten cases of wine for us when the O'Briens, who usually held the samples, were renovating. That hadn't endeared me to them since moving cases of wine around wasn't an easy job, especially at age eighty-plus. As I explained biodynamics, Mary gave me a very sceptical look. With this new twist she would not want me and my strange ideas – or my wine – to darken their door ever again. As I ended my explanation, however, she had a revelation and her face changed completely.

'You know, now I think of it, my granny used to do that and *she* was a very educated woman. The *Farmers' Almanac*, they called it. It had the lunar cycles and she used to work our vegetable garden by it. She went to one of the best schools in Dublin.'

We all laughed. The memory would be with me forever; a reminder of how as city-dwellers we were now often four or five generations distant from people who could identify with this strange 'new' idea of biodynamics. Monique was only one generation older than me but refreshingly connected to the concept. In rural France, *les paysans,* the French word for peasants but without the pejorative aspects of our English word, are people who work the soil themselves and are usually still in tune with these cycles.

In the last evening light, a field of wild flowers, a mass of colour that begged to be painted, punctuated the view of the village of Razac ahead of us.

I ploughed ahead talking about the use of natural plant- and animal-based solutions, sometimes in homeopathic doses and preparations, to help the vines' immunity from disease. 'We use stinging nettles macerated as a soil fertiliser, or dried and made into tea, as a leaf spray to help the vine keep the mildew where it should be – on the ground rather than on her leaves.'

'*Tiens*, that's what I do in my garden,' said Monique and we exchanged a smile of shared experience. Stinging nettle can provide a super tonic to us humans too. I often put gloved handfuls of it into soup in springtime.

We walked and talked for a while longer, then Monique strode off to attend to her guide duties. From that day we greeted each other with warmth, as though we understood each other deeply in spite of not knowing many everyday details about each other. It was still early days for us with biodynamics and I was far from understanding it all, but I knew with a deep-down instinctive sense that it was the way forward, a way to help us farm naturally. Seán and I had turned to biodynamics as a way to combat mildew, a fungal disease, but had found it offered far more than that.

We turned back towards Saussignac, the village floating enchantingly in the distance, lights twinkling. Soon moonlight and a few torches, brought by the well-prepared – not me – were all we had to see our way.

As we turned onto the last section of the walk, a grass path surrounded by moonlit vineyards, a small, white-haired man dressed in simple clothes and a beret stepped into the clearing just ahead. We slowed. He began to play a classic French bistro tune on the accordion slung over his shoulder, binding us together with the magic of music. When he broke, we burst into applause and he treated us to another. It was pure joy.

For the last kilometre, buoyed by the impromptu outdoor concert, we floated down the track, walking on air that was velvety smooth and warm. At the Château de Saussignac, tea lights flickered on the steps, lighting the way into the enormous stone hall. Settled at a long table surrounded by new friends, I was served a glass of merlot. The folks around me said the wine was *'très bon'* and I owned up that it was ours. For all the trauma of our first few years, we had produced something worthy of praise.

Other winegrowers' wines were on the table and I liberally tasted my way through them – for professional purposes, of course – as we munched on onion soup sprinkled with grated cheese and croutons. At the stroke of midnight a large slice of apple tart with a glass of Saussignac dessert wine was served. The unctuous apricot compote flavours, similar to Sauternes but better – *bien sûr* – complemented the tart perfectly, a grand finale.

Walking back alone in the dark I took in the quiet, the sky above me like a black velvet dome studded with diamonds, and felt deeply thankful for the enchanted evening. The house was fast asleep. I climbed the steps and fell into bed, exhausted but thoroughly rejuvenated by my *soirée insolite*.

Like the *Randonnée Nocturne*, the *Festival des Ploucs* was an unmissable event on the social whirl of Saussignac's summer calendar. The annual rock concert, held on the first Saturday of July and literally translated as 'The Country-bumpkins' Festival', promised kids' activities followed by live rock music, casual food and fun. In a corner of the festival field we found Ian and Brigit Wilson and their daughter Chiara watching kids' theatre in the scorching sun. Ian, a scriptwriter and entrepreneur, regularly helped me see things through a different lens with his wise views on life. He was Zen, while Brigit was beautiful, blonde and vivacious. Before moving to Pécharmant, the 'charming hill'

north-east of Bergerac known for its red wines, they lived in our village for six months and Brigit had become one of my running partners. They had proved many times for us Plutarch's wise words: 'prosperity is no just scale; adversity is the only balance to weigh friends.'

The makeshift stage for the children's show was surrounded by hay-bale benches filled with an eager audience. It was six in the evening but still roasting. I reached for the sunscreen in my bag and slathered more onto Sophia and Ellie as the clown started his act.

'He's coming, he's coming!' whispered Ellie, popping with excitement as she spied the clown's head bobbing up and down behind the stage screen. The anticipation generated by the crazy clown's simple motion was electric. He bounced onto the stage, gave a fart, looked totally surprised and pointed to individuals in the crowd... To shaking heads and great guffaws the show took off.

I tore myself away to hump a twelve-pack of our wine to the tent where participating winegrowers were selling local wines. En route I stopped every few steps to chat with someone I knew; it was a good feeling. When we first arrived in the area we knew no one; now we knew most of the local farming community. When I returned to the stage a half-hour later, the clown's show was over and the kids were roaring around the field freestyle while Seán kept watch and chatted with the knot of winegrowers nearby. Joel Evandre, sporting bright-coloured pants and waist-length dreadlocks, was an eccentric with a fabulous sense of humour. He was starting organic agriculture himself; one of the latest wave of organic conversions that helped keep our small appellation one of the highest concentrations of organic producers in France. A true joker, he was known to hide rotting steak under the mayor's car seat for a laugh and keep a loaded water gun in his *fourgon*, utility vehicle, at all times.

With him was Thierry Daulhiac, wiry, innovative and who, with his wife Isabelle, had become our best friends in the winegrower community. Thierry, a seventh-generation winegrower in the commune of Razac de Saussignac, had provided invaluable help and advice over the years. The animated discussion revolved around the current growing season that was proving difficult due to rain and consequent disease, like mildew. It was hard to believe at that moment, sweat-drenched under the blazing sun.

I took over watching the girls, eyes on them and ears on the discussion which turned to which tractor to buy. Thierry, like Seán, was looking at options for replacing his. He was well positioned to give advice on machinery as unofficial inventor and tester for a leading German manufacturer of vineyard equipment. Thierry had the heart of a mechanical engineer and spent hours working on his tractor and its associated tools. He was a true specialist.

'Seán, *pour moi*, for me, it has to have power. You know how many things I like to do at once,' said Thierry acting out working on the tractor with several different attachments doing different jobs at the same time. It was a complicated affair and had Thierry doing acrobatics in the vineyard that regularly drew chuckles from neighbours. We all laughed at Thierry's rendition. There was more theatre at this festival than the children's one advertised.

'But more power means a higher price, especially if you want the tractor to be small and relatively light,' he continued, then gave the price range for the kind of tractor and attachments we needed.

Now I wasn't laughing; I was trying not to hyperventilate. Even at a rock concert we were talking and thinking about our business. Our life was our work and our work was our life. We loved it but we could never get away.

Spotting Pierre de St Viance, a close friend and solid Gaulois who seemed to have stepped off the pages of an Asterix comic, zooming past, I took the opportunity to escape from the tractor conversation before it gave me heart palpitations. Pierre, a professional bottler who had bottled all our vintages, kissed me gallantly on both cheeks. With his wife Laurence, a close friend through running as Brigit had been, he owned part of the magnificent Château de Saussignac, where my night walk had begun a few days before. As a key organiser of the festival he didn't have much time to stand still, so leaving Seán tracking the small individuals, I walked down towards the winegrower stand with him to *causer*, chat, en route. It was almost time to take my 'turn' as barmaid. Barrels were set up as makeshift counters around the outside of an old army tent. Inside, winegrowers were opening bottles at a ferocious pace. After a few minutes' observation of how the system worked – serve wine, take money – I was frantically serving eager concert-goers too, elbowing colleagues that had helped us settle in, over access to the fridge and cash box.

My hour of duty done, we sat down on the grass with great plates of barbecued sausages and chips. The sun was setting over the vineyards to the north-west, a dazzling show of red and orange. The wine in our plastic cups tasted like nectar, the simple food like a banquet, and the music, a New Age rock band, was energised and bright. Chatting with Ian and Brigit and looking out over the crowds, I was filled with gratitude for our adopted community.

The music warmed up as darkness fell, but Ellie and Sophia were reaching the end of their tether. We packed up and said goodbye to our friends, feeling a little jealous of them being able to stay later with their daughter being a little older.

Seeing so many friends and acquaintances at the *Festival des Ploucs* reminded me of how much we had settled. And the festival itself was a revelation: a rock concert that attracted teenagers from miles around but also offered a safe and fun environment for young families and grandparents, so different to the feeling of rock concerts I had attended in cities, where the old and the very young are rarely seen. We'd be back next year for sure.

Along with heat and a packed social diary, the summer brought more visitors. Derek, Diane and their beautiful green Jaguar were looking for a few cases of red for a party. I took them through the wines on a rickety table in the shade alongside the winery.

'You don't happen to have a rent-a-row scheme, do you?' said Diane. 'We like your wines and Derek has been wanting one for a while.'

'We don't but I would be happy to start one for you,' I said, never one to turn a sales opportunity down.

We had seen rent-a-row in Canada's Okanagan Valley years before and it was on my ideas list when we arrived, but disappeared in the chaos of the first years.

'How much would it be?' she asked as I packed cases of wine into their trunk.

'I don't know. Let me think about it and I'll let you know in a couple of days,' I said and took down her email.

Starting a new product with a real customer was ideal and this looked like a great way to sell direct. Along with wine and special events like a harvest weekend, each 'owner' would have their name on an oak plaque on their row. I sent Di the weblink and she hit 'Buy'.

Perhaps it wouldn't come to much, or perhaps it would help our direct business. We had to grow that part of our operation to be able to make mission-critical investments like a new press.

For the previous two harvests the old press had cost more to fix than we made in a month. It was on its last legs and the repair money was throwing euros in the bin; we would never get it back on the resale. It was another long-term investment to add to the list. Selling wine to buyers like Jon was necessary but, at the prices we could demand in our appellation, and we were already at the top end, they didn't offer the margin required for ongoing winery investments. We had to generate more direct sales.

Chapter 4
Grape Skin Magic

We added the label with the Surgeon-General's notice about the dangers of alcohol, a requirement for all wines sold in the USA, and repacked the pallet of wine for our first American sale to Jon. That same day another American telephoned. Naomi Whittel introduced herself, then explained: 'I found you through your vineyard tours, where you say there are many organic growers in your area. I'm looking for organic grape skins for a new line of antioxidant products. We plan to extract resveratrol from the skins for my new anti-ageing supplement.'

We had taken our wine tourism site, French Wine Adventures, live a few months before and our first paying guests had visited around the time of the devastating spring frost. The site was bringing more than tourists, it seemed.

'I've had calls from academics looking for organic grape skins,' I said. 'Resveratrol is why a glass of red wine a day is good for you, isn't it?'

'Exactly,' said Naomi. 'My research team has been working in this area for years but recent press has put focus on it. The difference with us is that we are exclusively interested in developing products that are certified organic and biodynamic, in the tradition of great vineyards, such as yours, where nothing extraneous is added to the wine. We take great care to provide our customers with a natural product that is a reflection of nature's abundance.'

Naomi had a turn of phrase that made me feel like a marketing dunce. The academics had been the little league. I listened carefully.

'I like the pioneer spirit that I felt from your website. I have a long-standing regard for biodynamics. My grandfather was one of the first farmers to bring biodynamics to the USA and I was raised on a biodynamic farm. We are looking to establish an exclusive partnership with a vineyard such as yours, with outstanding quality and a vision that matches our principles.'

After the flattery, I was even more attentive. The only problem was that our own grape skins wouldn't be certified that year, as we were still a few months off full certification. Organic conversion took three years. I explained the situation then offered a solution, as I had learned to do back in consulting school with IBM almost two decades before.

'For this year, I can introduce you to a good friend who is certified organic,' I said, sure that Thierry 'Tractor' Daulhiac would be able to supply.

'Great,' said Naomi. 'I'll be over in six weeks for an investigative trip. Perhaps I can meet your friend as well. I want to start with a small sampling amount this year. For next year we'll need larger volumes.'

She was focused and precise. I felt a force and strength behind her words that encouraged me to visit Thierry that very afternoon. Château Le Payral's nineteenth-century farmhouse was resplendent, the climbing rose that covered part of its limestone facade like apricot jam and mint dotted on clotted cream scones. I found Thierry in his shed working on a tractor attachment for weeding under the vines, and described my conversation with Naomi. Thierry was intrigued. Adding value to a winery 'waste product' was a notion we could all do with developing in the tough wine market.

The organic road we had taken and the age of our vineyards – some sixty-five years old – meant higher quality but also lower yields, and a subsequent lack of return despite higher prices than most. Perhaps this new opportunity would help redress the balance.

Six weeks later Naomi arrived immaculately dressed in power-businesswoman style; beautifully tailored trousers, a red jacket and black patent leather shoes. In my torn jeans, paint-stained runners and a wine-splattered – despite many washes – harvest shirt, I felt like a farming hick. It seemed half the farm had made its way inside the house, against my best efforts with the broom. I felt embarrassed as she stepped into our humble kitchen but Naomi was charmed by the rusticity.

The vineyard looked better than the interior so I took Naomi around our vines explaining Terroir Feely. As we finished the tour, Thierry clattered into the courtyard in his old *fourgon*. Naomi stepped into the passenger seat and they took off to visit Château Le Payral.

On their return we settled into creaky chairs at our battered kitchen table with cups of organic coffee. Naomi explained that she needed the grape skins dry and food-grade. It wasn't as simple as digging the marc – the leftover grape pomace made of skins and pips – out of the press and handing it over at the end of vinification, the way we did when we passed it over to the distillery for industrial alcohol. There was work to be done to find the appropriate solution.

'Do you know of a manufacturing facility that could extract the polyphenols from the grape pomace?' she asked. Thierry, Seán and I shook our heads.

'Les Sources de Caudalie, the cosmetics business built around grape extracts, might know,' I said.

Naomi was a step ahead: she already had an appointment with them and with a professor at the University of Bordeaux. When she left, Thierry had us in guffaws about our shared feelings of being *ploucs*.

'Naomi, so smart in her beautiful city clothes in my *fourgon*, mud everywhere! The seat full of dog hair. *Ah, la honte*! (Oh, the embarrassment!) With my bad English I thought Naomi had said she was going to follow me in her hire car. If I had known she was catching a lift with me, I would have cleaned up. *Et en plus*, I have a cold, there were used tissues everywhere, on the seat, on the floor. When Naomi got into my passenger seat, I was so embarrassed. I expected her to grimace but instead she gave me the most beautiful smile.'

Thierry's misgivings about his well-garnished vehicle were mistaken. Naomi was smitten – charmed by Thierry, the fact that he was a seventh-generation winegrower, the wines and the stylish simplicity of their home, kept immaculate by Isabelle. I wondered how Isabelle did it; she had a full-time job, kids, a farm.

Cars, clean and dirty, old and new, were a major topic of conversation in general in our commune at that time. Pierre de St Viance, our friend the bottler, was turning forty. He and Laurence, who was studying to become a teacher, lived in the massive middle section of Château de Saussignac, and were also close friends with Thierry and Isabelle. Pierre was powerfully built for the heavy work he did, bottling wine all over the region of Aquitaine, with red hair and the temper and sense of humour to go with it. His passions were his family and cars. There was an ongoing joke about how many cars he had and the fact that Laurence didn't have a clue how many there were or where they were, since many were garaged with Pierre's friends. As she herself said, *tant mieux*, so much the better, because if she knew she would probably have a cardiac arrest.

Word had it the count was around twenty. We were planning to make it twenty-one. For Pierre's fortieth birthday, Thierry, Joel and a few other organisers of the *Festival des Ploucs* were making a collection to buy the ugliest, oldest car they could find. Emails flew: what, where, when. An invitation from Laurence to a party at Château de Saussignac arrived perfectly timed to save us from gatecrashing. Thierry said we were buying a '*quatrelle*'. I didn't know what it was but it sounded good.

Thierry thought the Renault 4L was an ugly car, but when I saw it for the first time I found it charming. We gathered at Thierry's vineyard to decorate the beautiful antique, covering it from top to toe in stickers for anti-nuclear proliferation, anti-genetic modification, anti-4x4, anti-rallying, pro-socialists and a few of my organic stickers to add a touch of green. For 400 euros we had a car that worked, if somewhat rusted and chesty.

A few hours later, as we lifted our glasses of champagne to salute Pierre's milestone in the great vaulted living room of Château de Saussignac, the sound of a sick vehicle drifted inside.

Laurence stopped her glass midway to her lips and said, 'I don't believe it.'

Pierre flung open the windows to better hear the sound. He could probably tell the age and make just by listening. The cream 4L burst round the corner, a cloud of grey smoke coughing in its wake, like some crazed scene in a comic book. It shuddered to a halt in the garden two levels below us. We galloped down the massive chateau stairs, two-metre-wide chunks of stone, to the cellar that led to the garden and the 4L work of art.

'It is exactly like the one I had when we were courting!' cried Laurence. 'Oh, it fills me with memories.'

After checking the engine and all other aspects of the superb addition to his car collection, Pierre declared, 'This will make a great rally car.'

Everyone roared with laughter. It wasn't going anywhere but to a parts shop. His real rally car, a Citroën parked alongside, was regularly pitted against the mountains of France and beyond.

This group of friends had become part of our stability in the new and unfamiliar world of France and wine when we arrived. To us nomads, living far away from where we grew up, like many people in the modern global village, they were like family.

That evening we talked with Thierry about Naomi's visit and the possibilities of the venture. With the frost damage we would need new revenue streams by the following year. It was early days. Naomi hadn't even finalised a business name. I crossed my fingers.

Chapter 5

Inhaling Grapes

Seán began preparations for our third harvest as I organised a multi-day wine tour for Chris, a client from Chicago. My research took me to top estates in Médoc and Saint-Émilion, including Château Pontet-Canet, a *grand cru classé* in Pauillac. I met the director, Jean-Michel Comme, a famous personality in the organic and biodynamic community.

Some estates were beautiful but the wines disappointing; others were rustic but the wine magnificent; and some, like Pontet-Canet, had a stunning estate and vineyard and delicious wines – a deep well of black fruit with a touch of spice, minerality and zest. Jean-Michel mentioned that his family property, run by his wife, was near Margueron, ten minutes' drive from our vineyard in Saussignac. The Saussignac appellation, part of Greater Bergerac, was on the border of the most easterly Bordeaux appellation called Sainte-Foy-Bordeaux, the location of his family vineyard, Champ des Treilles.

Taking up Jean-Michel's suggestion of a visit, I booked a tasting at Champ des Treilles. I loved orchestrating visits to give a flavour of the region, and the large corporate-style properties and *grands crus classés* contrasted with the smaller artisanal properties that offered a personal and authentic experience. Whatever the size, the vineyard had to strike a chord to be included. I had visited some of the most hallowed estates in the Bordeaux region and found them hollow, places I would not return to.

A few weeks of planning later, I welcomed Chris and setting off to Margueron offered the first opportunity to chat. 'Where is your accent from?' he asked as we made our way cross-country on small rural roads. Rolling hills covered in vines ran to the horizon, interspersed with trees and stone buildings. It was no wonder the southern Dordogne was sometimes called the Tuscany of France.

'It's a long story... a bit of an epic,' I replied. People were often curious about where we were from and how we ended up in this corner of France.

'We've got time,' said Chris.

I delved back to the beginnings of our vineyard dream some twenty years before. 'Seán and I met in Joburg in our early twenties. He was a journalist and I was a yuppie but a country girl at heart. For a while we played "we're just friends" but it was much more than that. He made me see life with different eyes.'

'True love,' said Chris.

'Exactly. We began to think of the future: we both had a back-to-the-land dream and we were passionate about wine. The logical step was to move to Cape Town, closer to where the vineyards were. About a year later we did just that. After searching for several months we were close to buying a small vineyard to work on weekends when the tech multinational I worked for asked me to move to Dublin. The Celtic Tiger was taking off and they needed skills like mine. Hence the accent – saffer with an Irish touch. Anyway, here we are, Champ des Treilles.'

I parked the car and promised to continue the story later. Corinne Comme opened the door of the *chai*, pronounced 'shay', meaning 'winery'. She was slight with long, dark hair and she had strong, delicate hands and the air of an artist and shaman, a wise woman. After introductions she walked us out into the vineyards explaining their approach.

Jean-Michel Comme, owner of the property and technical director of the only certified organic and biodynamic Médoc *grand cru classé*, was in the distance, working in an *enjambeur* tractor on his weekend off from Pontet-Canet. The tall machine looked like a strange insect mounted over the vines. An *enjambeur* tractor straddles the vine row rather than driving between the vine rows, a necessity in a very high-density vineyard like theirs, planted at around 8,000 vines per hectare. We made our way towards him, climbing a gentle slope covered in vines. Corinne stopped to touch them, almost stroking them, or to remove a wayward shoot every few metres.

'In spring we collect a sample of flowers from each parcel to see what the perfume is; that gives an early indicator of the aromas that will follow in the grapes and then the wine,' she said leaning in to inhale deeply from one of the bunches of grapes. I followed, breathing in the aromas. I had never smelled a bunch of grapes before; we always focused on tasting. I was astonished by the delicate perfume hanging in the air. It made sense – so much of a wine's character came from the aromas.

Jean-Michel stopped the giant insect and jumped down to greet us. He was fit and muscular, with a square jaw and determined eyes that explained why everything at Pontet-Canet was perfect: it was run with military precision. Corinne talked about the Champ des Treilles, their *terroir*: soil, climate, vines and how they farmed. The story started when Jean-Michel's grandparents emigrated from Italy to grow vines here in the

1920s. Their conviction to work organically and biodynamically was solidified when Corinne became sick from pesticides used by farms neighbouring their house. They had not been welcomed by the locals for their strange ways of natural farming, were even victims of tyre-slashing on their car in the yard. They had considered giving up and leaving but decided to stay, not be chased away. Knowing how she loved those old vines from the way she touched them, I knew it was not a consideration lightly made. Her story made me thankful for the generosity and openness of our Saussignac winegrowing community. Only ten minutes' drive away from Terroir Feely, this was another world. We walked back to the farmhouse, their vineyards glowing with health on the hills around us.

'During the harvest I have two months here on my own. My bedroom is above the winery. I listen to the wines talking to me in the night. If one is getting too hot, I hear it and I intervene. I don't like automated temperature control, I want to make the decision myself. In the evenings, during the harvest, I set my table in the barrel room, light the candles and have a quiet dinner there with my wines.'

I pictured the scene, enchanted. She was like a wine sorceress – full of intuition and deep spiritual knowledge of her place and her wines. At the back of the winery was an egg-shaped concrete vat that I felt an intense urge to stroke. My hand lifted and I looked up for approval from the master winemaker, then did. It felt good, its solid smoothness and geometric perfection comforting and satisfying under my fingers.

Talking through her winemaking, Corinne gave me ideas that would be useful for us, such as placing a little cup of sulphur dioxide to float in the vat and release its protective gas, rather than actually adding the liquid to the wine. We were preparing for our first vintage alone without a wine scientist giving advice.

It was exciting but also frightening. Seán felt confident and ready for it. He often disagreed with our wine scientist, who followed a technological, modern winemaking approach.

We were taking a different route, a natural, *terroir*-driven road that was filled with angst and risk, but also with character and joy. In modern winemaking many additives are used to decrease risk or increase volume. They mask the authenticity of the wine, creating factory wines that taste alike. At that time there were no European rules for organic winemaking. We were organic for the growing part in the vineyard, but once it was picked we could do what we liked.

Although there was no official obligation to follow natural winemaking for our organic status, we were slowly moving to it. This meant letting the grapes do everything naturally, including not adding cultured yeast. Indigenous yeast was in the air and on the grapes in the vineyard; there was no need to add foreign cultured yeast developed in a factory. Wild yeast offered more individuality, but also more risk. The fermentation was slower and sometimes that allowed bacteria to develop that could create bad aromas, increase the volatile acidity or even turn the wine to vinegar. Another key part of natural winemaking was lower sulphur dioxide levels in the wine, and the floating cup of SO_2 would help in that respect.

We tasted from the barrels, first a merlot, deep and plummy, then a pure petit verdot. Bordeaux blends are usually merlot, cabernet sauvignon and cabernet franc. On the left bank, such as in Pauillac in the Médoc, cabernet sauvignon is usually the majority accompanied by a tiny part of petit verdot, sometimes called the salt and pepper of the blend. The petit verdot from the barrel was spicy, tannic and acidic. It was the first time I had tasted it on its own and I could see how it would add to a blend. On the right bank in places like Saint-Émilion and Pomerol and where we were that day, merlot was the majority. It was all down to *terroir*: gravels on the left bank, hotter and better for cabernet; limestone and clay on the right bank, cooler and perfect for deep merlot with backbone.

Above us, impressed into the stucco of the stone walls of the small barrel room, were symbols for earth, water, air and fire, images to remind visitors of the importance of biodynamics. It was a magical place and I didn't want to leave but Corinne motioned to us to move into the house.

Inside, the bottled wines were as persuasive. The white offered acacia honey and floral notes and a long bright finish of vibrant acidity from natural farming. The petit verdot had left its trace on the red blend, pepper highlighting red fruit, and the lovely freshness I had come to recognise as a signature of natural wine.

As we said our farewells I felt I had made a connection with a wise woman of the south-west. After seeing their farm and tasting their wines I was even more excited about biodynamics. There was something here that offered more than just a healthy environment, something deeper. They were connected spiritually to their farm, their vines and their wines. I could feel it and it followed through in the taste.

'Wow, that was really interesting. I loved their wines,' said Chris as we took off.

I was surprised. He was a single, thirty-something go-getter working in investment banking with a freshly minted MBA from the INSEAD business school. I didn't expect his reaction to be so spontaneous and positive. He had felt the same magic as I had. 'So what happened in Dublin?' said Chris, reminding me to get back to our story.

'We settled. The one-or-two-year sojourn in Ireland turned into a permanent move. Our first holiday from there was to

France: the Loire Valley. My sister Jacquie Somerville and her boyfriend Ritchie came over from Canada to join us. He was a plastic surgeon, comic and wine fanatic. We visited artisan winegrowers up and down the river, falling in love a little more each day. And the cuisine! Duck breast and cabernet franc from Bourgeuil, apricot tart and Quarts de Chaume sweet wine. Our favourite everyday tipple was a 'blanc d'Anjou' that cost less than an hour of parking in Dublin. It was a *coup de coeur*.'

'It sounds like I should put a trip to the Loire on my wish list,' said Chris.

'Beware! You could land up smitten like us. A few years and many trips to France later, I said to Seán, "We need to write our vision of where we want to be in five years." He said, "That's chick stuff, I'm not doing that." I explained what I had read in O magazine: if we aren't clear about where we want to go, how will we get there? Who can argue with Oprah?' I glanced across at Chris and he laughed.

'Seán succumbed. Sitting in our enclosed balcony, looking at the drizzle out over the Irish Sea, we described our visions on a one-pager. When we exchanged, they were almost identical: winegrowing in France. The gauntlet was laid down. Almost exactly five years later we moved to France.'

'You are so lucky to have a shared vision, a shared dream that you are following,' said Chris.

He was envious, but he didn't know how tough it had been. Working together as a married couple brought new challenges. We almost split up as we began our second year of wine-farming, our relationship crushed by the pressure of changing country, language and job, and the precarious finances. Since then things had got better, but still not as rosy as it looked from the outside. Facing our third harvest I felt a familiar jab of anxiety. Harvest was crunch time, the culmination of the year's work. This was the first time that I would be juggling tour guests and harvest. Like a dose of petit verdot, it would add spice to the challenge.

Chapter 6
Vendanges!

The blue monster, our 'affectionate' name for the harvest machine, rolled into the courtyard a few hours before dawn. Three metres high, it had penetrating lights and a unique sound that meant we knew it was on its way long before it arrived. I greeted François, the driver, explained what was planned for the morning, then ran ahead pointing out the rows.

The process of indicating the rows to harvest was one of my favourite moments: the sky was usually bright with stars, the vines heavy with promising fruit, and there was a feeling that no one else was awake in the world. The perfume of the sauvignon blanc, always the first of our varietals to be ready, floated tantalisingly on the air. As I ran, I felt adrenalin pump through my body. The frost meant small harvest volume, so every litre would count. The lost buds meant we had half the grapes of a usual harvest in some parts of the vineyard. We had to be on top form. Harvest was dangerous and complicated, we could not put a foot wrong, not only for our safety but also financially. We could not afford the juice lost from a loose cap or a missed connection this year.

Philosophically, and for selection of the later-harvested varietals, we preferred hand-picking; economically, we preferred machine. A person hand-picking could assess quality and sort good from bad, which harvest machines could not do. This was why the Saussignac dessert wine, made from grapes attacked by a special rot called *Botrytis cinarea*, had to be hand-picked. But high labour costs in France meant the harvest machine, despite its high capital cost, was significantly less expensive than hand-picking on most vineyards.

Our organic vineyards surrounded the house and winery, allowing us to pick and process in record time in the cool dawn. This reduced the exposure to air and heat during harvest and transport, thus lowering the need for SO_2 to protect against oxidation.

Organic practices also help reduce the need for SO_2 in the first place. In the process of protecting themselves naturally through the season, the vines create additional elements that a chemically protected vine does not, like more resveratrol, the powerful antioxidant found in grape skins, which Naomi wanted for her new supplement. These elements also protect the grapes and the subsequent wine.

A key factor driving the SO_2 level required to protect a wine is the level of acidity. Ironically, chemical fertilisers used by conventional winegrowers contain a potassium dose that means the chemically farmed vines have lower natural acidity in their grapes and hence in the finished wine, so they need more sulphites. The lower the acidity, the higher the SO_2 needs to be. It is a direct inverse relationship, part of the calculation for the level of SO_2 required to protect a given wine at the final moment of truth, bottling. I had noticed that visitors were becoming more aware of and interested in this aspect of winemaking. On a visit a few weeks before to Nathalie Cuisset, Thierry Daulhiac's sister, who farmed with her husband Gérard a couple of kilometres from us on the opposite side of Saussignac, Jeremy, an English client, turned and asked: 'What do they use to preserve the wine?'

'*C'est quoi comme préservatif*?' I asked Nathalie on Jeremy's behalf, using the handy translation technique of 'take an English word and put a French accent on it'.

Nathalie, dark-haired, quiet and a strict Catholic, laughed uncontrollably for a minute and I wondered what was going on.

'*Préservatif* means condom in French,' she said, stifling another fit of giggles. 'We don't use any in our wines. We use SO_2 as the *conservateur*.'

We all laughed heartily as I explained my mistake to Jeremy and his entourage and blushed a deep shade of pink.

A little out of breath from galloping back up the hill after pointing out the rows to the harvest-machine driver, I found there had been no need to run. Seán was ready along with Ad, our close friend from Holland who helped harvest every year.

The previous afternoon Seán and Ad had walked the vineyard removing anything that was damaged or diseased. Since the machine was unable to select, we did a 'negative hand-pick', removing what we didn't want the day before the machine harvest.

'Are you sure everything is ready?' I asked Seán.

'Yes, the vats are connected to the pipes, the lids are on, everything has been checked and rechecked. All we have to do is wait.'

'I'll make tea for everyone, so,' I said, using 'so' like the Irish, a manner of speech picked up during our time in Dublin. We sat down at the old pine table in the kitchen.

'It is strange to be so calm on a harvest morning,' I said.

'You are right, Caro,' said Ad. 'How I remember the panic the first year or even the second. Remember when the trailer blocked and we had to hand-bucket the load from the trailer to the press?'

He laughed, a lovely rolling laugh, one we had come to know well. Harvest wouldn't be the same without Ad and his balding head, wide smile and generous spirit.

We sipped our tea and reminisced.

'I still feel on edge but so much more in control,' I said. Seán nodded, put down his cup and zoomed out to check where the machine was.

His head popped back round the door. 'He'll be up in a few minutes. We'd better get into position.'

The moment of calm was over. When the machine rolled back into the courtyard Seán lined up the trailer while I checked that the fruit bins would empty into it, indicating with hand signs to François, who watched me and the trailer in his rear-view mirrors. The fruit passed from machine to trailer without losing a drop. We were usually good with this step in the process. In our first year we had just one small spill, about 50 litres, in the transfer of a load of white grapes.

Sophia and Ellie loved the harvest, rising early – it was hard not to with the noise in the courtyard – to watch television. It was a treat; usually there was no TV allowed in the working week and none in the morning even on weekends. Strictly prohibited from stepping outside while the large machinery was about, their little faces waited patiently at the lounge window until I came inside to help them switch on our old fat television.

The last trailer was perfectly timed for me to take them to school. Sophia had overseen breakfast and getting dressed. They had successfully shod themselves and got their bags ready. Now six and four, they had to get on and be responsible. Harvest time was not for wimps.

After the school run I left Seán and Ad pressing the grapes and transformed from my harvest look of waterproofs and strong boots into smart pinstripe trousers, cotton shirt and pearls.

Chris and I were going to a biodynamic vineyard in Castillon, that of Clos Puy Arnaud, then on to Saint-Émilion.

Thierry Valette moved with fluidity, his lithe body relaxed but at the same time containing a taut energy. He had left a life as a musician and modern dancer in Paris to make wine at Clos Puy Arnaud. The vines around his beautifully crafted wood buildings were planted tight, the way we wanted to plant our vineyards when we bought the new tractor. Like us, he had left a completely different career, but he had a family history of wine going back four generations in Saint-Émilion. His explanation was passionate and moving: 'Wine is a reflection of the winemaker. They play the music, they play the terroir. You can have a grand terroir but if it isn't played it won't make music. We touch our vines about fourteen times a year. It's all that human activity, the care in the vineyard that makes great wines.'

Moving us into his new winery and barrel store, he explained the investments he had made in the facilities: 'Making a great wine takes three things: intention, investment and work. You cannot have it without all three.'

Chris asked him if he was satisfied; if pursuing his passion had brought the fulfilment he was looking for.

'There is no question, being a winegrower is tough. You have to have a sacred fire for it, a passion, and ideally a bit of money put aside since it always costs more than you expect and brings in less than you hoped. I think that if I hadn't pursued organic and biodynamic I would not have had the will to persevere.'

He had captured exactly how I felt. For all the difficulty of winegrowing – perhaps true for all small-scale farming – what kept us motivated and excited was the yearly advance towards a healthy soil, one that could reveal the true taste of a place. Each year brought better equilibrium in our vineyards and, for us, more experience in this complex profession. It was as if he was following the thoughts in my head.

'After working with Anne for six years, we work as a team.' He worked with Anne Calderoni, an oenologist – wine scientist – who specialised in organic and biodynamic. 'We don't even need to talk. I make the final decision but Anne is the driving force. She likes risk more than I do. She always wants to push the harvest date as late as possible. I like to be more cautious – I want to make sure I have something to harvest.'

Anne had saved us from stuck *malo* in our first year when we were in the *merde* with our merlot. *Malo* is shorthand for malolactic fermentation, a natural deacidification that takes place in most red wines. It is a conversion of malic acid, like green-apple acid, to lactic acid, like milk acid, to make the wine smoother. It usually happens naturally, although it is possible to encourage it with heat and lactic bacteria. When our first-vintage *malo* wouldn't budge, Anne was the angel that helped us work out what was going on and find a solution.

A barrel served as a makeshift tasting counter in the *chai*. I took the glass Thierry offered delicately by the stem, swirled the wine around my mouth for a few minutes and spat into the spittoon. The wines were delicious: clean and long. I preferred his second, less-expensive wine that had less oak, but could see how the first was still too young to drink. It had more ageing potential from higher tannin, which would be achieved through leaving it longer on the skins, from the use of new barrels and from longer barrel-ageing. It needed time.

After visiting Saint-Émilion village and another tasting, we returned to Terroir Feely as the last rays of evening sun splashed through the courtyard. Seán and Ad were finishing off cleaning the press and preparing to cold-settle the juice. Seán handed Chris and me a cup of pure sauvignon. He was justifiably proud. It was truly fine.

The only problem was the volume. When I later entered the figures into my spreadsheet I felt a ball of dread in my stomach; the frost had taken a heavy toll.

Deciding the date to harvest each parcel or part of a vineyard is a delicate and tough call.

Seán and I walked the sémillon vineyards together. The vines, planted in 1945, were gnarled and twisted like sculptures, their coif of green hair exuberant with summer growth and their grapes hanging down golden and rich. We had analysed a sample for sugar and acidity levels but nothing beat tasting – and smelling, as I had learnt with Corinne – the grapes in the vineyard.

Seán was two rows away; we had spread out to cover more of the vineyard.

'The skins are giving interesting aromas of peach and passion fruit,' he said looking over the vines to me.

'Yes, it's good over here, too. A hint of green apple, as well,' I said.

We kept walking. When we reached the end of the vineyard we talked through our impressions.

'The sugar and acidity are just right,' concluded Seán. 'We should pick tomorrow.'

I agreed and took out my mobile to book the harvest machine. It felt great being able to decide our harvest date on our own. In previous years we had been at the beck and call of our oenologist, waiting for her to make the final call. Over time we had realised that we were totally different to farms nearby; our vines marched to their own tune, their own rhythm. There were so many variables that contributed to this – the way we farmed, the soil, the slope, the age of the vines, the varietal… the list was endless. No one was better qualified to make the decision than ourselves, knowing our vines as intimately as we did.

The following day the harvest machine arrived in the courtyard fifteen minutes late and bearing a new driver. We introduced ourselves. I explained what we were picking and ran through the pre-dawn darkness indicating the rows. It was cloudy, there were no stars to marvel at, but at least it wasn't raining. The first load arrived faster than we expected. The guy was in a hurry.

As we lined up the trailer the driver tipped the first bin, not watching us at all. I yelled and waved but he couldn't hear above the noise and kept tipping. As part of our precious harvest tipped onto the courtyard floor I let out a scream of anguish that broke through the noise barrier and he looked in his rear-view mirror and stopped the tip. It felt like minutes but was just a few seconds – enough to lose about 100 litres of our precious grapes. The colour drained from my face in horror. Seán motioned to me to calm down and backed into perfect position.

I gave the driver a stiff thumbs-up but felt like giving him the two fingers. He emptied smoothly and I breathed deeply and counted to ten. Throwing a tantrum wouldn't help. Everyone was under pressure. If we sent this driver away we probably wouldn't get the machine for a few days. We had to get through this sémillon and then I would have a word with Serge, the manager of the drivers.

We could not afford to lose grapes with already low yields from the late frost. A bout of bad weather around flowering meant it was a vintage of double jeopardy. Ironically, this could be good for quality, as there were fewer grapes per bunch, meaning better aeration and less potential for disease. It was never good for our wallets, though, as the small increase we could demand for higher quality never compensated for lost yield. The rest of the morning the transfers went smoothly.

But pure plain sailing was not to be. Harvest was always guaranteed to include the unexpected, to raise the heartbeat a little. As Seán raised the pressure on the press to two bars on the last load, we heard a high-pitched whine then an ominous wheeze and a crunch. It ground to a halt. Seán and Ad tried a few adjustments and the machine growled, but would not spring to life. Ad was a retired mechanic, the perfect person to assess the damage. The failed part was a key component, part of the turning mechanism. We knew that repair would cost over four times what the press would be worth afterwards, since our regular mechanic, Monsieur Bonny, had provided a *devis*, a quote, when he warned it was looking worn.

The ancient press was finished. Lijda, Ad's wife, gamely donned cycling shorts and sterilised her feet, then climbed into the press to stomp the grapes in a vain effort to release the last of the juice. Fortunately most of the pressing on the load was already done, but losing this last bit of press juice was another small blow to already low yields and a new press was another investment we would have to make if we wanted to stay in the game.

When Seán walked the vineyards that afternoon they were roughed up, as if they had been through a storm. With a careful driver there was little damage, but a careless one could wreak havoc. Trying my best to keep my cool, I left a message for Serge that we did not want that driver again.

Naomi, the American grape-skin hunter, asked if she could visit to capture harvest on film. Progress with Naomi was good, a reminder that if you kept going in the hard times new opportunities presented themselves. If we hadn't stuck to our organic principles – against the economic odds and against the advice of vineyard 'specialists' – I wouldn't have received her call in the first place.

I invited Naomi to join us on any remaining harvest days; we had several hand-picks planned for our top reds and for the Saussignac dessert wine, including our first vine-shareholder harvest day. After starting the vine-share quietly with Di and Derek as our first members, it had taken on a momentum of its own and the harvest day had twenty people signed up. Since most of the guests were flying in specially, we set the date well in advance and prayed for good weather.

Thierry was fine-tuning the process of drying the marc for Naomi, using Gérard and Nathalie Cuisset's prune ovens. Gérard and Nathalie (Thierry's sister) dried their organic plums into prunes on their property, as well as making organic wine. In our centuries-old winegrowing community there were family connections everywhere. The Cuissets' equipment could be used without worrying about chemical contamination, plus they were geographically close to Thierry and ourselves. Each time I saw Nathalie she seemed to have a little smile playing on her lips, like she was remembering my preservative faux pas. With Thierry and Gérard's experiments, the process for drying the marc became reliable and repeatable and the new business opportunity with Naomi inched forward.

Chris left us to continue his voyage on to Burgundy and harvest hurtled forward. The next grapes ripe for picking were on the young merlot vines, the ones we used for our everyday red. I called to reserve the machine and Serge explained that the driver we didn't want was the only one available.

'Maybe we should wait until we can get another driver,' I said to Seán after sharing Serge's bad news.

'I don't think we can. The grapes are ready. Another few days and we will miss the window. Rain is forecast.'

We sat at the worn pine table in the kitchen debating the situation. We were torn.

'Better to pick at the right moment with the wrong guy than at the wrong moment with the right guy,' said Seán.

I called Serge back and confirmed for the following morning.

When our favourite driver rolled into the courtyard a half-hour late, Seán and I tried to be civil. Climbing high onto the landing outside the harvest-machine's door to catch a lift to the vineyard on the far end of the farm, my senses were assaulted by a haze of smoke and what seemed like a hint of alcohol. Convincing myself it was the smell of grapes, I pushed aside the worry about the renegade driver and focused on holding on. As we set off down the track a hare disappeared into the night then a deer. It was like a pre-dawn safari.

To reach the bottom vineyard we had to pass through a row of another of our vineyards.

'If I drive it I have to pick it,' said the driver.

'That's OK. We're picking this vineyard after you have finished the lower one anyway,' I said.

It was my first time on the machine while it was harvesting. I was stunned at the speed and the vibration, perhaps thanks to the driver, not necessarily the norm. We arrived at the vineyard that was first up and I carefully explained the rows to pick, requested he go slowly and take care, then took off back up the hill at a trot, leaving him to adjust the machine to the row width.

Turning to check if he had started, I saw him empty the contents from the harvest-machine bins, filled with the row he had just picked, onto the ground. The drivers sometimes emptied the bins before starting the picking of the day to be sure that water left from washing or rain en route was not left to mix with the harvest about to be picked. Today it wasn't raining and we had just picked a row of our precious grapes. I sprinted back down the hill in a futile rage. He was picking in the opposite direction, heading away faster than I was running and already way beyond my range. I stopped. The horror of already low yields and the incompetent driver flooded through me. Perhaps he *was* drunk. Either he had totally forgotten that we had already harvested a row minutes before or he had hit a wrong button by mistake; either way, I felt panic rising about what the rest of the day could bring. The row was short so the volume wasn't enormous, but we couldn't afford to lose anything. I forced myself back up the hill.

Seán dropped the pipe he was attaching to a vat and prepared to commit an act of violence on hearing about the chucked row. Now it was my turn to calm him; if we became aggressive, the man could sabotage what little harvest we had. I called Serge and got his answering machine.

When the renegade returned, I explained that he was not to empty anything until I gave the thumbs-up. He gave me a surly look but it went smoothly. A few hours later the rest of the young merlot was safely in the vats, but we were determined not to accept that driver again no matter what.

The low volume on the whites was a trend across the vineyard. The core red clocked in at a little over half our normal yield. As I filled the details into my financial spreadsheet I felt like giving up. The vintage would cost more to produce than we would sell it for, since the fixed costs would not adjust to the frost-battered result.

At least the machine-harvesting was over for the year. We felt a deep sense of relief. Machine-picking was fast but stressful, whereas hand-picking, while hard work, was human scale and more fun. The first of the hand-picking, our shareholder harvest day, dawned misty with a promise of sun. I had butterflies. Although I had organised events in my previous life, I felt out of practice and this was our first official client event. By 9 a.m., nineteen well-booted pickers had arrived, plus one, Maj, a good-looking forty-something, who was kitted out in sky-rise platforms. I made a mental note to include more precise instructions on footwear in future communications.

We gathered around the short rows of merlot at the top of the hill near the house, and Seán took us through how to place the bucket or basket under the vine so that you didn't drop your bunch onto the ground; how to cut close to the bunch but still avoiding your fingers (the first-aid kit was in the tractor, just in case); and then how to sort carefully to ensure only the best grapes were kept.

Maj, meanwhile, was struggling to exchange her gorgeous platforms for more practical runners. Holding onto her buddy, Mary, she laughed contagiously and gave a running commentary, banter that loosened up the crowd of people that had just met; ideal glue to solder the group. Seán gave a final word about how to tell a good grape from a bad grape, 'When in doubt, taste', and as the sun chased the mist back down the hill, we followed.

By the time we reached them, the merlot vines on the lower levels were dressed in dainty, lacy wafts of mist and golden rays. We split our pickers into pairs, one on each row. I ran up and down checking progress, giving advice and swapping full buckets for empty ones, while Seán and Ian ferried full grape bins to the winery with the tractor.

Ian 'Zen' Wilson, scriptwriter and entrepreneur, beautiful Brigit, and Chiara, their lovely daughter, the spitting image of her mum, were helping us organise the day. Like Ad and Lijda van Sorgen, our Dutch friends, Ian regularly helped us with harvest and bottling and knew the ropes of our eccentric winery. He was a medium-height fit fifty-something who looked like he was in his forties, his dark hair lightly peppered at the edges. Ian was one of those people who could make you talk about feelings without realising you were doing it. He had a cunning method of leaving gaps in the conversation that begged to be filled with deep thoughts.

As we worked, Chiara, Sophia and Ellie picked and ate grapes, getting their own sense of harvest rhythm. Hand-picking offered a special energy, a unique moment of human interaction far superior to that of a machine. I wanted to share it. This day was a way to do that, but perhaps there could be others. I pictured a day with Saussignac primary school, imagining what fun it would be to share this part of the harvest with local children.

The grapes were delectable, purple, ripe and delicious, and I was having a ball, like our guests, enjoying the banter and exertion in the autumn sun, my butterflies long gone. Maj and Mary picked like 'bejaysus', their non-stop quips keeping motivation levels high.

While motivation was high, though, energy was getting low. We needed sustenance: with a crunchy organic biscuit in one hand and a brick of organic orange juice in the other, we sat on the grass, chatting and feeling the bliss that comes from physical activity. To motivate the team, I promised wine rewards to the fastest pickers. An hour later we had finished the vineyard and the thought of a picnic drove our hungry stomachs back up the hill against the wishes of our groaning limbs.

Lijda and a friend made a German harvest speciality: *Flammkuchen*. With a delicious yeasty base, akin to pizza with a mix of onions and crème fraîche on top, they are traditionally served with *boru*, part-fermented white wine thought to be good for digestion and health. Our sémillon white, halfway through its ferment, was sparkly and zesty with a touch of residual sweetness, and a perfect match for the *Flammkuchen*. I took a deep draught, then sank my teeth into the luxurious yeasty crust and felt the cool wine relax my tired limbs.

Dave and Amanda Moore, aka Mr Greedy and Mrs Picky, the couple with a vineyard dream, had arrived to help with our harvest weekend and to learn winemaking with Seán for a couple of weeks. Our horror stories of frost-damaged yields and renegade drivers had not put them off. The farm north of Saint-Émilion that they hoped to buy was progressing, but was held up by a classic French-property transaction hitch – multiple family members unable to come to agreement.

I stuck my head around the winery insulation curtain to see Seán, Dave and Ian hoist the last harvest fruit from bin to vat.

'Try this,' I said, passing them three slices of *Flammkuchen*. 'With a sip of fermenting sémillon, it will change your life.'

They laughed and wiped their hands on their trousers to remove the juice before taking the slices.

'We need it!' said Dave. 'Bring more. This won't touch the sides.'

He was wearing his Mr Greedy T-shirt. I laughed and wondered just how many of those shirts he had. We had discovered that he was known for lifting food from kids' plates if there was a hint they weren't going to finish it. It had become a joke that the kids preferred not to sit next to him, especially if the food was something they liked.

'But won't you take a break for lunch with us?' I asked.

'We'll be here a while,' said Seán. 'We've finished loading but now there's all the cleaning. We must do it now or the juice will dry and be a nightmare to clean.'

'I'll bring sandwiches. *Courage les gars*!' I said, closing the curtain behind me.

At tables and chairs set out under the trees in the garden, Brigit and Amanda served cups of hot soup and laid out a feast of quiche, salad, bread, cheeses and pâté while I served wine just as fast. Our first vine-shareholder harvest day was going off in style: wonderful people, great grapes and good food, with wine and conversation flowing.

Remembering my promise, I ran back to the winery with a plateful of baguettes slicked with different cheeses and pâtés. 'About time!' said Dave, acting out a faint from hunger.

'You forget about us, did you?' said Seán.

'Better late than never,' said Ian.

'I'll be sure to keep you some apricot tart,' I said, focusing on the positive and avoiding admitting that I had momentarily forgotten them in the frenzy of serving lunch... I consoled myself with the fact that I myself hadn't had time to eat and ran back to prepare coffee and tea for the guests.

As the stragglers left the picnic site, I felt shattered. The fellas finished in the winery and we gathered for a cup of tea and apricot tart to dissect the day. The combination was a delectable reward after the non-stop activity; made all the more satisfying by the people collected on the pine chairs around the old table. As I made notes about ideas for the following year I felt deep happiness and a sense that this was the start of something important for us.

Phase one of the harvest weekend was complete and phase two was soon to begin: our first official harvest dinner, to be held at Domaine de Rudel, a chambre d'hôte at walking distance from us.

After the toasts, awards – for the best shoes, of course – and thanks, I handed over to Nadine, our dark-haired hostess. She served the *entrée*, a courgette and chèvre (goat's cheese) terrine with a tomato coulis, which was matched with our Luminosité dry white, the aromas of elderflower, peach and grapefruit perfectly enhancing the delicate flavours of the terrine.

In south-west France the most famous meat is duck breast. Nadine had prepared it *à point*, medium rare, in a fig reduction sauce as our *plat principal*. It generated exclamations of delight. Next up were local cheeses, including a white, chalky, flavour-packed young chèvre and a walnut-infused cow cheese called Echourgnac, paired with the first release of our barrel-aged white Générosité, made from old sémillon vines and reminiscent of a Burgundy chardonnay. This course is necessary, because the cheese, crusty bread and green salad are guaranteed to aid digestion in preparation for dessert. Our French harvest feast reached its finale with almond and pear tart paired with a Saussignac dessert wine – sourced from a friend since ours was all sold. Like old friends, despite having met only that morning, we hugged each other goodnight then staggered home.

A few days later, sitting on the terrace of the Wine Cottage with the sun going down over the vineyards, we toasted harvest. Two tiny sections of red grapes were left, one planned for Naomi's filming the next day. Seán appeared with a cake flaming brightly to celebrate my birthday and Dave and Amanda burst out laughing.

'I don't believe it!' said Amanda.

'How did you know?' said Dave.

It was Dave's birthday. They hadn't said anything, not wanting to disturb us when everyone was working so flat out. We celebrated our double birthday with a glass of our first-release *méthode traditionelle*, a champagne-style sparkling wine, fresh and fruity with a little brioche note from the second fermentation in the bottle.

'*Très bon, madame!*' said Dave with a flourish. We clinked glasses, set to be great friends.

The next day I rose with a little birthday hangover. An hour later, after a restorative cup of tea, I greeted Naomi, who was immaculately turned out as usual and accompanied by her cameraman. She seemed even slimmer than before, her dark hair perfectly set against her pale skin and open, honest face. Over tea before the picking, she gave us an update.

'It was destiny that I called you and you introduced me to Thierry. I had contacted many other organic growers and no one was interested in engaging with us in the production. Thierry has been incredible with his innovations and reactivity. Just days ago I discovered that one of the principal processing plants for extraction of resveratrol and other grape extracts is in Gardonne. Destiny. What more can I say?'

The factory where they would process most of the samples Thierry had prepared was 4 kilometres from our vineyard. Naomi gave me a wide smile with perfect red lips.

'We're doing an organic show in Los Angeles next March. Would you like to come over for it?'

I almost swallowed my cup. 'Who?'

'You and Seán and Thierry and Isabelle.'

'Wow. That sounds wonderful, Naomi, but the girls are too young to leave and they couldn't come with us.'

'Well, think about it anyway,' she said. 'We'd love to have you there.'

For the previous few years and the foreseeable future we couldn't afford to travel to the next region, let alone another continent. Naomi's offer sounded so good, a chance to see Los Angeles, to explore the wines of California and to see my sister, who lived in North America. But it seemed a step too far for us right then.

The pick that morning was a few rows of merlot for a new red cuvée based on our best berries: hand-picked, hand de-stemmed, and fermented with wild yeasts in oak barrels. Once in the barrels, to extract the colour and the tannin, we foot-stomped instead of pumping over, and codenamed it 'La Feet'. Foot-stomping, or 'punching down', pushed the cap of skins floating on the top down into the juice, and was a more gentle way to extract colour and tannin than pumping the juice over the top. Perhaps the real Lafite wouldn't be happy if we actually used that name on the bottle, but that would be a decision for a later date.

The next day we added a tiny yield of cabernet franc and cabernet sauvignon to the merlot in the oak barrels.

'Have no mercy!' I yelled. 'If there is the slightest hint of rot, throw it away!'

I was ruthless: waiting the extra days for the additional ripeness on the cabernets meant there was rot developing on some of the bunches. Ad and I carefully combed each bunch, rigorously removing anything faintly blemished. Now instead of half the usual yield we had about a third, but the quality was good. It had a wonderful, juicy, almost sherbet-like taste that characterised the vintage for me in any blind tasting in the years that followed.

Given that our old wine press had breathed its last in the thick of pressing the whites, we had to purchase a new one in time for pressing the reds. After some research we decided to purchase a second-hand basket press, one that would allow us to work with parcel-specific small lots in the artisanal manner we wanted. Although second-hand, it was a frightening expense that came with a lead-weight five-year loan.

Dave and Amanda threw themselves into winery work with gusto. They personally foot-crushed 'La Feet' twice a day and took on the larger-scale pump-overs, cramming as much experience as they could into their short time with us. They hoped they would be making their own wine the following year, but by the time they left, their offer on the vineyard north of Saint-Émilion hadn't progressed.

Our third frosted vintage, while small, was safely in the *chai*. With a kernel of friends around us, our roots were finding their way into our community. There was hope in the new opportunity with Naomi and we had made it through the first tightrope walk, balancing harvest and guests, intact. Each day we learnt more about nature and how to work with her. Biodynamics was doing more than changing our farming; it was changing how we viewed the world. But day to day our business was living life on the edge. Much as I loved what we were doing, I knew we could not continue this way forever. Between the vagaries of the weather and the trade buyers, our current situation was too uncertain.

A few years before, my sister had said to me that feeling your life was on the edge didn't mean you were going to fall; it meant you had to find the strength to keep on going. She said if you did you would grow wings, and then you wouldn't fear falling. Deep inside I knew we had to keep going and grow those wings.

Chapter 7
Animal Activists
and Amoureuses

Our laying hens had become part of the family at Château Feely, providing a protein anchor for our home-grown diet. They laid eggs with yolks like the setting sun and a heavenly flavour, so far from supermarket eggs, even the organic ones, that they were like a totally different foodstuff. The band of eight portly cream-and-red-feathered ladies usually stuck together in a tight-knit group.

One day during the previous winter, a dog the size of a Shetland pony had come loping through the farm, sowing chaos and panic. Seán, pruning in the vineyards below, heard a commotion and sprinted up. He saw the dog with a chicken in its mouth disappear below the winery heading for Saussignac village. With heavy pruning gear harnessed around him, Seán was no match for the monster long gone.

We looked everywhere for a sign of the chicken but she was lost. Sophia and Ellie cried bitterly. I felt intense rage at the dog and told Seán that I wanted to take shooting lessons so I could buy a gun to protect our livestock. I was stunned at the power and aggression of my reaction. Now I understood how a farmer could shoot a dog in his field of animals. Protecting the hens was a strong instinct: they were a part of our livelihood, but much more than that, they had become part of our family.

That night as Seán did the final check and lock-up, Blackie the hen – so named for the touch of black on her tail feathers – came limping round the back of the tasting room, near the old ruin that we hoped one day to renovate into a second self-catering house. Seán rubbed his eyes; he couldn't believe she was alive.

On closer inspection she wasn't in good shape, boasting a nasty open wound on her rear where the dog had grabbed her. Seán carefully took her to the hen house, where the rest of her brood was peacefully installed for the night. He created a nest of hay on the wood floor, gave her some water and grain and hoped for the best. The next morning the girls were ecstatic she had returned but we downplayed the chances of a recovery.

Blackie sat quietly and didn't move all day. We considered a trip to the vet but decided the trauma would probably kill her and the bill would probably kill us. We took her treats of cheese and leftovers; she was eating, which was a good sign. The next day she moved a little and two days later she limped out to forage with her friends. Within a week there was barely a limp and the only reminders of her recent trauma were missing feathers and a large scab. It was a chicken-run miracle. We rechristened her 'Lucky Blackie'.

Sunday's comforting routine was a run with my friend Laurence, followed by a visit to our local farmers' market with Sophia and Ellie. Gardonne, 4 kilometres from Saussignac, contained that market and offered such sophistication as a train station, a pharmacy, a bank and a convenience store. But, most of all, I loved the market with its familiar stallholders offering a range of vegetables, fruit and meat straight from the farm.

In summer the tomato punnets were draped with basil leaves that demanded lunch outdoors, and the perfume of the melons reached across the little square, just waiting to be matched with a thin slice of *jambon de Bayonne* as a simple starter. The strawberries sold by a tall and humble farmer had a clean and delicious flavour – the very essence of strawberry. The supermarket ones that I once bought in a moment of madness were so tasteless by comparison that I threw them away. Usually nothing was thrown away, but they tasted so toxic I couldn't even bring myself to give them to the chickens. I had read that strawberries were one of the products really worth buying organic – like grapes and hence wine – since, when conventionally farmed, they contained high chemical residues. I could taste it was true.

As Sophia, Ellie and I arrived at the market one morning in late autumn, the seasonal strawberries were no longer available and instead the delicious smell of farm chickens roasting on a rotisserie drifted across the square on the cold air. The poultry producer also offered uncooked chickens that looked healthy, their skin robust yellow, not the pale, almost fluorescent white of industrially raised chickens. Rows of them lay peacefully in the cold cabinet, their heads tucked neatly around their bodies with their eyes closed and their feet folded underneath them as if they were asleep. As we waited for the chicken I had chosen to be packed up, Sophia tapped me urgently on my side.

'Mommy, do they wait for the chickens to die before they kill them?' she said.

The chickens looked exactly like her friends, the hens at Terroir Feely, except they were dead and de-feathered.

'No, they can't wait for them to die, my Fia. They are raising the chickens for meat. But these chickens had a good life. They were allowed to run around outside, not like factory-farm chickens that are in a closed room, crowded in with hundreds of others, living in their poo, sometimes dying in it with no room to move,' I explained. Seán and I had watched Hugh Fearnley-Whittingstall's exposé of intensive production and it was something I couldn't be party to, no matter how tight our budget. Rather no chicken than industrial chicken.

I took my parcel off the counter and, as we walked away, Sophia realised what this meant. Her face crumpled and tears began to flow down her small cheeks. She grabbed my arm.

'But Mommy, they can't kill the chickens! That's not right. We have to stop them. Mommy, we have to stop the people killing the chickens!'

She was an animal activist with a mission, putting all the force of her small body into pulling me back towards the producer. I went down on my haunches so I was eye-level with her.

'Poppet, if we want them to stop raising chickens we have to stop eating chickens. If people want to buy them to eat then there will always be someone raising and selling chickens.'

As I tried to explain how the world worked it didn't seem so logical. I didn't want to create a scene so I led Sophia and Ellie firmly to the car to help them into their child car seats before the discussion continued. Sophia's blonde bob reached her waist; her beautiful, open face that was usually smiling was tear-stained and held a worried frown. She worked herself into a frenzy that overflowed as we took off.

'We have to find out who the king and queen are and make them stop the people killing the chickens,' she said.

One of the ironies of France is that, despite the revolution in 1789 which led to the demise of the monarchy, kings and queens and nobility are still entrenched in the psyche, the education system and the children's books; even more so than in countries where a monarchy is still in place.

'Sweetheart, it's not a king and queen in France, it's the government and a president,' I said. 'We would have to write a letter to them about the chickens. But even they can't do anything about the chickens. The only way to stop people killing chickens is to convince people to stop eating chickens.'

'But Mommy, we have to do something!' said Sophia exasperated. 'But I don't want to stop eating chicken. I like it too much.'

'You see, my Fia, that's the problem,' I said. 'No one else wants to stop eating chicken either so that's why the chickens get killed for meat.'

'But Mommy, if people are always killing the animals then the animals will turn against us and start killing us. We have to stop the people killing the animals.' After a Gallic pause, not satisfied with taking the animal farmers to the cleaners, she turned on the hunters: 'And Mommy, we have to stop the hunters from killing the animals. Otherwise there will be no more animals left on earth and then what will we do, hnh? Then what will we do?'

This was a nasal Gallic 'hnh?' rather than an American 'huh?' and it carried a good dose of French disdain just in the way it was uttered. Ellie, at three, wasn't all that sure what the stakes were but she joined in now regardless.

'Yes, Mommy, then what will we do, hnh?' she said, nodding her curly head vigorously. I caught her piercing blue eyes momentarily in the rear-view mirror and felt like a criminal in the dock. Despite her tiny size and shy personality, Ellie had a penetrating look that could stop an adult in their tracks.

I decided I had better get the crowd onto another tack, one with a more realistic target than stopping the entire population of France from eating meat.

'At least we eat chickens that have been raised in kind conditions and have had a good life until they get killed. There are lots of chickens that don't even have that for the short time they are on earth. That's what you need to fight for. It's cruelty to the chickens, not the raising of the chickens for food that we should be telling people about. But if you really want to stop animals being killed for meat you have to stop eating meat yourselves and then try to convince other people to stop too.'

Sophia was now crying freely again thinking about the poor dead chickens. Once we got home, Seán, who had stayed behind to garden, was brought into the debate to offer up his version of why people killed chickens and what we could do about it.

'We have to give the animals a good life, respect the animals,' said Seán. 'But you are right, Sophia, we should eat less meat or maybe we should give up meat. If we are not willing to kill the meat for ourselves, perhaps we should give it up.'

We had discussed this many times. We enjoyed eating meat but were too chicken to kill it ourselves. Brigit and Ian Wilson killed their cocks for meat when they wanted to have a Sunday dinner. They didn't cop out and go to the market. But neither of us was willing to do it. I could not imagine killing one of our chickens. Perhaps that meant we *should* give up meat. The beady-eyed analysis of my small animal activists and Seán's reflection made me see the world differently.

Somewhat guiltily, I started preparing the dead chicken I had bought at the market. Within minutes, most of our live chickens were up on the kitchen windowsill giving me a 'we *know* what you are doing' look. The previous time they had done this in such an obvious manner was the day I had brought a roast chicken home a few months before. They stared accusingly in the window and only left when Seán took the bowl of vegetable scraps out to feed them at the run. I made use of every single part of the chicken, down to boiling the bones for stock that we could use over the coming weeks. We weren't ready to give up chicken but we could reduce our consumption with thrift and good practice.

As the weeks passed we ate less meat and became more vegetarian. My animal activists wanted to stop eating meat at school, too. We decided that wouldn't be a good idea since there was no vegetarian option, but we asked Olga, the school chef, to offer Sophia little or no chicken when that was on the menu.

From the age of two and a half, as part of the full day at school, French kids are served a three-course lunch complete with such adult flavours as radishes, endives and olives. On a few irregular lunchtime visits to the *école maternelle* – the pre-school – I was amazed to see the small groups of tiny people talking in a civilised fashion over plates of *boeuf bourguignon* or *poisson pané*. Seán and I felt a hint of envy as we perused the menu provided each month. Not only did it sound good, it clearly tasted really good too. I regularly heard 'This is not as good as Olga's' as I served up my pale representations of the dishes she created.

'Olga: can we get someone fired for being *too good* at their job?' teased Thierry as we waited at the school gate a while later. 'I have had enough of hearing "Oh, Olga's *haricots verts* are better than this", "Oh, this *hachis Parmentier* (cottage pie) isn't as good as Olga's", "Oh na na na, na na ni, na na na." *Ça suffit!* (Enough already!) Can't you do something to make the meals you give these kids *less good*?'

All the parents laughed conspiratorially. Their cooking didn't make the O.L.G.A. grade either. I was relieved it wasn't only me.

Seán took ownership of our 'new' press the day we needed to press the reds: we had become specialists in doing things just in time. As part of the purchase arrangement the supplier removed the old double press.

'I can't believe how big it feels, how much space there is,' said Seán, walking into the half of the winery that had been occupied by the old press and pulling the Karcher pressure washer into position to give it a good scrub down.

As Seán power-hosed, I swept the floor with a squeegee and a broom. Neither was very efficient. The concrete floor was worn and full of tiny craters. There was still so much we wanted to change: the floor needed to be relaid or tiled, the roof and insulation needed doing. At least the wiring had been taken care of, removing the risk of electrocution, a serious threat when we arrived.

Seán finished hosing and moved the Karcher out, then pushed the red chassis of the new press into position.

'Wow, you can move it on your own! At last, something human scale,' I said, feeling it was instantly more us, better suited to the small-lot, plot-specific wines we were making.

The main U-shaped body of the press had a metal plate in the centre that used hydraulic power to press down into the oak cage that was like a slatted drum, fitted over a stainless steel tray that fed the juice out of a spout into a receptacle and then on to the relevant vat. We had purchased two of these cages so we could fill one, press the grapes, and then, when the pressing was finished, the cage and tray could be removed and replaced by the second, which could be pressed while the first was being emptied.

The next step to free up space in the winery would be the removal of two enormous vats – each the size of a minivan standing on its rear, too large for our individual vineyard wines.

That would have to wait until we had the time and money to do it.

Seán had released the 'free run' wine from the vats overnight, getting up every few hours to check everything was OK. With the reds, this step released about 80 per cent of the total end wine, since the fermentation process had extracted most of the juice already. The last 20 per cent would be released by pressing with our new press.

The final quality of a wine is determined by an almost infinite set of factors, of which the press is one. Our new press was the 'caviar' of presses, a basket press. It pressed gently, which meant that it did not crush the pips and release the bitter oils within, and it did not mangle the grapes, which could release harsh tannins that we didn't want either. Basket-pressing is seen by some winegrowers as significant enough in terms of quality to be included as information on their front label.

We usually kept the press wines separate and then mixed them into the final blends as required a few weeks before bottling. They brought structure, body and grip through their strong tannins. There are many different types of tannins. Strong tannins are different to harsh tannins. Strong tannins can be smooth and bring power, but harsh tannins rasp and grate the tongue. For our long-ageing reds, we wanted strong as opposed to harsh tannins. I left Seán to the pressing and prepared to welcome guests for a day tour.

When I looked in at the end of the day after saying farewell to my guests, Seán passed me a tumbler of dark red liquid. I tasted.

'Beautiful wine. What is it?' I said.

'The press wine,' said Seán.

'No way!' I said.

'This press makes a difference,' said Seán smiling proudly. 'We don't get as much volume but the quality is significantly better. *Au revoir*, rustic press juice, hello *jus fine*.' To celebrate, Seán appeared from the cellar bearing a bottle of Chambolle-Musigny Les Amoureuses 1999, a *premier cru* from Burgundy. *Les Amoureuses*: The Lovers. It had a lovely ring to it. I had seen the name a few times in ETS Martin, a wine shop that had become a favourite to visit with wine-tour guests. The name alone made me want to taste it.

I had read that this *premier cru* vineyard in Burgundy's prestigious Côte de Nuits region was about twelve acres divided among thirteen different owners. To put that into perspective, it was half the size of our vineyard then divided into thirteen parts. There were many suggestions about where the name came from; perhaps it was the place where young lovers went to explore their passion. The explanation I preferred was that after rain, the clay of the vineyard would stick to your boots, clinging on like young lovers.

This bottle was one of Seán's secret purchases from our previous lives as professionals in the city. Back then we didn't have a shared bank account and his acquisition of a 'few' special wines only came to light much later when they required several times the capacity of his brother's large family car to bring them from London to Saussignac. It wasn't only Seán who was inflicted with the wine lovers' disease. A newspaper article revealed that many wine lovers had a second, hidden credit card to feed their habit of purchasing wines that their partner would consider way too expensive.

I had seen the affliction in action when two couples from Wales visited Saint-Émilion with me. On a tasting visit to ETS Martin, the ladies made it clear that the Bordeaux wine made from white grapes planted at a *grand cru classé* estate in Saint-Émilion, while delicious, was one of those in the 'way too expensive' category. Saint-Émilion is a red-wine-only appellation, so even if it is made there, a bottle of white cannot refer to Saint-Émilion. With this one retailing at around eighty euros, I could totally see their point. The men tasted and drooled but were not allowed to buy. Mark emailed me the following week with a little secret. He and Peter had revisited ETS Martin without the 'girls' (their lovely wives), had drunk an entire bottle of the forbidden fruit in Martin's vaulted cellar, then bought six, plus six more reds. Though Mark and Peter did own up to the 'girls' later.

Now I was delighted Seán had engaged in his illicit shopping, since Les Amoureuses was a crystal glass of pure joy; a cherry symphony with a hint of coffee and a swish of minerality in the finish. A journalist once coined the term 'iron fist in a velvet glove' for Burgundy pinot noirs and this was exactly that.

Enjoying each other's company at mealtimes was sacred. Sophia and Ellie actively participated in dinner conversations, providing amusing contributions.

Picking up the *amoureuses* thread of the conversation, Sophia said, 'Today Inés teased Pierre that he was *amoureux* with Coralie.'

Ellie looked bashful. Pierre was her best friend. Perhaps she would be a little jealous if he was *amoureux* of someone else. Seán quickly diffused the situation.

'For whom are you *amoureuse*, Ellie?' he asked.

'Juan,' said Ellie without a blink.

'Wan?' I asked.

'Yes, the Juan with the blonde hair,' said Seán. I was clearly being left out of the loop on school affairs.

'As in Juan Carlos, King of Spain?' I asked.

'Yes, he's the one with short hair. The naughty one,' said Ellie.

'The Juan who's best mates with Jean-Philippe,' said Seán.

Ellie nodded sagely and Seán and I exchanged a glance. Jean-Philippe was another 'naughty one' in the three-year-old pack.

Ellie had come home with a few scrapes thanks to him. I didn't want our kid mixed up with him or this new blonde-haired 'Don Juan'. The *Les Amoureuses* in my glass was one thing, that was quite another. I took a long draught. It was light but deep.

'When we make a truly elegant wine like this, we have to put it into a Burgundy-shape bottle,' said Seán.

We were always thinking about the business. Not even this incredible Burgundy could draw us away from it. I worried about our relationship. Since arriving in France we had been consumed by the business and keeping it afloat. Wine was our passion but perhaps making it our livelihood would end by suffocating us as a couple.

We had taken out a loan for the new press, and when the first payment and monthly insurance fee left our account, reality bit hard. It was the end of November and Seán had also signed the contract to purchase the new tractor. The five years of significant annual payments that accompanied it and the new press were a serious responsibility. We still weren't seeing the sort of revenue required to cover them and the other commitments necessary to keep the business afloat. Despite working long hours trying to sell to trade, I was having little success.

The buyer in the chain of wine shops in Ireland that had been a staple for us for two years had left and our relationship with his replacement was not looking positive. She was never available to meet when I was in Dublin. Other potential buyers I contacted in the UK and the US already had Bergerac suppliers and often an organic one from Saussignac. They were not interested in hearing about another. It was a buyer's market; the wine crisis – created by too much supply relative to demand – was in full swing. Over 50 per cent of producers in our appellation were organic, something I loved but which was also proving an Achilles' heel.

When we'd bought the farm we didn't know we had purchased in an enclave of organic producers. We instantly identified with them, despite being foreigners without a clue, and our fears of being left out as newcomers in rural France had been thoroughly quashed. We were welcomed with open arms by people like Thierry Daulhiac, but there was a commercial price to pay for us all being of one mind.

I bemoaned how difficult trade sales were proving when I visited Thierry that week to plan our trip to Millésime Bio, the largest organic wine show in the world, held in Montpellier each year. Seán and I had decided I would do a recce to help us decide whether to make the investment in a stand the following year. Thierry had kindly offered me a lift since we only had one car. He would drop me and a friend, Gabi, who was staying with us for December and January, at our hotel. Gabi planned to explore Montpellier while I did the show.

Thierry and I were seated in his tasting room. Local stone and tasteful tiles were matched with furniture that Thierry had made from 'junk': two beautiful bar stools with dainty legs and old Massey metal tractor seats welded on top, a counter welded from bits of a cast-iron bed and a large desk chair made from a wine barrel.

'Caro, I have found that export trade contacts usually take about three years of work to deliver sales,' he said.

I felt a jab of adrenalin in my stomach. With our new loan commitments we didn't have that sort of time. Selling direct was clearly the way to go; that way, we were in direct contact with the end buyer and there was less risk. But it was a lot more work, and building that would also take time.

Thierry described his experience selling to importers in the US and UK. Despite the apparent saturation of those markets, they were the obvious choice for us, since they were significant and English-speaking. I had tried contacting high-profile large-scale supermarkets like Waitrose, whose literature seemed to support artisanal producers, but for one order of a single wine they needed volumes that were equivalent to double our entire production; clearly not our level of artisanal. Our targets narrowed to specialist importers and small chains of shops.

I had a breakthrough sale to a small chain of specialist delicatessen shops in Ireland that Christmas. They were happy and so were we, but they were relatively small.

The exchange with Thierry was helpful but grim. There was no shortcut in the wine game. It was a play of multiple years, decades, even generations.

Isabelle arrived home as I was preparing to leave.

'Did you put your application in for the aid for the frost?' she asked.

'What aid?'

'FranceAgriMer is offering aid to those who were badly hit by the spring frost. It's not going to cover all your losses but it will help. You have to hurry. I think the deadline is tomorrow.'

The next day I was at the mayor's office as it opened to pick up the form. I filled it in and made copies of all the relevant documents that offered proof that our yields were way below normal, then registered the application with the mayor minutes before the final deadline. I didn't know what the aid package would bring but we needed all the help we could get.

I felt frustrated that after four years we still were not 'in the loop', despite signing up with all the necessary agencies at the start of our adventure. With the plethora of bureaucrats that control the lives of winegrowers in France it was hard to know who to target in the maze. I sent an email to our local federation, demanding they verify we were on the list for communications of this nature. Moments like this made me realise how much we had increased the challenge of transforming our lives from urban to rural by also moving country, culture and language.

Gabi was dark and alluring, of Greek parents, with a naughty sense of humour and a contagious laugh. A friend from my Johannesburg days, she was planning to stay in the Wine Cottage for a couple of months en route to the UK to avoid quarantining her dog, which was too old to put through the trauma. Her beloved Labrador foiled her plans by dying just days before she and he were due to travel. Since all her travel arrangements were made, she stuck to them, thinking the calm of rural France would provide her with the time and energy to write her second novel. But she was struggling to adjust to life in our isolated environment, very different to the exciting chaos of Johannesburg, and she desperately missed her furry friend. A week before Christmas she knocked at our kitchen door with tears pouring down her cheeks.

'I'm so lonely, Caro.'

We walked up for lunch at the Lion d'Or. It was my first girls' lunch in three years. We laughed and talked, enjoying the delicious fresh pasta served by François and Pascale, the couple that ran our local restaurant. Somewhere between the pasta and the pear pudding we decided to start an exercise routine – removing the canes that Seán had cut from the vine trellising.

It was great to be outdoors. All the green wands that had waved delicately in summer were now hard and brown. Clinging to the wires with tendrils hard as iron, they had to be forcibly removed. Gabi's wicked sense of humour changed forever how I would see the practice of *tirer le bois*, pulling the wood.

Despite our exercise routine and the planned trip to Montpellier, Gabi was depressed. The winter weather didn't help, bringing cold and damp totally unfamiliar to a girl used to the Highveld of South Africa. To make matters worse, the toilet kept blocking up. I called our plumbing merchant, the good-looking but generally unresponsive Monsieur Lambert, and explained the urgent situation. To my amazement our old friend Jean-Marc, a muscular and jovial plumber with a shaved head, who had helped us through many plumbing crises in the past, appeared within hours.

'What have you broken for me today?' he asked with the usual twinkle in his eye. Over the years we had been a top-performing client, breaking things like our boiler by not turning it off when the fuel was refilled, or our copper pipes by not emptying them before the winter freeze. Our 300-year-old farmhouse was not like the house we'd had in the city.

He checked the toilet and then began digging into the earth around the pipe. The stink confirmed a significant problem.

'We have to dig down to unearth all the piping between the house exit and septic tank entrance,' said Jean-Marc. 'It will take a long time.'

'How long?' I felt a familiar twist of panic that accompanied each unplanned cost we had encountered since arriving.

'About eight hours,' he replied.

I made a quick calculation – his plumbing rate was almost four times the minimum wage. Without factoring in the stench and conditions of the dig or how many daylight hours were left, I blurted: 'We will do it ourselves. You can come back tomorrow morning and it will be ready.'

'I'll help,' said Gabi.

'No way, you're our guest,' I argued feebly.

Soon Gabi and I were kitted out in our oldest clothes, rubber boots and gloves. We covered our noses with headscarves. When Seán came up from pruning at dusk he thought we were two bandits up to no good. Drenched in sweat and exhausted, we had a new appreciation for plumbers' work. In a couple of hours we were far from complete.

After a day of hard-core pruning the last thing Seán felt like was digging a couple of tons of poo. But Gabi and I needed a break, dinner needed to be made and the pipes had to be ready by morning.

When we moved from the city I had envisioned beautiful sun-drenched vineyards and wonderful wines. I hadn't foreseen clearing blocked drains, digging tons of C.R.A.P. – we never said the word, only spelt it, so the girls wouldn't pick up bad habits – and months of hard labour doing jobs like pulling the wood. At least it was great exercise. I could feel my arms were toned from three hours of digging. We set up industrial spotlights usually in service only at harvest time and Seán took over the digging relay.

Several hours and curses later, the pipes were unearthed, crushed in several places, and the work area was ready for Jean-Marc. The pipes had been laid on a bed of rocks instead of sand, ensuring that this was bound to happen over time with the natural movement of the earth. The work also gave us the opportunity to spot another serious problem: our septic tank was angled the wrong way, sloping towards the house instead of away.

The next morning we debated whether this was a problem that had existed since it was first laid, or one that had resulted from earth movement, but avoided discussing the only solution, which was to remove and replace the tank at the correct angle.

After the previous afternoon and evening's experience, I wasn't volunteering. For a short time we would have to pump it regularly instead. These challenges were part of having a house that was centuries old. As a friend said, 'You don't own it, it owns you.' At least the toilet was back in order.

In the first week of December, after one of the biggest dailies in Ireland recommended our vine shares as a Christmas gift in their weekend's pull-out Gift Guide, there was a flurry of purchases via the Internet.

As the weeks progressed the sales gained momentum; the guide was clearly something people held on to and it kept giving. Not only was each purchase a new potential customer for longer-term wine sales, it was also much-needed cash in the bank. As I created vine shares and photos deep into the night on the cranky old PC and inkjet printer that we had brought with us from Dublin, I cursed and felt relieved at the same time. Each photo print meant a sale but it took about an hour on the dinosaur machine. As the orders kept coming I knew I could justify – and could not live without – a new PC and printer. The vine share that had been a chance new product for us that year had turned to gold.

On the first day of the Christmas holidays I set out bread, salad and ham on the table.

'Ham isn't meat, is it, Mommy?' said Sophia.

'Yes, it is meat, my poppet,' I replied.

'What sort of animal is it?'

'A pig.'

She looked at me like I had sprouted wings, and exclaimed: 'There is no way! I have never seen such a flat pig!'

Seán and I cracked up and Ellie and Sophia joined in. We discussed giving up ham but Sophia enjoyed her ham too much to consider this route. We explained that we must only eat good organic ham to be sure the pigs were raised correctly. Although we had not seen a Hugh Fearnley-Whittingstall-style exposé of the plight of factory-farmed pigs, we knew it was as bad as or worse than the plight of chickens. Pigs were so stressed in intensive farming that researchers were trying to genetically modify pigs to remove the stress gene; that way the conditions could be as horrendous as they liked and it would have no effect on production. Thinking of it made me nauseous.

Something inside me said genetic modification spelt Frankenstein-style disaster. It felt wrong, like feeding cows meat, an act that ended in the horror of mad cow disease. Rudolph Steiner, the founder of the biodynamic method of farming, had predicted that feeding meat to cows would create madness, explaining the science behind it about eighty years before – never expecting it to actually take place. Greed and thoughtless industrial agriculture had taken it beyond hypothesis. I wondered what he would say about this new madness.

Sophia wasn't giving up ham but she had stopped eating chicken. Under pressure from her, we stopped too, including the tradition of Sunday roast chicken.

It was deep winter and being super-busy kept seasonal depression at bay, but for Gabi the intense human and animal contact of her previous life was sorely missing. I knew a dog would help her, especially during the ten days we planned to be in Ireland in February, when Gabi had volunteered to farm-sit for us. Sophia had been asking for a dog. Christmas was around the corner. If there was an ideal moment, this was it.

I had been against our getting a dog, although I loved them, worried that we were not ready for the time and commitment required. We worked such long hours, particularly in spring and autumn, we barely had time for our daughters; I couldn't see how we would have time for a dog. But, on the other hand, we worked from home so we were around a lot. Using this and Gabi's immediate needs as my argument, I quashed my misgivings and contacted a local rescue centre. Two days before Christmas Seán walked into the kitchen and released a honey-brown furball from a carrier box. She ran around the kitchen sniffing and Sophia and Ellie scrambled onto the bench. They had never been around dogs. By the end of the evening they were ecstatic. They made a nest for the puppy with an old baby blanket in a basket. She cried at night and I was desperate to go to her but Seán wisely stopped me. She settled.

In France the dog's birth year determines the first letter of their name and our pup's was D. All dogs born that year would be named with a name beginning with D, the following year it would be E and so on. When she proved herself to be an explorer, Dora, after the kids' TV programme *Dora the Explorer*, seemed apt. In a sheltered corner down in the limestone amphitheatre she stumbled unwittingly into a field of stinging nettles. Stung all over her soft velvety tummy, she sprinted around the courtyard non-stop for almost four hours, double the time she usually stayed awake. We researched cures on the Internet and tried them all, from lavender oil to watered-down urine. Each worked for a few minutes, and then she was off again, circling the courtyard. For all her pain, Dora never snapped, growled or showed aggression. She was honey-coloured and honey-natured.

That Christmas Sophia lost her front teeth and Dora discovered snow for the first time. We had worried that a pup would cause problems for the chickens, who roamed freely in the vineyards and garden; but having arrived after the chickens, she saw them as top dog. Already I could not imagine life without her. Arriving at the Château de Saussignac for New Year with Pierre and Laurence, I felt we too had settled. The magnificent 400-year-old vaulted room flickered evocatively in the light of the fire that roared in the massive hearth as we greeted Thierry and Isabelle and other friends gathered to celebrate.

Laurence fed the hungry children then it was our turn: succulent scallops, seared to perfection, and conversation that flew like lightning. Thierry and another winegrower friend, both great raconteurs, entertained us until my stomach ached from laughing.

This feeling of being part of the community hadn't happened overnight. On Christmas Eve the previous year, I'd found Seán listening to an Irish ballad at the kitchen table with tears rolling down his cheeks. We deeply missed Ireland and our friends there. This New Year's celebration was also the first time Seán dived into the conversation, participating in the fast dinner flow rather than staying quietly on the side. His French had been non-existent when we arrived, but now he felt confident enough to join in, despite spending most of his days in silent commune with his vines and wines. Now we were putting down roots, part of a strong band of friends.

Part Two

Leaf

In biodynamics we talk of a leaf day when the water forces are powerful. It is a good time to plant a leafy plant like lettuce or to use foliar sprays to feed the plant or to enhance the plant's resistance to fungal disease. It is a time when I feel open to new ideas, like water that takes on the aroma of anything that passes through it.

Leaf days occur when the moon is in the water constellations: Cancer, Scorpio and Pisces.

In our wines we find that leaf elements, like fennel or mint in certain reds and fresh grassy or herbal notes in the sauvignon blanc, are reinforced on leaf days.

Our instincts don't play it safe. Trust them.
Jacquie Somerville, www.jacquiesomerville.com

Chapter 8
A Seed is Sown

When Gabi returned from London, she could not believe there was a puppy to spoil. A few days later I had to tear her away from Dora as we set off to the Millésime Bio wine show in Montpellier with Thierry and Gérard, his brother-in-law, discussing everything from the wine crisis to local celebrities. The four-hour drive offered a chance to understand some of the deep undercurrents in our centuries-old wine community. From dirty business deals to love affairs, we traversed the gamut of life. As they dropped us at our hotel, Thierry invited us to a dinner presentation on biodynamics at their accommodation the following night, then proposed lending us his car the following day so Gabi and I could go exploring. His generosity amazed me.

At the show my first meeting was with the Klurs, winegrowers from Alsace. Francine Klur had sent a circular email looking for partners for an organic wine tourism association, inviting interested parties to meet. The website Klur.net showed a vibrant operation similar to ours in its mix of wine and tourism, but on a larger scale and with about four centuries of winegrowing history.

Francine's husband Clément was on their stand, a compact, fit man with an infectious broad smile, apple cheeks, curly greying hair that was receding slightly, and a beard; a dead ringer for Bacchus.

'Francine is flying around networking and deal-making,' he said, shaking my hand.

He offered me a taste of their wine, pouring from a classic tulip-shaped Alsace bottle with a striking modern label. The wine was deep and divine: lime, acacia and a mineral touch like a hint of the sea.

When Francine arrived she talked fast – with the slightly clipped French accent of Alsace that helped me to keep up – moved fast, and zapped from idea to idea like a cauldron of electricity. With Jean-Jacques Paire, an easy-going winegrower from Beaujolais sporting a cowboy hat, we gathered at a conference table and talked about how we could work together to promote organic wine tourism to the media and to clients, tourism products we could offer across vineyards in the association, and how we could share ideas and information on subjects ranging from regulations in France to ecological packaging.

Klur was biodynamic, interesting for us as we prepared for biodynamic certification with Demeter, the same organisation they were certified with. Francine was a powerful force with infinite energy and enthusiasm and a deeply rooted organic ethos. Meeting these two inspirational winegrowers alone made the trip a success. But real success would be selling our wine to the buyers who were patrolling the hall.

Since I wasn't officially presenting I signed up under the name of my tourism website and snuck about to present our wines. I found a few spare glasses and a table in a rest area and organised my space for meetings. Zooming back and forth between this unofficial space and my clandestine cooler box, kindly stored at the stand of a friend, I offered tastes of our precious wines with a glass as spittoon and a surreptitious pitch, one eye on the wine and one eye scanning for show organisers on the hunt for poachers like me.

Although we had rafts of positive reviews I felt nervous when people tasted our wines. I poured tastes of the whites for one buyer and he tasted, nodded, chucked, and moved quickly on to the next. He barely said a word while I was pouring the three whites. I poured the rosé.

'There is more work to be done on that. That isn't what the market is looking for in a rosé,' he said disdainfully after spitting.

'Maybe,' I said. 'Our rosé is always savoury, almost salty, because of our limestone, plus we leave no residual sugar so we can have low sulphites. It isn't your usual semi-sweet or off-dry rosé.'

He appeared to ignore my comments and I poured the reds and saw him proceed in the same manner as the whites. Given the experience of our meeting so far, perhaps no comment was better. I ended with the Saussignac dessert wine.

'I like that. The problem is no one buys dessert wine any more,' he said. 'Let's catch up next year.'

Like hell. I watched him do his rounds and realised his arrogant approach wasn't reserved for me. It was a buyer's market. His attitude made me question again why we should work through the trade.

The afternoon meetings brought another type of buyer. Mary Pawle was an Irish importer and Ivan, her English husband and collaborator, a professional musician. They were delightful. They tasted through the range asking relevant questions about the vineyard and the winemaking as I poured the different wines. Nearing the end of the tasting I poured the La Source red.

'It's our last tasting of the day and I'm not spitting this one,' said Mary holding the glass in her hand like a precious baby.

'Don't worry, Mary, I'll get us home,' said Ivan tongue in cheek. We all laughed.

Seeing how she held the wine, and given the exchange we were having, I knew Mary had respect for the work that went into our products. This was what being in the wine business was about, working hard but also having fun. I felt like I had made two new friends.

Gabi and I set off in Thierry's red *fourgon*, the mud-splattered one that Naomi had had the pleasure of experiencing, to explore the city. As I pulled up to the ticket dispenser of a city parking garage, I spotted a sign with a large warning and exclamation mark '*Hauteur maximum*: 1.9 m'. I was sure Thierry's van was at least 1.9 metres. It seemed a little late for the warning given there were six cars jammed into the feeder lane behind us. It looked frighteningly close but there was no option but to try. With Gabi guiding, I inched forward, praying that we wouldn't return Thierry a cabriolet.

The van made it with barely a centimetre to spare. Still mildly worried that there might be a lower section at the exit to the garage we walked into the city. Central Montpellier spread out from the Place de la Comédie, a giant square surrounded by eighteenth-, nineteenth- and twentieth-century buildings. Standing in the luxury of its grand open space in the midst of the city made me feel good; it was like a great lung bringing fresh air. The city was vibrant with students and well-heeled citizens. The old town with tiny cobbled streets hemmed in close by medieval stone buildings reminded me of parts of Barcelona. A charming, dark-haired George Clooney lookalike at the tourist office helped us discover ways to lose ourselves in the city for the afternoon, and we did.

Inching out of the exit, we escaped the garage in one piece and made for Thierry's gîte for the biodynamic presentation dinner. The accommodation was in a *garrigue* landscape, wild herbal scrubland, surrounded by small craggy mountains that reminded me of Montagu, a favourite place in South Africa. As we got out of the van we were engulfed by the dry herby perfume of the Languedoc, the same notes I associated with her wines.

Thierry introduced us to the group of winegrowers and we settled in a large dining room in the old stone *mas*, farmhouse. Pierre-Abel started with a slide showing a mass of stars spread across the heavens. He then went on to talk about how and why the biodynamic calendar worked and about the preparations used in biodynamics. His presentation moved from a snapshot of the history of biodynamics to the theory and on to his practical experience on his own farm down the road from us in Bordeaux. I was riveted. It was so much more than the scientific reductionist agriculture we heard from the likes of the Chamber of Agriculture. It was an agriculture that realised that the farm was a living entity, not a factory. We had already been using herbal cures like the stinging nettle and the willow to combat mildew, a fungal disease; now we were gearing up to do full biodynamics across the whole farm. Reading books was one thing, but real experience was better. The talk left me fizzy with excitement, keen to return to Saussignac to share the insights with Seán.

Dave Moore 'Mr Greedy', the Yorkshireman on a quest for a wine farm, apprenticed himself to Seán to learn the ropes of pruning for a couple of weeks that winter. Their offer on the vineyard near Saint-Émilion had fallen through, family wrangling over the property having held up progress for a year.

In the process Dave and Amanda had learned more than they wanted to about French property transactions but it had given them the time to sell their house in a market that was a little slow. They had now made a new offer on a farm ten minutes from us. It was progressing so well that Amanda joined Dave midway through his two weeks with us, and we accompanied them to translate their negotiations with the seller's agent.

Chateau Bonté was located on a hill, the courtyard surrounded by stone buildings in need of love. Like Terroir Feely, it looked like it could be a life's work, perhaps even more so.

'You think you have a problem with your septic tank sloping the wrong way,' said Dave. 'This has no septic tank.' He laughed nervously and pointed out of the window. 'The outpipe sends the waste directly into the field out there.'

The only toilet on the property was located in the far corner of the large room where we were standing. The room looked like it was used for everything from drying meat to washing clothes.

But the buildings were beautiful, old and authentic, with original tiles and woodwork that offered enormous potential. Dave's background as a builder was perfect. After looking around the property, we talked through a few final points that needed to be resolved, and we helped to translate where necessary. By the end of our visit all the sticking points in the negotiations were resolved and the purchase was ready to go ahead. Dave was already planning where his new septic tank would go.

Sophia and Ellie were getting to know Dave and Amanda, seeing them more frequently than they saw our own siblings. Chatting over dinner on the last night of their stay, Amanda told me about the Wine Spirit Education Trust course they had completed a few weeks before. Seán had passed the first three levels when we were in Dublin so I knew a little about it.

'WSET are looking for people to offer their education programmes, particularly outside the UK. You should think about it, Caro. You're already offering your own wine education.'

Like our Kiwi friend Kerry Guy's suggestion that we offer the wine classes and tours two years before, Amanda's words sowed a seed. With the debt repayments looming and sales to trade buyers stagnant, we had to find other ways to make money. The wine education and tours almost sold themselves, while selling wine was an uphill battle in spite of excellent reviews.

Being part of an internationally recognised network of wine schools would be good for credibility and create another revenue stream. But there were some key requirements that we didn't have. First, it was necessary for me to have the WSET qualification, and second, the current tasting room, renovated from a caved-in building soon after we arrived, didn't have a toilet facility and was too small. It could take groups of six but more was a squeeze. I had turned away larger groups for visits the previous year and knew we would have demand if we had a larger space; WSET school or not. A better tasting room would also help sell more wine direct.

Taking a step towards our plan, Seán set about renovating a low stone building next to the tasting-room terrace to create a facility so that guests didn't have to come into our private house for the toilet. Managing the working, public parts of the farm separately from our private family space was something we needed to learn. Setting the boundaries was up to us.

With no previous building experience, Seán elevated the stone walls *à l'ancienne*, raising the building two feet using stones gathered from our fields. Then he constructed the roof and fitted a new door and window in their respective cavities. I was in awe. Seán had transformed from certified financial analyst to winegrower *and* builder.

In the intervening years, within a 5-kilometre radius of us, three winegrowers had died, two asphyxiated by carbon dioxide given off by the fermentation process, and one from falling off a vat. Our new life's work was dangerous. Within a 20-kilometre radius, yet more had died in tractor and harvest-machinery accidents. The local strawberry grower, one of my favourite farmers at the Gardonne market, committed suicide. I was filled with a deep sadness; I read that in our modern economy, suicide amongst farmers was double what it was for other occupations. I also felt very frustrated that the accidents were usually the result of fatigue caused by farmers working long hours because they could not afford help. Like the suicide, they were a result of the environment. In modern farming and rural environments, with the scale required and enabled by machinery, there is less community, making it more lonely; and there is more debt because of the capital machinery and equipment required to survive, creating more stress for the farmer. Building work could be dangerous, too. Seán had learned to take care, but I still worried.

In a forested enclave in the north-east of the Dordogne we bought a composting toilet from an eco-warrior to complete Seán's *chef-d'oeuvre*. The loo was constructed to separate human waste, thereby making it easier to process in an ecological manner. The urine from this special loo and all the grey water from the shower and basin of the new washroom went into a moveable tank we could use for watering plants. The 'dark matter' fell into another section and, since it was kept dry, it did not smell – much. It had to be removed manually every six months and composted for a long time before it could be used on decorative plants.

This new contraption was cheaper than installing a septic tank for a 'normal' toilet and gave us the opportunity to test it for potential use in future renovations. At last guests didn't have to trek to our house. In my sign for visitors I included instructions and the amazing facts that the waste was safely composted to be put to good use, and that each visit to this toilet would save 5 to 10 litres of water compared to a normal toilet. The facts were very convincing, but I didn't know if I was up to the challenge of manual removal of the dark matter – only time would tell.

Seán and I admired the new toilet now installed, then walked out along the small stretch of scrubby grass and rubble between the tasting-room terrace and the cliff down to the limestone amphitheatre. I gazed back onto his renovated building, wedged between the terrace and the stone ruin behind the winery, and was filled with pride. Helen and Derek Melser, a Kiwi couple, had uncovered this area two years before in a Herculean forest clearance that revealed expansive views. At last we were starting to make use of it.

The vines were hibernating, their forces gathered back into their roots for the dark cold winter. Below us, rows of leafless stumps, some like porcupines with their brown canes pushing up in all directions, others already pruned neatly back to one or two, ran down the hill towards the lower part of the valley, a natural forest scrubland we called 'Where the Wild Things Are'. At night the sounds reminded me of Africa, with hooting owls, barking deer and many others that we couldn't identify.

We made our way back from the ruin to the tasting-room terrace.

'But even with the new toilet we still don't meet the requirements for the wine school,' I said.

'How come?' said Seán.

'The room has to be large enough to sit people double-spaced for the exams, and it has to have an anteroom attached,' I said.

'Hmm.'

'I always wanted Helen and Derek's ruin to be a second gîte, so we can't put it there,' I said.

'Maybe we should make the tasting-room terrace into the wine school,' said Seán.

We stepped onto the terrace and I looked out. The views were almost as good as they were from the ruin.

'That's a good idea,' I said.

'But we have to renovate the ruin into an ecological gîte at the same time. We can't do it later as the access will be blocked by the new tasting room.'

'That will cost a fortune,' I said.

'But it will also make good revenue. We have to cost it to know,' said Seán pulling me towards him and giving me a hug. We stood for a moment and looked out at the vines together, feeling that this could be the start of an exciting new step in our adventure.

Armed with broad estimates from a few local artisans, I created a spreadsheet. It revealed that with the second accommodation unit, and more visits and sales from a new tasting room, we could turn the corner. We might just say goodbye to the knot of financial angst that had been a companion since arriving in France almost four years before. The ideas took form in our minds: a lodge within the stone walls of the barn ruin and a new tasting room backing on to the current one and taking the place of the terrace. The two ideas burgeoned like two leaf buds at the top of a rooted seed. It sounded like nirvana, but it was hard to see how the two buildings would be financed.

Setting aside that problem, I looked into getting my WSET qualification for the wine school. Some study followed by an intensive course and exam – if I passed – combined with the wine educator course would qualify us to offer the courses that made up the first two levels for WSET. I made an inquiry about availability for the end of the year.

Seán's new tractor arrived. Along with a significant outflow of cash, its arrival meant we could plant the acre of cabernet sauvignon in the old peach field. We had money to make the first payment on the tractor and the deposit on the new vineyard plantation, thereafter was a hole that led to red.

Farmed organically and biodynamically, our new vines could live for a hundred years. They could be there for our great-grandchildren. We needed to be sure we were choosing the right thing. Vines, like many fruit trees, are grafted, and the specific fruit varietal you want is implanted into the ideal root for your soil, a different strain of the same family of plant. When choosing vines, the winegrower must select the specific clone – or pre-clone cutting, as we would discover – of the varietal, the specific rootstock necessary, and the nursery to supply it.

Cécile, the vineyard advisor who had helped us survive our first few years, stopped by to talk us through the options. She was supportive and friendly, and had dark curly hair and bright eyes. We sat down together at the old pine table in the kitchen, the heart of our house, where all our key discussions seemed to take place.

'You see, Seán, Caro, you need to look carefully at the qualities, the pros and cons for each of the clones available for the varietal you want,' said Cécile. 'Are you sure you want cabernet sauvignon? Perhaps you should consider cabernet franc?'

Seán shook his head. I explained that he had researched extensively and was sure that the small vineyard we were about to plant was the ideal place for cabernet sauvignon on our farm. It was a flat limestone plateau with excellent drainage that received full sun all day and the rows would be planted north–south ensuring even more sun on the trellised leaf surface.

'OK. If you are sure of that, then the next step is to look at these cabernet sauvignon clone descriptions and decide which best suits your needs.'

Her finger traced down the page in front of her.

'You see, this one is bred for volume, this one for quality of flavour, this one for disease resistance. You need to decide which characteristics are most important for you and make your choice. I can leave this document with you.'

'Thanks, Cécile. We want quality first and disease resistance as well. What do you recommend?'

Cécile marked a few clones on the page.

'You also need to select the right rootstock. Given the results of the limestone test, you have to go with fercal. It is the only rootstock that can handle this limestone plateau. Have you decided who you will buy the plants from? Remember buying from a nursery, rather than taking your own cuttings, is *obligé* if you want to receive aid for the plantation.'

Armed with Cécile's advice, we invited three nurserymen to visit and quote for supplying the vines. When we finalised our decision, the lucky winning nurseryman looked at us as if we had three heads when we explained our detailed requirement.

'You want to order three different clones for this tiny vineyard?' he said, incredulous. 'Usually I supply one high-yielding clone for multiple acres.'

We were adamant: we wanted biodiversity. It was key to flavour and to disease resistance. Knowing what we know now, even selecting three clones wasn't enough; for biodiversity we need massal selection rather than cloned vines. This meant for future plantations we would take cuttings from individual uncloned vines. Since the 1980s, when cloned vines became the norm, disease resistance has been dropping. With modern cloning we have lost the biodiversity that helps a particular plant species to stay strong. We still had a lot to learn. Fortunately, it was a single acre rather than all twenty-five.

As we finalised our choice, Cécile announced that she had bought a vineyard of her own about three hours from us and would be leaving her job at the Chamber of Agriculture. We were sad to see her go. She was a familiar figure who had been a patient and supportive teacher through the years. I liked to think she had discovered a different perspective on her journey with us, just as we had been nourished by her technical expertise.

Now we were on our own in the vineyard, as we were with the winemaking. We felt ready.

My clandestine meetings at Millésime Bio in Montpellier had brought us an importer. Mary Pawle, the longest-established organic wine importer in Ireland, was keen to represent our wines. She and her husband Ivan were the kind of people we wanted to work with. Their ethos, ethics, philosophy and size fitted with ours; and, just as important, I really liked them.

This success convinced us to sign up for a stand at the organic 'off exhibition' to be held at the time of Vinexpo in Bordeaux in June. Vinexpo was one of the biggest wine shows in the world, attracting around 50,000 professional buyers. The 'off exhibition' shows that took place on the periphery, like the one we would be part of, were less expensive than Vinexpo itself, but the cost still made my head spin.

With the down payment on the tractor and the deposit on the new vines paid, I worried about how we would survive the next few months. Mary planned to order when she redid her catalogue, but that was a while away. I had to make sales and I had to make them fast.

Thinking about it all one night, I wound myself into a frenzy, ate several squares of dark chocolate, then couldn't sleep. Given the insomnia I decided to continue researching potential importers for the show. I worked into the early hours of the morning, sending requests to meet at the Vinexpo 'off-show'. Some responded but none were planning to be there.

As I descended into a deep depression, however, the pitiful balance on our bank account astonishingly grew. It was the aid payment for the frost-related losses, a silver lining to the panic of that frightening day. The cloud over my head lifted as we pulled back from the precipice, thankful for a minor miracle made possible by Isabelle.

Chapter 9
Roller Coaster

Expressions Bio, the off-Vinexpo organic show, was held in the old German submarine base in Bordeaux, a dark underground venue that felt damp and was filled with a sense of violence and sadness. The bunker was cold and cavernous, the nearly 10 metres of solid concrete roof contributing to the feeling of weight inside. The World War Two U-boat pen felt haunted not only by the violence of what it housed, but by the violence of its construction; I later read that six thousand prisoners of war worked on it and many died from exhaustion, drowning or falling into the concrete. But even before I knew this, I could feel the lingering presence of its history. There was nothing organic or joyful about it and I wondered how it could have been chosen as the location for this show. Fortunately Clément and Francine Klur were on the stand next to mine, offering a lift to the mood and non-stop conversation. We discussed wine, vineyard accommodation, tourism, eco-friendly living and our new association Organic Wine Tours. They were super-ecological, using their apartments as a way to share their organic ethos, even requiring their guests to compost waste.

'I'm not sure our visitors would do it properly,' I said. 'We aren't very good at it ourselves. We leave our compost bucket until it is full to bursting or until the smell forces us to empty it.'

'Oh my God!' said Clément in mock horror in a supremely English accent to tease me. 'We leave ours until it stinks *and* seeps fermenting gloop.'

'*Tiens, autre chose,*' said Francine, interjecting the equivalent of 'hey, and another thing', as she often did, tumbling one thought after another in a frenzy of ideas and energy. 'You should visit us. We'll visit you next time we come to Bordeaux. Everyone in the association should visit each other, it will make us stronger.'

We made a loose plan for us to visit them *en famille* for a week in December. Given Francine's fresh ecological thinking on everything from wine labels to construction, I was sure a visit would be a shot of inspiration.

At the end of the first day I had poured less than half a bottle of each of our wines, about eight tastes, to 'tyre kickers' – people who were there for their wine club, students or – worse – trying to sell *me* something. I discovered the label Bergerac did not tempt wine buyers to stop and taste. On the second day I hid the organiser's sign that had Bergerac in bold and left a sign with the name of our vineyard. More people stopped, but most were looking for wines priced well below what we could produce for.

The kind of low prices they mentioned would only be possible with intensive conventional viticulture, prices that appeared cheap but which did not factor in the long-term cost of desertification of farmland, the pollution of water sources and the degradation of the health, or even death, of vineyard workers.

The large sales I had pinned on the show, critical to paying the looming second payment on the basket press and the balance on the plantation, did not materialise. I didn't even have any promising leads. Meeting the cost of the show alone required selling a pallet of wine – six hundred bottles. At the end of the last day I was thoroughly depressed. The show had been an opportunity for networking, meeting like-minded growers and brainstorming with Francine, but it had delivered nothing in sales.

Seeking wine to drown my sorrows, I left my stand to go exploring. Wandering the aisles I saw a Bergerac winegrower I hadn't met before and introduced myself. Athanassios was a delightful Greek man, another import to the region like us. Stunning to look at, a physique like a statue from antiquity *and* entertaining, he was the perfect antidote to my dark mood. He owned and farmed an organic vineyard in Pécharmant, the 'charming hill' red-wine appellation north-east of Bergerac, where Ian and Brigit Wilson lived. His wines were fabulous and I glugged back with abandon, happy that Thierry was giving me a lift home. I asked my new friend what he thought of the show.

'Never again! I don't need to come here to be insulted by arrogant wine buyers who walk past with their noses in the air or who stop and taste then say, "I like it but I'll never sell it because no one's heard of your appellation," or who want wines for less than two euros. No! A total waste of time! Never again.'

I felt the same way. Selling direct to end-consumers was more fun, faster, and they paid before taking the wine. Trade could be arrogant, as Athanassios said, demanded payment terms of two to three months and even then many required significant follow-up to get them to pay. Applying Thierry's estimate of three years of work to sign them up, only to lose them because the buyer changed, made it even less attractive. But the investments we had made needed to be paid for. Planting new vineyards was expensive. One acre put us back several thousand euros and required loving care for five years before offering a yield that *might* help pay for the outlay if we were able to sell it.

The Irish financial crisis was biting hard and our direct sales to end-consumers had fallen off a cliff. If we hadn't had the vine-share windfall at Christmas and the frost aid, we would have been in dire straits. I arrived home thoroughly dispirited. Seán listened to my gloomy prognosis. We had pinned big hopes on that show.

'Don't worry, Carolinus. You'll find a way. You just have to work harder.'

He was teasing me, knowing that I already worked long hours and saw few weekends or holidays. Riling me to anger was better than seeing me totally deflated, sapped of energy by the disastrous expo. I stomped outside to hang washing on the line and tried to gain control over my pointless fury. Only we could make a difference to our future. The state of the market was not in our control but we could succeed by changing the rules. I would not be a punchbag for arrogant buyers.

Like Athanassios, if we wanted to be in this wine business we had to be rebels. We had to stand out and change the rules to suit us, rather than succumb to the rules of a game set by large buyers, a game doomed to be lost by small producers. Wine buyers were only reacting to the market conditions of too much supply.

I dumped my bag on the bed in my makeshift office, threw my paltry contact notes onto the desk in disgust, then logged on to check my emails. Sitting at the top of the inbox was an email from Damien, the wine buyer for the small chain of delicatessens that had bought from us before Christmas. My heart sank: it had to be a problem. Through the years I had found that wine buyers seldom emailed to express niceties alone, and never for unsolicited orders.

Proving me entirely wrong, the email contained an order for four pallets of wine – a significant chunk of our annual production. And the shops were chic, exactly the kind of places we wanted to be associated with. I let out a whoop of glee. Usually orders were the result of months or years of information and negotiation. The order would pay the looming press loan repayment, the balance on the new vines and some.

In the positive glow of Damien's order, I signed myself up for the WSET Level 3 course for late autumn. Passing the exam would take us a step closer to being qualified to run a wine school.

Over the next few days we planted our first new vines, the acre of cabernet sauvignon, taking care to time it with the planting time zone defined by our biodynamic calendar. The Maria Thun calendar plotted the movement of the moon, stars and planets relative to the earth over time and we could use this information to determine the ideal moment to do different work in the vineyard. The transplanting zone was a two-week period per month during a descending moon. This is the ideal time to transplant – what we were doing when we planted new vines – because when the moon is descending the sap of the plant rises less, thus it will be less stressful for the plant and it will recover and re-root faster.

Talking to Gérard Cuisset, a long-time organic convert, a few weeks later, he said: 'We planted a field of vines last year; half of it at the right moment during the planting zone, then we had an urgent order so we stopped for two days and then continued with the other half. By that time we were outside of the planting zone. The difference was incredible. The half planted at the right moment took beautifully; the other half is not looking good.'

Two years later Gérard started the process towards biodynamic certification, making us two in Saussignac. Our own certification was well into its first year at the time. We had welcomed the Demeter certification representative a few weeks before. He was impressed with our free-ranging insect-eating chickens and with Seán's vineyard work, and particularly interested in our experiments with the Maria Thun compost in the vegetable garden. We had planted cabbages on one side of the garden path in simple composted cow dung, and on the other in the Maria Thun compost that Seán had made by composting the same cow dung with the biodynamic preparations inside old oak wine barrels dug into the ground. The resulting cabbages were like night and day. In the standard compost the cabbages were leggy and spotted with fungal disease and holes from insect attack, and in the barrel compost the cabbages had tight heads and were healthy and disease- and insect-free. It was so stark it seemed like witchcraft, but it was about the food value of the compost for the plant. The preparation-boosted compost was like a healthy vitamin drink and the straight cow dung merely left to break down for a year was more akin to a sugar-water carbonated drink.

After the formal checking of the paperwork for our certification and a tour of the vineyard, he joined us for lunch and we exchanged ideas as we crunched on coleslaw and home-made bread. We needed to find better ways to dynamise and spray our preparations. We were mixing by hand and Seán was spraying them with a 50-litre copper backpack on his back. After doing 10 hectares like that, he needed a week off to recover. Our Demeter man promised to send us information sheets on alternative solutions.

Our cabernet sauvignon plantation was a major milestone. If Seán's analysis of the location was correct, the vineyard would produce stunning wine in a few years. We were excited.

Now the vines were planted, they needed love and water. There was no irrigation allowed in an *appellation d'origine contrôlée* in France once the vines were producing fruit. Watering was allowed on young plants pre-fruit only, so there was no point in a permanent irrigation system. In the blistering heat we watered 2,500 baby vines by hand. Seán drove the tractor at a snail's pace with a vat of water on the forks at the back, stopping every few metres and I watered with a hose behind. This slow and painful method was the most efficient we could devise.

The main thing we had to be careful of now was the rabbit problem; the nurseryman had told us that rabbits were a catastrophe. They could wipe out a vineyard in a night.

'Should we get an electric fence for the vineyard?' I said to Seán, wiping the sweat from my brow as we turned into the last row nearest the treeline where the rabbits hung out.

'Dora is our secret agent,' he said, pointing.

To the horror of Sophia and Ellie, Dora had a baby rabbit in her mouth. It was gory but better than losing a vineyard investment worth thousands.

Summer brought ferocious heat, a blur of visitors and gîte guests, the rapid approach of our fourth harvest and an email from a Niall Martin in Dublin. He asked if he could stay in our gîte, learn about harvest and film it to use in a show for the Irish national broadcaster. I tried to contain my excitement: a slot on television would be the marketing coup of our vineyard's short history.

The Christmas gift article had doubled the guests booked for our harvest weekend. It would stretch the boundaries of my event-organisation skills. I wasn't complaining. We needed the bumper turnout and the sales it would generate.

The bottling costs always left the account early summer, giving us a nasty shock no matter how much planning we did for it. Our most significant outgoing of the year, it was frightening but necessary. While a million-bottle, bulk wine operator could bottle a wine for a third of a euro, for an artisan outfit like us, a quality bottle, label and cork cost a euro or more.

Bottling involved a minefield of decisions. The five dry components – bottle, cork, capsule, label and box – needed to be specified and ordered, plus mountains of paperwork for each individual wine had to be filled in, all within specific time limits.

The cork alone offered myriad choices, from plastic to metal to real cork, and then within these categories even more choice. I was constantly asked about the cork versus screw cap question in the tasting room.

As organic producers, we couldn't consider plastic, the cheapest option, or screw cap, not so cheap but with elements we didn't want. Screw caps are metal and not, therefore, a renewable resource, whereas cork is. The metal cap is also usually lined with a plastic inner. As with the plastic cork, this is bad for long-term storage as the wine can take elements from the plastic over time, not just taste but potentially dangerous chemical elements like endocrine disruptors. For wines that are going to age in the bottle like ours, we absolutely could not select either of these.

Cork is harvested every seven to eight years from trees that live for hundreds. Not only is it renewable, but buying it encourages growth and maintenance of forests, important for our planet's ecosystem. For wine quality, cork offers breathability that allows the wine to age optimally. The key negative with natural cork is the potential for cork taint, caused by bacteria; making wine smell of wet dog or damp basement. To combat this we bought DIAM corks, manufactured using a process that guaranteed no cork taint and Forest Stewardship Council (FSC) approval. Each year at bottling we reconsidered all the options and latest research but came back to this one. The price of the stopper alone could run to over a euro for a high-quality natural cork, compared with a couple of *centimes* for a plastic one. The corks we used constituted about a third of our bottling costs.

The wine was selling well with the chain of delicatessens but they had enough stock that they wouldn't be reordering for at least a year. Even with professional buyers like them and Mary Pawle in the pipeline, we needed another boost to the direct sales to keep our boat afloat. Niall's television show could be it. I replied with a casual suggestion that our harvest weekend would be the ideal time to visit.

Chapter 10
The Last of the Summer Wine

The mist was thick outside my window as I sat drafting *Grape Expectations*. I had a few children's book manuscripts in the bottom drawer and dreamed of being published. Seán's gift of *The Maeve Binchy Writers' Club*, a how-to guide for new writers, provided the motivation for me to get on with the manuscript that had been in draft since we had our first firm thought about moving to France. Now each morning from 5.30 a.m. until the house woke at 7.30 a.m., I relived the previous years, marvelling that we were still on the vineyard after such a precarious journey.

Taking a break from writing, I opened my emails and found Niall's reply. He loved the idea of filming the harvest weekend. Within a few weeks he had flights booked, a cameraman organised and it was all systems go.

Now there was even more pressure for the harvest weekend to be a success. I threw myself into planning mode. Laura Bolt, a young chef I'd met at Ballymaloe Cookery School in Ireland when giving a talk on wine and biodynamics a few months before, volunteered to do the picnic. Brigit and Ian agreed to cater the dinner. I booked the magnificent main hall of the Château de Saussignac, owned by the commune and available to its inhabitants for the entire weekend for the cost of a dinner out, and clicked it off my to-do list.

On the Friday of the harvest weekend, the murmurs of a waking household tore me from my writing. Ellie still needed help getting ready for school. Laura and I skipped from recipes to notes of what we needed to buy to timing as I served Ellie's breakfast and crunched on organic home-made muesli and yoghurt. In a whirl the girls were gone and Laura and I were flying along the Route des Coteaux to Bergerac, a million checkpoints flashing through my brain like lightning.

Shopping done, we installed tables, chairs, settings and candles in the chateau and prepared as much as we could for the picnic, then Seán raced me back to Bergerac to collect the minibus for the TV crew.

As I drove to Bordeaux along the familiar D936 that ran through Castillon and passed Saint-Émilion, I mentally checked through the weekend plans again. The mist of the morning had lifted and autumn sun bathed the vineyards along the route in gold. On the hills of Saint-Émilion, hand-picking crews scuttled up and down the rows like ants. Machine harvesting had almost totally replaced humans in the rest of the Bordeaux vineyards. Only the most prestigious could afford the luxury of hand-picking, given the minimum wage, and yet, ironically, it could help solve the grave unemployment situation in France if the practice were widespread.

My mind drifted to the wine tours I had done that year. I had met wonderful Saint-Émilion characters through them and got to know the appellation almost as well as my own. The tours were becoming a lifesaving revenue stream, a fulfilling aspect of what we did and a way to share our organic ethos.

Arriving at Bordeaux airport, I found the Aer Lingus flight from Dublin had landed. Maj and Mary were the first to burst through the security doors. I felt warmth flow through me. We had only met once, the previous harvest weekend, but, along with the other second-timers in the group, they were more friends than clients. I loved this convivial aspect of wine, how it brought people together. Two men loaded down with filming equipment came next: Niall and Ronan Hand, his cameraman. They gripped my hand firmly in turn and I introduced them to Maj and Mary as Ronan unpacked his camera. He filmed the arrival of the rest of the group and the hustle of suitcases and banter that ensued. Then, walking backwards down the glass corridor to the parking exit, he filmed us as we made our way out and chatted excitedly about the plans for the weekend. I led the throng through the car park to the minibus and packed the suitcases, doing a quick mental check that I hadn't forgotten anyone or anything. I felt a little overwhelmed and we hadn't even got out of the airport.

With Ronan sitting next to me filming and Niall behind me talking non-stop accompanied by a stream of wisecracks from Maj and Mary, I tried to tune out to concentrate on leveraging the bus out of the car park and pointing it in the direction of Saussignac. Getting film crew and clients lost in France would not be a good start to the weekend.

The cobbled main street of Saint-Émilion signalled the last leg to Saussignac, a road I could drive blindfolded I had taken it so many times. Ronan wanted to capture the bus leaving Saint-Émilion. I turned the cumbersome minivan around and took off again three times so he could catch the rear end and the sign in the perfect shot. My nervousness rose with each turn. I was unfamiliar with the large vehicle and I needed to get home to continue preparations for the harvest day.

But Ronan knew what he was doing; third time lucky he captured the perfect shot that formed part of the trailer for the television show.

Laura had taken over as majordomo, leaving Seán to his all-consuming winery work. The house was peaceful, the girls' homework complete. The guests were settled into their accommodation nearby and making their own plans for the evening, leaving family and film crew to the dinner of lasagne with cream, home-grown *potimarron*, a gourd-shaped bright-orange pumpkin with a sublime nutty flavour, and home-grown walnuts that Laura had concocted. Seated cosily around the kitchen table with Niall and Ronan, candles flickering, we toasted good health, fine food and the harvest weekend with our *Générosité* white, then tasted in silence before recommencing our chatter in hushed tones to match the heavenly food.

Ellie was wary of men except her papa but there was an instant connection with tall, handsome, charming Ronan. There was magnetism about him. Soon all the girls, not only the small ones, were hanging on his every word. When Sophia and Ellie went up to bed, Ellie asked if her 'adult friend' could come up to say goodnight. Ronan's charisma had won her over in a couple of hours.

Before dawn, Niall and Ronan were crunching across the gravel of the courtyard, setting up the camera to capture sunrise over the vineyard. I brewed strong coffee and we planned the day. They would accompany me to our local bakery to collect the bread and apple tarts, then film Seán demonstrating how to pick; then it would be freestyle. En route to the bakery, Ronan's camera over my shoulder, I drove and talked non-stop about our love of France and being winegrowers despite the challenges we had encountered.

'You're a natural!' said Niall as we parked at the *boulangerie*.

It was easy to talk about our life and our passion. As we left the bakery loaded with twenty-five baguettes and two enormous apricot tarts, the next shopper raised his eyebrows and said: '*Oh la la, il y a du monde!*' (Oh my, oh my, you have a lot of guests!)

He was right: fifty to be exact. Ashley and Rob, the couple that had buoyed me up at a low point soon after the frost, were with us for their first harvest weekend. We embraced warmly. Golden sun chased the wisps of mist away as the rest of the pickers arrived.

Seán demonstrated how to pick and we were off. Running up and down the rows I checked quality and plastered snipped fingers while Seán and Dave struggled to keep pace with the processing required at the winery end. Their production line of grapes from bucket to de-stemmer to vat was like a film on fast forward in their race against the speed of our fifty-strong picking crew.

Three hours later all the vines were picked bare and the hungry gang tore into Laura's picnic, a feast of salads that people talked about for days and quiches that had guests clamouring for the recipe. Somewhere in the afternoon's blur was the highlight of stomping grapes to the tune of *Riverdance*.

I felt like I was in a high-speed shuttle. Laura and I arranged the aperitifs in the chateau then sprinted for a shower. Flying back after cleaning ourselves up, we found the guests, smartly dressed in evening wear, already gathered in the courtyard of the chateau. We celebrated the achievements and faux pas of the day with awards and glasses of *méthode traditionelle*, revelling in the hard work and hours of sunshine that epitomised hand harvesting in perfect conditions.

Niall and Ronan put their film equipment away to relax and enjoy. A delicious fig and goat's cheese starter served with the dry white *Luminosité* set the tone for the feast that followed. In the early hours, we all exchanged a high-five before Laura and I delivered a heavy load to the recycled-glass containers behind the chateau.

As the weekend progressed I realised that Niall was worried that, despite our Irish ancestry and citizenship, perhaps we wouldn't be well received by the *RTÉ Nationwide* audience since we didn't have Irish accents. He said nothing direct, but I understood the momentary concern I had seen flash across his face when he asked about our background on our trip from the airport.

I was beyond exhausted; managing the event for a group of fifty people, coupled with the pressure of the film crew, had drained my usual energy. We finished the cleaning and clearing and I fell into bed to sleep like the dead.

The following evening was so deliciously warm that we sat on our terrace, the vineyard and valley stretched below, as we chatted with Mary Kennedy, presenter of *Nationwide* and an Irish celebrity. Niall had organised her trip to Bordeaux to film the vignettes that would set the scene for the show. The weather kept playing ball and Laura kept the kitchen rolling, working with Seán to turn out duck breast with home-grown figs and *potatoes dauphinoise*. Sophia and Ellie demanded that Ronan read the bedtime story, his position as Ellie's first 'adult friend' now firm.

Ronan filmed beautifully evocative shots of Seán punching down our red wines by hand, a stone wall as background, illustrating artisanal winemaking on a small farm in stark contrast with the factory-size, mechanised stainless steel wine production often portrayed on mainstream television. He ended with scenes of Mary and me chatting in Saussignac, showing off our quintessential French village and its beautiful chateau in Monday's early morning light.

Looking back on the weekend, it had passed so fast and yet been so packed it was hard to reconcile the two. It was over to Niall to produce fifteen minutes from hours and hours of film.

A few weeks later, the red grapes harvested on the vine-shareholder weekend finished fermenting and we dug out the marc, pressed it and prepared to dry our first load for Naomi. Following Thierry's instructions to the letter regarding the strict procedure required to keep them in perfect condition, we took the grapes from the press to Gérard's ovens. The immediate low-temperature slow drying meant the skins would keep their food value and stay in food-grade condition for years.

Seán was having one of the most difficult years ever in the winery. With our natural-winemaking and minimal-intervention approach, the high sugar and low acids of the vintage had created some problems. He clumped into the kitchen in his heavy winery boots looking haggard.

I passed him a print of the latest analysis just in on email from the laboratory, a little knot of anxiety in my stomach. Natural yeast struggles to work at high alcohol levels so, with the high sugar levels that year, the yeast wasn't always able to finish its job of fermenting the wine. Seán, therefore, had vats that had stopped fermenting part way through the process.

'Thank God the *pieds-de-cuve* are working,' said Seán, quickly assessing the numbers set out in neat columns on the sheet. When we first arrived we had little clue about what they meant, but now reading the details was quick, almost instinctive.

Three vats had stopped fermenting and needed to be coerced into continuing. To restart the fermentation Seán had taken a small amount from each of these vats and placed it into new containers. To these he added cultured yeast to encourage the wine to restart fermenting. Once he was sure each small batch was fermenting actively he increased the batch gradually, checking that the fermentation had taken properly with each addition before adding more. This process, called creating a *pied-de-cuve* (literally translated as 'the foot of the vat'), took almost constant observation and regular laboratory analysis, as well as hours of pipe-work to control the temperatures and regular changing and cleaning of vats to accommodate the changing volumes.

'Oh feck!' said Seán after turning over the page to look at the analysis of the other vats. 'The volatile acidity on our biggest vat of red has gone through the roof.'

I felt a jab of fear in my stomach. The volatile acidity, or acetic acid, had rocketed – our wine was turning to vinegar. We researched the problem deep into the night, thinking we would lose it all. Along with learning about what we could do, we discovered that, if arrested in time, this acidity could add complexity to a high-quality wine. The hallowed 1947 vintage of Cheval Blanc, a *premier grand cru classé* in Saint-Émilion, was widely recognised to have a high level of volatile acidity. It consoled us a little, but we were still worried sick. The following day I called Thierry for his advice.

'You must stop it as fast as you can. Give it a good dose of sulphur dioxide and sterile-filter it, but *ne t'inquiète pas!*' Don't worry, he said laughing. 'Most winegrowers with a bit of experience have been where you are. You don't hear people talk about it much, though, it's one of those taboo subjects.'

I felt even more consoled but as soon as I put the phone down I went searching on the Internet for a company that could do sterile filtration. We had never done it to any of our wines, preferring to do a light paper filtration, if anything, so as not to damage the wine.

By the end of the week Seán had the fermentations under control and the volatile acidity stable. We worked out that the vat concerned had completed its malolactic fermentation in record time, even before the alcoholic fermentation finished; a far cry from our first vintage, when the malolactic fermentation had taken a year. The lower-acid environment this left in an already low-acid year, coupled with the high sugar content, had allowed bad bacteria to get to work on turning our wine into vinegar. It was an unusual confluence of factors and we would know to take precautions if we ever experienced another vintage like it.

We had arrested the problem by taking Thierry's advice, but we were still on tenterhooks. The level of volatile acidity was just a few milligrams below the cut-off allowed for our appellation. We decided that we would have to sell that vat to a wine trader, or *négociant*, so it was critical that it stayed within the appellation limits, as this would ensure us a higher price on the bulk wine market. We had never sold *en vrac*, in bulk, before.

Seán worked late and started early, doing everything he could to save the vintage. He hadn't worked such long winery hours since our first harvest and the stress was taking its toll.

The worry about our accents damaging viewership proved unfounded. The fifteen minutes of airtime Niall called 'The Last of the Summer Wine' was watched by a few hundred thousand people. Orders began to flow in while the show was on air. By the following day I had so many vine shares to send, I wished for a more automated process. Even with the new PC and printer purchased earlier that year I couldn't keep pace.

Our friend Barry in Dublin recommended writing a programme to take the order as entered on the web, transfer it to a certificate and photo and print it automatically. I said no; I couldn't remember how to do that, and anyway handmade and hand-painted oak signs, each carefully photographed and then printed, were part of our differentiation, what made us special.

Between processing the orders I studied frantically, preparing for the wine course that would take us closer to being a certified wine school. The waves of orders kept coming. As the days progressed the funds grew, at first enough to cover the loan repayments the following year, then the bottling. We began to think of the project to create the wine school and a second gîte, the 'Wine Lodge'. If the orders kept flowing, they could turn that dream into reality.

Chapter 11
Wine-tasting Boot Camp

The sky was a mass of stars and the courtyard silent but for the wheels of my suitcase on the gravel. The week-long Wine Spirit Education Trust course was in Languedoc, four hours away. I was looking forward to the drive, an opportunity to listen to the radio and lose myself in my thoughts.

I closed the car door and started the engine, breaking the silence. A few hours later a magnificent sunrise splashed over the medieval citadel of Carcassonne as I crested a hill before turning onto a small country road for the last part of the journey through the *garrigue* that permeated the air and covered the hillsides of Limoux.

At Domaine Gayda, Matthew Stubbs, the wine-school proprietor, showed me to my room: old oak furniture, a view onto the courtyard and an enormous bathroom that had a claw-foot bath, a large walk-in stone shower and double basins. Luxury! If only Seán had been with me.

I was excited about the course. I had read the textbook and felt ready for the theory, but I was a little frightened of the blind tasting. I dropped my bag and went to have coffee with Matthew and the students, a vibrant group that included a Canadian, a New Zealander, a few Frenchmen and two Englishwomen.

In the classroom we whizzed through a quick introduction then dived into tasting six international wines, setting the tone for the week. We voyaged across the planet: the Americas, Australia and New Zealand, South Africa and Europe; and into lesser-known winegrowing countries and grapes, from Austria's Grüner Veltliner with citrus notes and intriguing hints of pepper and tobacco to a white Spanish Rías Baixas from the Albariño grape with notes of apricot and peach, a luminescent colour that was almost green, and a high acidity. I was learning the definitions of the different wines, and the aspects of wine that helped to define them, two things indispensable to blind tasting. It was fascinating and the time flew: I loved the diversity, complexity and intrigue.

But as the week progressed I became even more worried about my blind-tasting ability, mistaking a Médoc wine from an estate I had visited for an Italian red, and a New Zealand sauvignon blanc for a Spanish white. The stress of blind tasting made me forget to follow my instinct. The textbook knowledge became jumbled in my head. I felt like I was back in final-year exams.

The group were A-type achievers, taking the course seriously; even those doing it for pleasure. The first two nights we ate together, taking our time tasting through the wines, relaxing and enjoying meeting other wine lovers. I offered tastes of our red La Source and our Saussignac dessert wine.

'That's delicious!' said Lori as she tasted the Saussignac. She was my housemate, a tough thirty-something Canadian businesswoman who was filling in a few weeks between jobs by learning about her hobby.

The group was impressed with the dessert wine but found the red too tannic and dry. Taking criticism about wines that were so much part of us was an aspect I found difficult. It was like taking criticism of your children: sometimes useful, but always hard to swallow. Like many reds from our region, it needed a few more years to mature.

Matthew was a great teacher. He was the guru but he was humble and recognised the specific knowledge of individuals on the course, offering the floor to the tall New Zealander when we discussed New Zealand wines, and asking me for my perspective on organic and biodynamic farming. Seeing Matthew at work offered me insight on how to run our wine school. In the evenings I studied with Lori, the blonde Canadian, in the comfortable lounge area of our shared house.

'What is the Hungarian wine known as "bull's blood" made of?' she asked.

'Kadarka,' she answered before I could.

She rattled through another volley of questions machine-gun style, leaving me ricocheting like a punch-drunk loser in a boxing ring. She seemed to know everything, using honed exam techniques from a recent MBA. It was so long since I'd studied for an exam I had forgotten how. I realised I needed to up my game and followed her suggestions on how to fix the info into my brain that felt like it had gone soggy from years of lonely farming and motherhood. I didn't stay late after dinner, and got up early to revise. On the last night we ate quickly then reviewed wine regions and styles deep into the night.

I wasn't confident about the blind tasting, and failing it meant failing the course. To get the accreditation I had to pass the tasting as well as the theory. I phoned Seán and told him I was sure I was going to fail. He assured me I would not.

Despite his assurances, when we gathered for the exam the following afternoon I was a bundle of nerves. Some nerves were OK but too many would cloud my judgement. I told myself to get a grip. The first part, the theory, flew by; though after writing almost exclusively with a keyboard for two decades, the freehand on the pages was unfamiliar and spidery. I wrote until my hand felt ready to fall off, revelling in all the detail that poured out instinctively, the years on a vineyard and the grinds with Lori paying off in spades.

We left the room then returned to find a glass of dark red wine on the tasting mat in front of each place. The format was something we had practised during the week but my nerves still jangled. Getting closer to the glass I caught a familiar aroma. It was a wine we had tasted on the course. The options on the page left me in no doubt and a wave of relief flowed through me. I would have to wait a few weeks to be sure but I was confident I had the right wine.

I felt sad as I said farewell and invited all my co-students to visit if they were in Bordeaux. We had experienced an intense week together, learning and tasting nearly a hundred wines. My journey back to Saussignac offered time to think about the wine school and what ideas we could use from Matthew's set-up. By the time I reached my sleeping household, a vague idea of what ours could be like had formed.

It was good to be home. The Christmas card from the president of the Aquitaine region had a photo of a pristine mountain and lake, followed by a one-liner from Mahatma Gandhi: 'Live simply so others may simply live.'

It was a reminder of what was important: love, health and simple joys; hugging a kid; fetching eggs; feeling good and tired after a hard day's work. We lived in a socialist country where social charges and taxes were high but ensured everyone received a minimum of care and education no matter how little they had. While there were times when I was driven nuts by aspects of our new country, it was helping me see life in a different way.

Overall I was happy. Seán, on the other hand, was frustrated. While I enjoyed a relatively warm office and three-course lunches with paying clients some days, he was knee-deep in winter pruning.

He didn't want to do the trip I had planned back in the glow of summer, a five-day December break at my new friends Clément and Francine Klur in Alsace, followed by two nights in Burgundy. He wanted to be gloomy in his vineyard and winery all on his own. It was a classic case of the man and the cave; ironically the French word for cellar being *cave*. One vat was still fermenting and he was worried about the vat with the high volatile acidity and about finishing the malolactic fermentations on the other reds that hadn't completed this step. We were ultra-anxious to ensure that the vinegar bacteria didn't get a chance to start on any of the other vats. But the trip was long booked and I was keen to visit these two key wine regions. Alsace was the most advanced of all the French wine regions in terms of biodynamics and promised to be a good learning-ground for us. We needed to research equipment and my taste for wine touring had been given momentum by the WSET course.

News that I had passed both the theory and the blind-tasting exams with distinction brought ecstasy – but Seán's grumpiness quickly deflated it. He harrumphed around the house, never speaking directly to me or using my name. Something was going badly wrong. We spent more time together than ever before and yet I felt further from Seán than I had when we first moved in together. It was like we were going in different directions.

I lost myself in work from before dawn to late at night, creating vine-share photos, certificates and letters to keep up with the orders that were still flowing in. On the back of the television show I had secured a few good mentions in print media coming up to Christmas that helped keep the sales rolling. Now in the thick of that marketing windfall I didn't like to leave, but Seán and I needed some time away from the business.

Chapter 12
Snowed-in in Alsace and Burgundy

We took off in pre-dawn darkness, hoping to reach Alsace for a late lunch. The envelopes of the share orders that had come in before nightfall the previous day, a wedge of about twenty, were in my bag ready to post in Alsace. New orders would have to wait for our return; there was Internet at the Klurs and in Burgundy so I could acknowledge receipt.

At Brive-la-Gaillarde, about two hours from Saussignac on the autoroute, snow began to fall. Soon we could only see about ten feet in front of us and slowed to a walking pace. There was no one on the road. The old Renault bought second-hand when we arrived wasn't in prime condition and the tyres were at the limit of acceptable. We had two small children, it was well below freezing and we hadn't seen a person for what seemed like hours.

'What if we stall?' I said.

'Don't be stupid!' snapped Seán. 'Of course we won't stall. Just keep your eyes on the road and help me navigate.'

I was shocked. His harsh outburst chilled the atmosphere in the car more than the weather outside. The next few hours we crept forward in silence, the fresh snow making a strange mumbled crunching under the tyres and the flakes swirling into the windscreen. We reached the gateway to Burgundy after seven hours, a journey that should have taken four, filled the car with fuel, and bought −30 °C antifreeze for the windscreen wipers and a bite of lunch.

Neither of us had experience driving in snow. Every few kilometres we passed yet another accident caused by the horrific conditions. The road news was 'crash central'. Sophia and Ellie were mute for the first time ever on a long journey, frozen by fear and the rapidly falling temperatures. We would be lucky to arrive in Alsace by nightfall. Our lovely holiday – the first in more than three years – had started on the wrong foot and Alsace felt far, far away.

We crawled onward, hoping the conditions would improve, then picked up speed as the sun dropped towards the horizon and we saw the Vosges mountain range and classic Alsace A-frame houses for the first time. The car's atmosphere warmed with the clearing sky. We were on holiday; it felt great to be away, to be in such a different place.

Alsace is a long valley running up the top right side of France, bordered by Germany and a small part of Switzerland. After a turbulent history of ping-ponging between France and Germany for a few hundred years, it is now a magical cross between the two, and totally unlike our province of Aquitaine. Katzenthal, home to the Klurs since time immemorial, turned out to be a charming village a little larger than Saussignac. As Seán parked outside a building with a copper sign that held the familiar spiral Klur logo, a fresh flurry of snow fell.

The Klur winery reception was a masterpiece; glass double doors were nested in a wood-clad arrow-shaped entrance, with the arrow in turn set into a section built of natural stone. The

137

tasting room and reception area looked like it had grown out of the original wood building behind like a living thing.

We announced ourselves to Régine, Francine's right-hand woman, and she showed us to our apartment in the old traditional building next door, where six of their nine self-catering units were housed. It was so beautiful – magical – I felt I needed to whisper so we wouldn't break the spell. Carved wooden stairs adorned with regional Christmas decorations led to a landing sparkling with star-lights, furnished with a comfortable reading chair, an enormous mirror and the door to our apartment. It was an Alsace fairy kingdom.

Inside, the living room was toasty with natural colours, wood panelling, an inviting sofa, a four-poster bed and a thermal mass wood-burning stove sculpted in rounded shapes and earthy tones. The small galley kitchen led to a dining room, shower room and two bedrooms. I put our small box of shopping, bought at the Biocoop en route, onto the kitchen counter. Sophia and Ellie were exhausted, fear having kept them wide-eyed throughout our eleven-hour journey. Spotting curly kale in the box, I grabbed one and put it on Ellie's head.

She caught a vision of herself in the mirror on the wall and giggled for the first time that day. I snapped a photo.

'Me too, me too!' said Sophia.

Seeing herself, she giggled like Ellie and I snapped a few more shots of them modelling the stunning green hats.

We descended the enchanting staircase to fetch more bags and Clément appeared. He gave me a hug and kisses on both cheeks.

'Oh my God,' he said in his teasing proper English accent. 'All this snow! You are not in the Dordogne anymore.'

Feeling instantly at ease in Clément's familiar, positive presence, with his relaxed attitude to the scary white stuff, I introduced him to Seán. His invitation to taste in the winery was manna from heaven, just what we needed to disperse the stress from a day of snowflake hell.

We dropped our bags and followed him through the tasting room into Klur's ecological winery. It was built in a spiral design using the principles of biodynamics and felt like a womb; safe, peaceful and cosy. The central circular room was surrounded by oval oak vats, the signature of Alsace. Some were simple; others had Bacchus-style figurines carved into them and around their taps. In the middle of the winery was a wood-burning stove for natural heating.

Clément drew samples and we enjoyed a voyage of Alsace aromatics. The Klur Riesling was mineral and lime; the pinot gris was tropical and fruity with a lovely richness on the palate; the Gewürztraminer had wonderful lychee and rose notes; and the pinot noir was a cherry bomb. Clément was a tonic with his light touch, sense of humour and a dash of humility despite his heritage and reputation.

We could have stayed tasting his beautiful wines deep into the night but our small girls needed bed. Ellie, usually such an upbeat little character, hadn't smiled since the curly kale. Seán and I went to tuck them into bed, then settled down to chat.

'It is so good to be on holiday!' I said, clinking glasses with him.

'But what are we going to do this week?' asked Seán.

'We have the visits with three biodynamic winegrowers booked,' I said. I had asked Matthew Stubbs, the Master of Wine that took my WSET course, for his suggestions and researched online to come up with these visits.

'But we need to do activities with the girls, this is their holiday too. I think three wine visits is too much,' said Seán.

'We need to see practical biodynamic farms, though, and I need to become familiar with regions like Alsace to run a credible wine school,' I countered, feeling mildly irritated that he didn't show any appreciation for the research and organisation I had put into the planning of the trip.

The next morning I disappeared to catch up on emails at the guest computer. When I returned, Seán was furious; I had been away too long. I was shocked and hurt. I hadn't done anything but respond to the orders that had poured in over the previous thirty-six hours. Clients needed a response. They needed to know their gift vine shares would be with them in time for Christmas. Seán was spitting mad and so was I. Neither of us could see the other's point of view.

I had to get out. Sophia, Ellie and I walked down to Katzenthal's commercial centre hoping to find a post office to post the vine shares and a bakery to buy treats. We left Seán fuming and researching things to do as a family.

Katzenthal was a winter wonderland. The snow covered the contours of the houses like icing sugar and outdoor Christmas trees were decorated with little bread men like something in a Christmas fairy tale. In the bakery, the language spoken by the people coming and going was a fascinating mix of German and French. Loaded up with traditional pastries for a late breakfast, we returned to find Seán simmering.

It was not that I wanted to work on our holidays; it was the reality of owning a small business, the choice we had made. I wondered how much more of Seán's bad temper I could take.

Alsace in December was heaven for kids: Christmas markets, twinkling lights, ice rinks and enchanting merry-go-rounds, where life-sized horses rose up and down serenely to funfair music before a puff of snow was blown into the rider's face as they cantered into the final section. Sophia was ecstatic; she was desperately keen to take up real horse-riding.

With Sophia and Ellie filled with chips and magical rides, we wound our way along the Alsace wine route to Domaine Deiss in Bergheim. The entrance and the tasting room were strangely modern, and I felt ill at ease. The dark-suited man on the tasting room floor was more sommelier than winemaker. He switched on a metre-wide screen and pointed to an interactive map of the different *terroirs* of the domaine. I preferred walking the *terroir* to looking at a screen, but the tasting room and winery were on the main Alsace *Route des Vins* in the town of Bergheim, not on the edge of their vineyards, and this offered a high-tech way to see them.

Mathieu Deiss, newly appointed chief winemaker and son of Jean-Michel, the owner at the time, arrived. I immediately felt better seeing him dressed in wine-stained jeans and sweatshirt, a hard-working farmer rather than a sales person. He was fit, with dark hair and a charming smile and spoke in a quiet, considered manner. Sophia and Ellie settled at a tasting table to watch a DVD, the office secretary promised to call if there was an emergency, and we disappeared into the labyrinthine Deiss winery.

The main pressing room and reception part of the winery was a modern block that felt impersonal rather than the birthplace of great wines. As the visit progressed, though, I realised there was more to them and the winery. Mathieu spoke of their *terroir* and winemaking with depth and inspiration. We descended into an old section constructed of stone, more sensual than the concrete, where oval wood vats aged their white aromatics. Further down, brick vaults that housed *barriques,* small Bordeaux barrels of red wine, felt even better.

'We don't rack the reds, we prefer to leave them undisturbed, in peace to decant naturally and make their maturation journey,' said Mathieu.

Leaving him and Seán to discuss the finer points of red maturation and racking, I dashed back to check on Sophia and Ellie. They were still happily watching a Kirikou animation film.

I found Mathieu and Seán again by following the echoes of their voices. Mathieu explained some of their machinery innovations as we climbed back up the steps.

Back at the tasting room, Mathieu poured a sample for each of us.

'This part of the range is called *Terroir*. It's grapes from fields with mixed vines so the blending is done in the vineyard rather than the winery.'

He swirled and sniffed then sipped and contemplated before spitting expertly into the spittoon.

'What is surprising is that when we plant them together the vines mature together. Grapes that would mature at different rates planted in single-variety fields come to maturity at the same time. It's the power of shared experience, a kind of crowd mentality,' said Mathieu.

We had old parcels for Saussignac dessert wine planted this way. Perhaps the old-timers knew more than we gave them credit for. Rudolph Steiner, the father of biodynamics, had defined the five hormones that drive a plant's activities fifty years before modern scientists 'discovered' them, and it was one of these hormones that created this crowd behaviour.

We progressed through the tasting, offering the girls sniffs of the different wines so they could start to hone their noses for the future. We loved the *Terroir* wines and the two *premiers crus*, Schoffweg and Engelgarten. Each *cru* vineyard had a meaningful name: the 'sheep's road' since it was sited on the route where the sheep travelled in the old days; and the 'angel's garden' where the local children used to play.

We left loaded with a few bottles. I had never dreamed of visiting Alsace as a wine destination until I met the Klurs and took the WSET course, but I was smitten. We promised the girls more Christmas markets, a trip to the ice rink and a visit to the toy museum the following day... and a tiny wine visit in Pfaffenheim in the evening.

It was a visit of medieval magic. From the rustic wood-panelled tasting room Jean-Pierre Frick, a lanky, quirky figure, led us along a set of outbuildings to dive down, down, down, like Alice in Wonderland, into an intoxicating cave of treasures.

Starting with a two-year-old white wine from one of the Alsatian oval vats that I found so beautiful I wanted to hug them, he said:

'I don't know what to make of this Riesling that is still fermenting.'

I tasted and was transported to heaven. The wine was filled with golden bubbles and tasted of apples and nuts. It was the essence of what I realised was signature Frick.

'Each wine is an individual. We let it follow its own pace. This one decided to take a very slow fermentation. We'll leave him to continue and see what happens.'

We moved further into the winery and he pointed to a flowform, a set of specially shaped interconnected bowls that made patterns in liquids as they flowed through, a way of dynamisation, another biodynamic method.

'We dynamise a wine by passing it through this flowform if we think it needs it. It is up to each individual wine, to what it needs. We don't use any additives, very little or no SO_2, no fining agents, just a light filtration before bottling.'

He was like a druid; I was enchanted. As we tasted through the wines I experienced a clear style so unique I could pick it up blind forever after. Years later when I tasted his wines I was instantly transported back to that place where he worked his magic. It was like time-travel back to the day in Alsace when we visited him.

There was much more to Alsace than we had time to see. We would have to come back to explore the things we missed, like Riquewihr, a town minutes north of Katzenthal, where we circled the medieval walls and saw captivating glimpses of a restored heritage centre within but didn't have time to stop. Although Alsace was widely bombed at the end of World War Two, there were a remarkable number of historic buildings still standing.

At Zind-Humbrecht, our last winery visit in Alsace, another biodynamic vineyard with a surprisingly modern building, a secretary welcomed us to a fancy glass-and-steel waiting room with views onto the vineyard. Each of the visits offered ideas for our own project, stealthily forming in the back of our minds.

Olivier Humbrecht, owner and winegrower, looked fortyish and was very tall, standing a good 5 centimetres taller than Seán. We walked out to the sleeping vineyard. Everything was perfect, the courtyard was clean and organised; the vines were neat and well maintained.

Pointing to the soil, Olivier said:

'Avoiding soil compaction is a priority for us. Compacted soil has no air and hence no life. We use caterpillar tractors and equipment that is as light as possible.'

Seán took notes while I tracked Sophia and Ellie running around on the grass. We realised that despite his reputation and that of his wines, Olivier was unassuming. He was one of the first Frenchmen to achieve the Master of Wine designation, a qualification requiring a fine tasting palate and many years of experience and study; he was a mover and shaker in the world of biodynamics in France. Despite this and a weighty family wine heritage, he talked to us as equals, sharing his insights and asking our opinion.

Leaving Sophia and Ellie watching another DVD in the waiting room, we entered the tasting zone, a mezzanine floating above the winery, surrounded with photos of their steep vineyards with such intriguing, hallowed names as 'Clos Saint-Urbain au Rangen de Thann'. Some were more like names I would expect to find in a Tolkien novel than on a vineyard. Zind-Humbrecht created so many single vineyard wines that the tasting table was a sea of bottles.

'We use gravity to move the wine, there is no fining and the wines are usually aged on the lees,' said Olivier as he poured the first sample.

Even with spitting, when we hit sample twenty my head was spinning. It was a rainbow of taste from dry and mineral to sweet and luscious with a diversity of *terroir* that could be seen on the map and tasted in the glass.

We selected a few wines to buy but Olivier would not hear of it, requesting a swap instead. We swapped six bottles of our La Source red for a six-pack of wines equivalent in value to about six cases of ours. I wanted to give him more wine but he insisted it was bottle for bottle: each bottle requiring as much love and effort regardless of the price. He was a gentleman; I felt honoured to have met him.

The timing of our visit to Alsace had been perfect. Seeing Klur's tasting room, the spiral winery, their ecological apartments with sauna and spa, gave impetus to our ideas for our own new tasting room and Wine Lodge. As the vine shares kept pouring in we could see a financial seed for the project emerging. As Naomi would have said, it was our destiny.

Feeling sad to leave, we set the GPS to head south-west to the Côte d'Or in Burgundy. Sawday's *French Vineyards* guide had yielded a B&B owned by Anne Gros, a celebrated winegrower. When I booked the rooms I organised a tasting with Anne for 5 p.m. on the day of our arrival. Leaving Alsace at 11 a.m. for a trip that should take three hours allowed a massive margin, until the snow began to fall. We tuned into traffic news: crash central once again. The car inched forward, the highway jammed with traffic blocked by gruesome accidents. At times we stopped so long we turned off the engine, but then we got too cold. Through the hours the snow continued to fall, making the journey ever more treacherous. I vowed never to travel north again in winter.

At five o'clock we entered a car park in Beaune for a toilet break. In perfect conditions it would have been around fifteen minutes from there to Vosne-Romanée, the village where Anne's B&B nestled alongside *grands crus* Romanée-Conti, La Tâche and Richebourg. In these conditions I estimated an hour. As I hung up from announcing this news and apologising to Anne, Seán pulled slowly into a parking space but the brakes didn't hold in the icy snow and we slid in slow motion towards the neighbouring van. It seemed like minutes but it was seconds. I knew we would hit but prayed fervently we wouldn't. We stopped a hair's breadth from the vehicle and I felt faint, drunk with relief but even more cautious about the treacherous snow.

Witnessing two more accidents on the last stretch didn't dampen our excitement at being in the heart of Burgundy for the first time. Travelling at a snail's pace, we took in the views of the steep vineyards up to our left, home to names and producers that we had only heard of – usually in hushed tones – or read about.

As night fell we came to an unplanned halt. The 20 centimetres of snow was too much for the grey monster: our fat-bottomed Renault refused to go any further. After several attempts to get her out, me pushing and Seán yelling and gunning the accelerator, I called Anne. Fortunately we were only about a kilometre away and she arrived in minutes in a snow-tyre-clad Audi, a knight in shining armour.

Grabbing the essentials and a basket of leftovers from Alsace we leapt into the plush car. Despite the late hour, Anne gallantly offered to do the tasting. The two girls happy in the well-supplied playroom, we descended into her new underground *chai à barriques*, the storage area for her oak barrels. The vaulted space was reminiscent of a cathedral. Anne was intrigued by our story and impressed by our courage taking on a vineyard in France with no experience.

'How many vintages have you done?' she asked.

'Four,' replied Seán.

A look of intense emotion, almost like a longing for a loved one, crossed her face, like she was pining for vintages missed.

'I have completed twenty-two vintages and I wonder if I will have enough time to achieve what I want to with my wines. There is still so much to do.'

We had started late but at least we had started. For all its ups and downs it was an incredible journey being a winegrower. Thinking about it still gave me goosebumps.

With Anne we progressed in our tasting through the 'lesser' vineyards of Hautes-Côtes de Nuits, to Vosne-Romanée, to the *grands crus* like Echezeaux. Seán's wonder was palpable.

I ran back to check on the girls, suddenly panicking that if they took off into the snowstorm to look for us they could be lost forever. All was peace and warm in the house, however, and they were engrossed in toys and books. Locking the door behind me, I returned to taste Anne's Richebourg *grand cru*: a sensation of cherry fruit, spice, rose and minerality that evoked powerful joy and infinite depth. It was a classic, a pinnacle; a wine that helped me understand why these tiny pieces of land called *grand cru* in Burgundy carried such gravitas.

Anne had given up part of a precious Friday evening to share her wisdom and wines with us. We were deeply grateful. She disappeared into whirling snow saying she would ask her cousin to help extract our car from the snow the following day. In a warm embrace of *grand cru* inebriation we returned to our daughters and a cosy kitchen to dine on leftovers and read the feast of Burgundy wine books.

The blizzard did not stop the Côte de Nuits *boulanger*; we found croissants and baguettes in the baguette box outside the front door in the morning. A glance at the road confirmed that *we* weren't going anywhere in the car, though. The forecast on the Internet made it clear we weren't leaving the next day either. Madame Gros, Anne's mother, opened the front door in a blitz of snowflakes and introduced herself. I asked if we could stay an extra night or two.

Research on our laptop showed no shops or restaurants in Vosne-Romanée and we needed to eat, as the leftovers from Alsace were wearing thin. Seán set off valiantly to search for the nearest food shop. After a long, cold walk he bought key supplies in Nuits-Saint-Georges. As he loaded them into our backpack at the checkout someone tapped him on the shoulder.

'You're courageous,' said Madame Gros with a smile. 'But I think it will be better for you to take a lift with me back to the house.'

Michel, Anne's cousin, was ready to pull the grey monster to safety with his 4x4 when they returned. He towed it up and Seán parked in the yard. We still weren't going anywhere, but at least we had our gear.

Although the sun was out, snow was falling; flakes like a million floating sparkles suspended over the white-blanketed vineyard. Wrapped up warmly with hats, scarves, gloves and thick coats, we walked up the lane that led from Anne's B&B to the vineyards, passing the entrance to Domaine Romanée-Conti, one of the most hallowed wine estates in the world, en route. Within a few minutes we were in the vines.

The stone walls were stark, the famous names etched on them edged in frost: Richebourg, La Tâche, Romanée-Conti, Romanée-Saint-Vivant. The stalwart vines within were reaching for the sky but drawn back to the earth by the onset of winter. Snow-clad vineyards ran to our left and right, surrounding the village of Vosne-Romanée below us, and smoke wisped out of chimneys in the snowy roofs of ancient stone houses. There was something exciting about discovering these world-famous vineyards in snowy glory; no one but us in the white silence. Ellie and Sophia ran off up the hill and we followed, revelling in the view over the Côte de Nuits.

That evening as I cooked Burgundy-style meatballs that would be perfect with one of Anne's pinot noirs a little later, Seán spluttered a mouthful of her *Hautes Côtes de Nuits Blanc Cuvée Marine* chardonnay across the table. He pointed to a photo in the guide he was reading.

'That was THE Michel Gros that pulled me out of the snow.'

In the book we discovered he was recognised as one of the top producers in Burgundy.

'He was such a nice guy. He seemed genuinely pleased with the bottle of La Source I gave him as a thank you. I feel so inadequate,' said Seán.

We laughed. Being snowed in, we were meeting the who's who of Vosne-Romanée. That evening we enjoyed Anne's divine wine, pleased there was no chance of it running out while we were staying at the vineyard. She had a waiting list of clients wanting to purchase, and I promised myself one day we would be like that.

When the snowstorm eased enough to step outside we made a snowman, setting a carrot as the nose and two pebbles as the eyes. Two days later we had explored everything that could be reached on foot with two young children and I began to feel trapped; desperate that we were so near and yet so far from the biodynamic growers I had hoped to see.

Each day I logged in to find more vine shares had mounted up, adding to the pile that had been building since we left. With Christmas now days away, the chances of buyers receiving hard-copy photos of their rows in time was remote. My stress rose with the centimetres of snow, matched by Seán's stress about the difficult vintage he had in the winery and the pruning of the vineyards: each day signified lost opportunity. Madame Gros said it was the worst winter she could remember.

By the time the roads were declared safe and we could escape, we were like two wild animals that had been trapped in a cage rather than relaxed after a holiday away. Back home, we dived into our work. We were both worried about our respective responsibilities; he to make wine in this difficult vintage and I to make sure our clients got the gift vine shares they had ordered for *Christmas* and not for New Year. To cap things off, the heating had stopped while we were away and one of the pipes had burst.

Something, I don't even remember what, then sparked the worst fight we had ever had. It was a culmination of everything that had been building, and we lost the plot. It was the first time we had fought so ferociously in front of our two daughters. I was crying, they were crying and Seán slammed the door and disappeared into the cold, black night.

I tried to comfort the girls, but we were shaken to the core. I retraced the build-up to the explosion, trying to work out what had happened, but could not. Since moving to France we had been so consumed with keeping our business afloat that we had not taken care of our relationship. Now the success of the vine shares had put us onto a positive financial footing and things should have been better, but instead they were worse. Perhaps it was our feelings of inadequacy from meeting winegrowers who were confident and at home, their families having grown wine on their vineyards for hundreds of years; perhaps it was simply years of relationship neglect. Whatever it was, something had tipped us over the edge.

The fight destabilised our daughters' world and was indelibly etched on their memories. They saw that no relationship was safe; even one that appeared strong like ours could dissolve. I buried myself in vine shares and Seán disappeared into long days of pruning in the vineyards to catch up on the time away. With the memory of the fight like a wall between us, we prepared for Christmas.

Dave and Amanda Moore's purchase of Chateau Bonté was finally going through. Expecting to be settled in France by February, they generously offered to look after the girls and Dora so we could take up Naomi's invitation to visit California with Thierry and Isabelle in March. I was torn. Our girls were still very young. Ellie was five and Sophia nearly seven, but it was a once-in-a-lifetime opportunity.

Naomi had offered to pay our airfares to Los Angeles and hotel and expenses for the show. It was a chance to visit the Napa Valley and Sonoma wine regions, and to see my sister whom I hadn't seen in years. Confident in Dave and Amanda, and knowing that Sophia and Ellie would be only too pleased to spend ten days with their two daughters of similar ages, we decided to go.

The Moores expected to move onto their new farm days before we were due to leave for the trip. If the move-in date was delayed, they could house-sit for us. They were planning to stay with us for a week or two before anyway. It was the perfect solution.

Hardly daring to believe it was actually happening, I spent hours researching Californian organic and biodynamic estates, drawing on contacts I had in the area for the best places to visit. Seán and I had made an uneasy peace. Between Christmas and New Year we visited Thierry and Isabelle for dinner to plan the finer details of our trip to California. We swapped notes, discussed routes and had a good laugh. The trip would be educational, a chance to deepen our relationship with Naomi, and fun. Our tickets from Naomi arrived. It was real.

The *Terre de Vins* magazine described pruning as '*parfois pénible mais cruciale*', meaning 'sometimes painful but crucial'. Pruning 25,000 vines at Terroir Feely took a couple of months of hard labour. Working in cold and sometimes damp conditions, Seán had to grit his teeth and get on with it, despite a sore back and a strained wrist.

Tough as it was, though, Seán also found it a joy. When the cool winter sun poked up over Gageac hill and lit up the vines under a clear blue sky, he found a meditative rhythm, a time to commune in the silence with the frosty vineyard. In biodynamics this was a key moment to talk to the vines; they were in a state of hibernation, not concentrating on starting the new season's buds as in spring, growing canes and leaves at Formula-One speeds as in summer, or maturing fruit as in autumn. They were quiet, unoccupied, and able to listen.

Françoise Bedel, a biodynamic champagne producer, had told me the story of how one winter she told an underperforming vineyard if it didn't buck up and produce more volume the vines would be grubbed up. The following year yields were up about 25 per cent and they weren't across the whole property. She was convinced the vines had listened.

The agricultural workers' social services organisation, who took close to half of our income every year and sometimes a lot more, said they were alarmed by how much injury and sick-leave pruning generated. Seán grew a thick beard to protect his face from the elements. When Ellie did a skit of him that winter, she acted out a heavy-footed Neanderthal.

Looking back at the previous year, setting aside the big fight, I felt happy and excited about the future. Biodynamics was becoming part of us, changing our thinking and keeping us motivated.

Meanwhile, the children were growing up. Sophia started reading and learning piano. The French education system meant she already recognised some classical music and art that I didn't even know as an adult. Ellie loved music, too, and would sit on an old beer crate set up as a bench in the kitchen, creating gritty, off-the-cuff songs on her toy guitar.

Our stereo, a sixteen-year-old purchase from our days in Johannesburg, had sung its last song back in the summer. Feeling buoyed by the response to the TV show, we bought a new hi-fi as our Christmas present to ourselves. Seán finished setting it up on New Year's Day and put on Vivaldi's *Four Seasons* as I said goodnight to the girls. Sophia turned to me as the music rose up the stairwell and said, 'Now that, that makes me very happy.' We went to sleep with joy in our hearts and music in our ears.

Chapter 13
A Taste of California

Two months later Thierry and Isabelle picked us up pre-dawn, their sons settled with Joel, their neighbour and an eccentric winegrower, who was now sporting bright red hair rather than dreadlocks. Our girls and Dora were safely installed with Dave and Amanda on their new farm. The previous night they were so engrossed playing with Martha and Florence by the time I left that I received a desultory wave instead of the difficult farewell I had expected.

It was Thierry's first trip outside Europe. We were all excited but he was bursting with it. The D936 had almost no traffic, little wonder given the early hour. As we descended a single-lane ramp connecting one road to another, a dark Alfa Romeo flew past on our right. The driver attempted the same thing on a large truck just ahead, but the hard shoulder narrowed and he found himself wedged between the truck and the road barrier. As the car ricocheted between the truck and the barrier, the driver struggled to keep it upright, bits ripping off with each impact, bouncing every which way; the bumper, a part of a light, a hubcap.

'*Oh la la la la la la!* Des Girondins! *Mais quel idiot!*' yelled Thierry, navigating the flying debris. The other car was clearly marked '33'. The rivalry between the more powerful Gironde region, the home of Bordeaux wines, and the smaller Dordogne, home to Bergerac wines, was legendary. *Girondins* were said by the *Dordognais* to be arrogant, proud idiots – as we had just witnessed. Miraculously, the Alfa Romeo didn't flip and once on the other side of the bridge they pulled over to assess the damage. We had a plane to catch and since there were no injuries we were quickly on our way.

Arriving into Los Angeles about twenty hours later, we were logged by an eyeball-scanner, grilled by the immigration officials and sniffed by vicious dogs that let out intermittent blood-curdling howls. We felt unwanted, but as we passed the security gates everything changed. We were in the land of bigger and better; of smiling customer-service agents and massive cars.

At the car-rental office Thierry wanted a Mustang, but after a safety scare on the Toyota Camry in the US they were renting the Camry out cheap – although the safety issue had apparently been resolved – and we were skint; if we were to go ahead with the building project we would need every penny from our windfall and a lot more besides.

'Regardez les bagnols!' Look at the cars! said Thierry as we took off, him driving, Seán navigating and me and Isabelle back-seat driving. Every car and truck on the jammed six-lane highway heading north to get on the I-5 to San Francisco was enormous; many were 4x4s with a single suited person inside. Our large family sedan felt small. Alongside the cars were monster trucks with metre-plus noses pushed way out in front to contain the engines required to pull gargantuan cargos. When we stopped to overnight at a rundown motel we still had not seen a single small car. It became a game to find one.

The hotel breakfast was sweet muffins, pre-sweetened instant oats and sugar-coated cereals. We opted for coffee and orange juice, then hit the I-5 on the hunt for small cars and cowboys. Thierry wanted to experience what he had seen in the movies.

Instead of cowboys out on the range, though, we saw endless green pastures void of grazing cattle. What we did see was intensive cattle farming. We began to recognise the initial sign: a terrible smell. A couple of kilometres later cattle would be jammed into a pen one against another, knee-deep in slurry. The stink would follow us for another few kilometres.

It didn't seem logical. I reflected on what could be behind this phenomenon and could only deduce that it was because fossil fuels were cheaper than human labour. The grass could be baled by a machine more easily and at a lower cost than managing herds on the prairie with personnel. This was in stark contrast to the health and animal-welfare issues on the other side of the coin.

Beef provides omega-6 and omega-3 fats, both essential to our health; we need a balance of about three to one. Over four to one and we start to experience health problems. I had read that, whereas grass-fed cattle had omega-6 to omega-3 ratios that were around the recommended level of three to one, after 200 days in a feedlot, grain-fed cattle had ratios exceeding twenty to one. The contrast was even starker for intensive eggs compared to free-range eggs. I realised then that our home-grown eggs didn't only taste better, they were way healthier too.

Even as an organic farmer totally wired into all of this information I still sometimes bought whatever my local supermarket proposed, handing my conscience over to buyers driven by quarterly results, not concern for my health or animal ethics. Reading books like *Fast Food Nation* and *Food, Inc.* had opened my eyes and made me more vigilant, but I sometimes strayed because I was in too much of a hurry to read the fine print. Seán would demand that the offending product be returned, but that wasn't easy in France where the customer is *never* king and *seldom* right.

We hopped off the I-5 to take a district road to Santa Cruz for our first winegrower rendezvous. It was early and we were making good time so we stopped at a coffee shop in Paso Robles. The car park was filled with 4x4s.

'All the cars look new. How do they keep them so clean?' said Thierry. We laughed, reminiscing about Naomi's trip in his mud-encrusted utility vehicle and thinking how much of a shock it must have been for her, coming from this culture of gleaming chrome and bright paintwork.

Hoping for a coffee similar to those experienced from the same chain in Vancouver years before, I ordered a cappuccino. As we sipped our drinks, Seán ragged Thierry about the pink sweater he had on, warning him not to wear it in San Francisco. Seán would not be seen dead in pink. In Dublin I had once made the mistake of buying him a stylish black T-shirt from Eden Park for his birthday. There was a tiny pink bow-tie emblem on it, barely visible, but the spot of pink meant Seán would never wear it. I tried inking it black but the ink washed out each time and Seán rejected the shirt outright. Eventually I gave it to the local charity shop. I should have given it to Thierry. My small coffee was so large I couldn't finish it. It wasn't as good as I remembered.

A while later we arrived at Santa Cruz, a small city of around 60,000 people known for its surf, and becoming known for its wineries. Philippe Coderey, director of viticulture at Bonny Doon and a biodynamic specialist, was a tall, eccentric mix of French and American traits. He grew up and worked on vineyards in France then moved to the US, first to Pennsylvania then to the winelands of California. From newly furnished, modern but ghostly empty offices on the ground floor, he whisked us upstairs.

'Bonny Doon has been having a tough time financially so many people were laid off,' he explained. They were going through a change of strategy from bulk branded wines to quality estate-grown wines, but it was a tough transition.

His office and sensitive-crystallisation lab was a comfortable, shabbily furnished attic. I felt more at home there than in the stark offices downstairs and could see he did too. He emptied his heart to us: his crystallisation work; problems he had with his back from too much driving to see all the growers; his relationship with Bonny Doon's founder and leader, Randall Grahm, self-described as the 'original Rhone Deranger', and, according to their own website, described by his staff as 'particular'.

Philippe talked non-stop for several hours, delighted to have a chance to speak French. His crystallisation work included wine but also vineyard earth and earth from other places. One was a comparison of blank dust from Death Valley and dust from an American Indian tribal-dance ring that was vibrantly alive, like a biodynamic wine. Both original dusts looked identical, but their crystallisation told a whole other story about their quality.

Randall parked his red Citroën outside. Looking down at him from the attic window, he was smaller than I imagined. When Philippe introduced us, he seemed quiet, not the court jester I had read about. He made his reputation with good wines but also with marketing stunts like a mock funeral for cork, burying a real cork that he called 'Thierry Bouchon' in New York's Central Park, capturing the imagination of journalists at the height of the cork versus screw cap debate. The opposite of us, he believed screw cap was the only way and had milked the media angle.

The cellar and offices behind were empty but the tasting room and restaurant out front had a full staff. No expense had been spared. A biodynamic flowform water feature had pride of place at the entrance, there were nooks made of massive oak casks that housed private tables, chandeliers made from wine bottles, bar counters made from old barrel staves, and posters explaining biodynamics. It was beautiful and packed with clever ideas and unusual features. We ordered the biodynamic wines; the Albariño white and a red. The wines were delicious and the food imaginative, local and finely prepared. Philippe was fascinating but the experience was marred by his frustration.

'*Mais c'est que du bluff!*' (Their talk about biodynamics is marketing hype), said Thierry as we left the winery.

I described an advert I had seen for a large organic wine producer a few years before. It proclaimed they had the largest organic compost heap in the USA – with the tag line 'our neighbours might not like it but our vines sure do!' Their heap may have been the largest but it implied everything from them was organic, whereas I read that only about 15 per cent of the grapes under their brand name were organic at that time. It was the kind of marketing confusion that would not be tolerated in France.

Isabelle reminded us that we could not talk wine all day every day. She wanted to sightsee. The following day we explored southwards: Monterey, the setting for John Steinbeck's *Cannery Row*; the evocative seascape of 17-Mile Drive; Pebble Beach and Big Sur. It was totally California. But I wanted to visit the winelands, having seen most of this before on a year working and travelling round the world in my early twenties.

We were feeling nervous about our budget after the hefty dinner bill at Bonny Doon. If we ate like that every day we wouldn't have funds for the week. Between sightseeing we picnicked on the beach in Carmel then dined at a cheap Mexican restaurant a couple of blocks down from our hotel. The hotel, selected for proximity to Bonny Doon, wasn't fantastic and the restaurant even less so. I woke up retching in the middle of the night and stayed at the toilet bowl through the early hours.

We had ordered different things; luckily the other three were unscathed. Feverish and miserable, I tried not to vomit in the car as we drove from Santa Cruz to San Francisco.

'*Regardez!*' yelled Thierry as we came into San Francisco city.

Looking up from my nauseous haze I saw a hip new Mini, our first small-car sighting. San Francisco was a different world to LA; instead of gas-guzzlers there were Minis and Toyota hybrids, though still no cowboys.

I felt like death, unable to stomach anything but a little water. Even that made my gut unhappy. I prayed the upset would be over the next day when we hit the winelands. The cheap food now didn't look so cheap.

Missing our clean, home-grown food, I dragged myself around San Francisco trying not to let the team down, then fell into bed in our hotel, escaping my unhappiness by diving into a good book. Seán watched over me, adamant he would not leave me alone to accompany Thierry and Isabelle to Chinatown. For all the food-safety laws in the US that meant Roquefort and other unpasteurised cheeses were illegal, I had never had food poisoning in France or Ireland.

It was the longest time we had spent in an English-speaking country since leaving Ireland, but, travelling with Thierry and Isabelle, we had never spoken more French. It was fun. The next day we crossed the Golden Gate Bridge, setting the GPS for Ceàgo Vinegarden, founded by Jim Fetzer, former president of

Fetzer Vineyards, long since sold and now owned by a massive conglomerate. Some of the money from the sale had seeded his new Ceàgo venture, a biodynamic farm.

About halfway to Ceàgo we saw a sign to Chateau Montelena, the winery made famous in the 'Judgement of Paris' in the seventies, and more recently in the film *Bottle Shock* that tells the story – *Bottle Shock* and *Sideways* had been on Thierry and Isabelle's pre-trip 'watch list'. *Bottle Shock* tells the story of an American city professional, Jim Barrett, who went wine-farming in the Napa Valley before it became famous. On the opposite side of the Atlantic, a Paris-based wine-shop owner and now famous English wine journalist, Steven Spurrier, was concocting a way to improve sales by bringing in high-quality international wines. He decided to raise the prestige of his shop and his new line with a competition between top French and top international wines. On his trip to Napa he meets Barrett, who wants nothing to do with the competition, but his son Bo slips Spurrier a few bottles. In the meantime, the wine concerned did a volte-face and went brown. Barrett drank himself into depressed oblivion and gave it all away. In these scenes *Bottle Shock* so perfectly captured the angst of being a winemaker, I felt it was a masterpiece. Meanwhile, on the opposite side of the ocean, the bottle given to Spurrier hadn't turned brown and wins the competition against famous *grands crus* chardonnays from Burgundy. The wine changes back to its normal colour in Napa, Bo gets the girl and they get the wine back. I loved the film and demanded we stop to pay homage.

Thierry did a U-turn and we took a winding road up through a forest that led to an entrance that was a mix of old-chateau style and modern Japanese garden.

I was keen to taste the chardonnay on which they had built their reputation. It was only available as part of a flight of four wines for twenty dollars per person, the lowest-priced tasting they offered. We didn't have time for four wines plus we were told the chardonnay was not grown on the estate, it was bought in. The estate only grew red grapes. The chardonnay wasn't even from the same vineyard as it was when they won the tasting in Paris back in the seventies. It was a shock to our French perspective, where the word 'chateau' on a label guaranteed the wines were exclusively grown and made on the estate.

Ceàgo Vinegarden was a hacienda-style winery with a boat-landing on Clear Lake, and a lavender, olive, sheep and vine farm. Barney Fetzer, a twenty-something, thick-set, bearded farmer dressed in checked grey shirt, muddy chinos, boots and a cap struck a chord with Seán and Thierry, his secateurs hung on a belt at his hip. *At last a real winegrower*, I could see them thinking, *not a poncy winery owner.*

The field hands in the vineyards we had seen from the roadside on the trip so far had their heads stooped and faces hidden by hoodies pulled low, as if they were embarrassed by what they were doing, instead of proud. Next to the field would inevitably be a flatbed truck with two chemical Portaloos on it, effectively saying: 'You are not worthy even to leave your C.R.A.P. here on our land.' I was sure it was a legal requirement, but nonetheless its implication was scary.

The modern, industrial economy denigrated manual labour. Since changing our own lives, I knew it should not be so. Rough working hands should be celebrated, not hidden in embarrassment. People who worked with their hands, who were passionate about what they did and were respected for it, were the happiest in the world.

Barney knew his vineyards. He worked his land; his hands told the story. He pointed to a stack of cow horns in the biodynamic preparation tower. Biodynamics uses plant sprays like the dried stinging nettle, but also more complex preparations created to improve the health and life of the farm. The most important is 'the 500', cow manure fermented in a cow horn, buried and overwintered in the soil before being dynamised – mixed into water in a special way – and then sprayed onto the soil. Barney explained that on the lower level they stored the horns and the preparations, and that on the upper level was the dynamiser, so that the preparations could be moved to the sprayer by gravity.

The manure acts like a starter culture for soil fertility. A tiny dose – 100 grams per hectare, about a handful per football field – is like placing a drop of yoghurt starter culture in a large bucket of milk. It creates a massive change, promotes root activity and stimulates microbiotic life in the soil. While the preparation sounds crazy when you hear it explained – who would have thought of putting cow dung in a cow horn for six months? – it has been proven to create a powerful tonic, with nearly a thousand times more microbiotic activity than the same cow dung placed in a clay pot for the same period.

The other key preparation, 'the 501', is ground quartz – silica – mixed with rainwater and packed in a cow horn, buried in spring and then dug up in autumn, the opposite timing to the 500. It enhances the light metabolism of the plant and her photosynthetic processes. Again, a tiny dose generates significant results. The microparticles of the quartz are like mirrors bringing light and heat into the vineyard. Instead of spraying as night falls, onto the ground, as we do the 500, the 501 is sprayed at dawn skywards, into the air above the vines.

When we first started biodynamics we dynamised our preparations in rainwater in a large, smooth-sided, hard-plastic black bin. Wood, copper or concrete are better, but we didn't have the budget. Stirring about 100 litres of water for an hour was a great workout – to do our whole vineyard required about 400 litres. Seán and I each had two bins, working one at a time. I tried doing both at once but found it impossible to co-ordinate. Doing this process a few times not only convinced me that a mechanical dynamiser was necessary, but also how important the dynamisation itself was. At the start the water was like normal water from a tap with a fine smattering of cow dung through it. By the end the water was smooth as silk, languid and soft, totally transformed by the process. If we had had the budget to buy the dynamiser straight away, I would not have understood or experienced this. I was grateful.

'We have to be careful with the 501 since we already have a lot of heat and light here,' said Barney.

We could see: the buildings were beautiful, with warm curved walls in natural tones and beautiful tiles, but organised with large overhangs and terraces to protect from the heat, like a Mexican hacienda. In their grand event-room, the ceiling was a ladder of wood beams, great black-and-white photos decorated the walls and the furniture was handmade by Barney from oak barrels. Tasting in a room that was invitingly warm in temperature and colour, filled with books and gift items, we discovered their wines. They were beautiful and hot, the high alcohols almost impossible to avoid with the climate they had. Their challenge was too much sun, while ours was sometimes the opposite.

I felt inspired. It was idyllic, well planned and beautifully constructed. Like Bonny Doon's tasting room, it gave Seán and me ideas for the professional tasting space that was forming in our heads. But before we could get back to the Dordogne and start planning the project, we had more Californian vineyards to visit and a couple of days with my sister. I was bursting with excitement to see her. It had been too long.

Chapter 14
The American Dream

It was drizzling as we headed up Napa's Golden Mile to our next destination. A door or two up from Opus One, the joint venture between French wine royalty the Rothschilds and American wine royalty the Mondavi, was Cakebread. No showy entrance, just a tiny wooden sign near the mailbox that we nearly missed, understated but chic.

'Wine and food pairing' visits were on my wish list of activities to offer at Terroir Feely and this trip to the US was a chance to see what innovative winemakers were doing. Research had led me to the Cakebread Cellars wine-and-food-pairing tour, but it was only available in season on certain days and our visit was out of season.

I had a vague recollection of the name; Jack Cakebread had been on a course at Stanford with my dad back in the eighties. My dad was a 'neat freak' and very organised – when we first moved to France he called our house a 'corridor of crisis'. Now his organisational trait was paying off; he still had Jack's contact details, despite not having been in touch for years. On receiving my dad's email, Jack's wife Dolores had generously offered us a complimentary tour and a private visit.

The style was American farmhouse with wooden barns, the tasting room set up rustically between oak barrels and pallets of boxed wine right in the centre of the working zone. It was the lowest season possible but there were clients passing through constantly.

White blossoms on the miniature cherry trees and daffodils in full bloom announced spring in the central courtyard garden where, Dolores explained, they held their wine-club events. The Cakebreads achieved a homely family feeling despite being a large operation with six full-time staff working on wine-club marketing and organisation alone. They had begun as a 'Mom and Pop shop', working a small parcel of land at the same time as holding down their day jobs in San Francisco. The first year they produced just one barrel of wine. From one barrel they went to two barrels, and so on.

Dolores introduced us to Ted, a wine guide, to continue our tour through the barrel-storage barn, stacked higher than I had ever seen, into another section of wood-panelled rooms with large panoramic windows and doors onto the vines. Sliding wood partitions could disappear into the walls to open up several small rooms into one large room. It was clever, simple and stylish.

On a dark, solid-wood table looking onto their hibernating vineyards were four settings with four aperitifs and a number of different-shaped crystal glasses. Prawn marinated in mango was paired with Cakebread's top sauvignon blanc; the Reserve Chardonnay was matched with a teeny tasty pie; the smoky zinfandel was so perfectly matched with a smoked sweet potato I would never forget it; and Cakebread's best cabernet sauvignon was paired with a tiny nugget of venison.

Wowed by the genius and delighted that my dodgy stomach was holding up, we followed Ted back to Jack's office via the kitchen, where we met Brian Streeter, one of two professional chefs employed full time. The pairing triumphs did not happen by chance. They were the result of hard work and investment. Brian and his team were testing the recipes for their second recipe book that was about to go to the publisher.

Jack had been a bomber pilot in World War Two and now, in his eighties, he still came to work at the winery every day. Most of the activity had been handed over to his two sons but he was still the figurehead, overseeing things from his magnificent light-filled office with views onto the vineyards and garden, surrounded by awards, accolades and photos with famous people. The Cakebreads were icons of the American dream, an example of how working hard and smart – with a bit of luck thrown in – could pay off.

Before we left I bought a copy of the first recipe book, and that evening I became engrossed in their story of how it all started with a little piece of land on what had become Napa's Golden Mile.

From Cakebread we headed west to Sonoma to meet Kathleen Inman. She farmed next door to a vineyard owned by a colleague from Dublin, who had become a lecturer in San Jose. His vineyard wasn't organic and he outsourced the farming then sold the grapes, but he knew his neighbours and had highly recommended Kathleen, knowing our organic bent and her skill. How lucky that turned out to be.

Kathleen's wines were powerful, but with a feminine touch and finesse that was ethereal and magic. They had *terroir*. Her organic vines were offset by a background of lime-green spring growth, carefully hoed beneath the vines and mowed between the rows. Across the road my colleague's vineyard made me want to cry, his old sculpted-trunk zinfandel vines surviving in a herbicide desert.

Kathleen had organised a comparative tasting of her wines alongside her other neighbour, DeLoach, an organic and biodynamic estate owned by Boisset, a powerful Burgundy family. Their single-vineyard pinot noir from Maboroshi vineyard on the Sonoma Coast hills was, like Kathleen's wine, true *terroir*. Even Thierry was impressed. But the *terroir* wines were not budget; nothing was under fifty dollars. Wines selling at less than twenty dollars from these cellar doors were typically bulk wines sourced from conventional growers. Our own single-vineyard, *terroir*-driven wines were worthy of higher prices – they cost more to produce, but we hadn't worked out how to sell them for what they were worth. We debated how to achieve this en route back to Sonoma town.

Mid-discussion we spotted a sign for Benziger Family Winery; it had been on my wish list so we took a detour. The farm was nestled in a beautiful valley bowl surrounded by vineyards. I ran inside and tried my best charm to wangle a free tour from the tasting-room staff. They called the vineyard manager on an internal phone.

Dave arrived looking tired. He explained that they were doing double time since vineyard staff had been cut as part of a cost-saving initiative to cope with the recession. Even a haven like this was not spared. The vineyard hands were the first to go. He flicked his hand towards the tasting room, still bursting with staff, and his face said it all. Clients saw the front face, not the vineyard.

He organised a visit for us the following day, followed by a special reserve tasting – all on the house. '*Caro, le tour guide extraordinaire!*' said Thierry as I shared the news.

The following day, part way through the tasting, one of the Benziger brothers joined us. I gave a brief introduction to ourselves and the Daulhiacs.

'Thierry is a seventh-generation winegrower?' asked Bob.

'That's right,' I said.

'You sure?' he asked. Thierry nodded; this much he could understand – many of the American accents we had encountered on the trip so far had had him and Isabelle foxed.

'Seventh generation! Wow, that is really something. Here even the oldest wine families can boast three at most.'

We tasted the Tribute Red Meritage Bordeaux-style blend, rich and full-bodied, then a pinot noir farmed on the coastal hills.

'That is beautiful wine,' I said.

'But it's not seventh-generation wine!' he laughed. 'How long are you staying? Do you have time to join us for a barbecue tomorrow?'

We had to decline since we were leaving the next day. We were discovering that Americans were very hospitable, but we were also realising that the US was about marketing and brand. Many of the wineries were selling conventional, organic and biodynamic under the same brand name, sometimes talking about biodynamic as if it applied to all their wines when it was often only true of a small part of the range. It confused the customer, just like the advert I had described earlier in the trip.

In France the whole farm, and hence the whole brand, used for the estate wine had to be biodynamic. We could not use one name for conventional, organic and biodynamic estate and non-estate grown wines. It was seen as too confusing and made our fraud squad upset.

The only biodynamic place we visited that didn't appear to be doing both was Ceàgo, although looking at their website later I found a pinot noir under their brand that was from elsewhere and not certified biodynamic. Perhaps even they were tempted to take this path following the huge swing to pinot noir created by the film *Sideways* – another sign of marketing and fashion's power at work. *Sideways* is a hilarious wine lover's cult classic that lambasts merlot and deifies pinot noir. After the film's success, sales of merlot-based wines in the US dropped significantly – some articles suggested by a third – and pinot noir sales rose even more than that, though some of the wine sold as pinot noir was not pinot noir. Vineyards take several years to grow, and the world's stocks of pinot noir vineyards versus merlot vineyards could not have changed overnight the way the stats had.

The American wine buyers and consumers drinking the fraudulent wine had no complaints about the product. It was discovered by the *Direction Générale de la Concurrence, de la Consommation et de la Répression des Fraudes*, a department of the French government with a dedicated police force (the fraud squad). Part of this department's role was to validate labelling so consumers could be sure that what they bought was what it said on the label. A loose marketing statement could land you in jail. Selling a blend of merlot and shiraz – or syrah, as shiraz is called in France – as pinot noir resulted in a suspended jail sentence with a fine of over €50,000 for the wine professionals in Languedoc-Roussillon that masterminded the fraud.

Visiting Whole Foods in Sonoma that evening, a chain that we thought was exclusively organic, we estimated the wine shelves had at most 10 per cent organically grown wine. I was disappointed and depressed. If this haven of organic products wasn't offering organically grown wine in a serious way, perhaps we were fighting a losing battle.

But I knew it was a worthwhile battle. If wine lovers knew about the dangers of pesticides, herbicides and systemic fungicides that were rampant in some conventional wines, they would be demanding organic. A study in France based on a hundred randomly selected French wines showed that the average wine had 300 times the level of pesticides that are allowed in our drinking water, and one of the samples had 1,650 times the level.

Mainstream resellers and journalists were not educating the wine buyer; they had too much to lose if they weren't selling conventional wines or advertising them. Almost every visitor to our vineyard, however, left with a new perspective, saying they would seek out organic – the only way of being sure your wine is not host to chemical residues.

Staying in Sonoma we found a classic American diner open early 'til late. They offered the full breakfast, complete with maple-syrup pancakes. From there we could see a traditional yellow school bus pass each morning. The timber houses on the street opposite had large porches out front and mailboxes next to the gate on their white picket fences. It was classic America. As we cleaned the last morsels off our plates, Thierry lamented once again, *'Mais où sont les cow-boys?'*

We still hadn't found a cowboy and time was running out. After being on the road back to LA for a few hours that evening, we agreed it was time to stop. The GPS said the nearest town was Paso Robles. That suited us perfectly, since it was a famous wine town.

The GPS found a few hotels and we stopped at the first. It was a little expensive but looked good. They were fully booked, however. The next-door hotel looked OK and fit the budget better, so we waited at reception to check availability. Behind us we heard 'clink, clink, clink'. We turned to find two cowboys kitted out in hats, chaps and spurs taking up a spot in the queue. Behind them a crowd of cowboys was gathered in the car park. It was surreal. Seeing our surprise, the receptionist pointed to the poster behind her.

'It's the State Cutting Horse Championships. That's why the hotels are full, but luckily I have two rooms left.'

Thierry and Seán exchanged broad smiles. Cutting horses are trained to cut specific cattle away from the group; a key part of being a cowboy. It was effectively the state cowboy championships.

'Can we visit?' I asked.

'Sure, anyone can go and watch. It's in the showgrounds up the road.'

She pointed to where we would be able to see more cowboys than we imagined possible.

At the steakhouse across the road the mechanical bronco was bucking non-stop and almost every seat held a cowboy. When Isabelle ordered a beer she was asked for her ID to prove that she was over twenty-one. Thierry, Seán and I reached to offer ours. The waitress shook her head. Unlike blonde, apple-cheeked, fresh-faced Isabelle, we looked like we were well over the limit. We laughed, then discussed having a go on the bronco. I went up close and read the warning sign, then returned to announce that it was too dangerous for oldies like Seán, Thierry and myself but OK for a youngster like Isabelle.

Before the cutting horse championships we hit the local cowboy shop. The Boot Barn was a warehouse selling everything cowboy from rhinestone hats to pink cowboy boots. Seán bought a pair: definitely not pink.

The arena contained a large knot of bullocks being herded tight by one of the organisers. We scrambled over a barrier of iron bars, crossed the animal walkway filled with perfectly groomed horses and climbed into the stands. The speaker above us announced the next competitor. A beautiful, young, blonde cowgirl cantered into the ring on a bay horse. She dropped her reins, leaving the horse and marked bullock to dance like two world-class footballers in a classic set of dummy moves. We were gripped. I got chatting to the lady next to me. She owned a ranch nearby and explained the sport, deflating our cowboy bubble.

'No one is a cowboy any more. This is all about the money. The best cutting horse wins and the person who can afford the best cutting horse has the most money. Most of the top contenders out there are wealthy lawyers or dentists or bankers who do this for a hobby. A real cowboy couldn't afford to do this sport. These horses can dance but they probably couldn't survive one harsh night out on the range.'

We watched a few more contenders, including a slight, older, dark-haired lady and two older men. They were good and their horses better, but they weren't the young cowboys with rippling muscles I had expected. There were indeed no real cowboys left.

But American hospitality was large; my new friend invited us to visit their ranch outside Paso Robles that afternoon. Unfortunately, we had to get to LA. On our way out, the beautiful blonde cowgirl was walking along the dust track just ahead of us.

'What I wouldn't give for a photo with her!' whispered Thierry to me.

I asked the gal if she wouldn't mind making my French pal's day. She was delighted to oblige. She wasn't a real cowboy on the range, but she was Thierry's dream come true.

Chapter 15
Fire!

As we left cowboy country, back in Aquitaine Dave and Amanda were preparing a casual supper with their two daughters and our temporarily adopted two. Their semi-ruin had no central heating so to survive the winter they had installed two wood burners. Dave casually tossed a piece of cardboard into the living-room burner to rekindle it and they continued their evening preparations.

'What's that smell of smoke?' asked Amanda.

'The wood burner,' said Dave.

'It's much worse than usual,' said Amanda.

'You're right,' said Dave. 'I'll check outside.'

Seconds later he yelled, 'Get the kids outside; the house is on fire!'

There was smoke billowing round the chimney and flames licking the top. He sprinted inside for the phone.

'Who do we call? What's the emergency number?' Dave shouted as he ran back outside, phone in hand and adrenalin racing through his body. The fire looked more serious by the second.

'My God! 911? No, 112! That's the Europe-wide emergency number, dial 112!' yelled Amanda as she herded the kids outside.

In halting French, Dave explained the emergency to the operator and gave his address details. Amanda huddled with the kids in the courtyard, her mind racing about what this could mean for them. They were not the owners yet; they were renting the place until the transaction completed in a few days. They didn't have insurance as the policy on their house and effects would only come into effect when the transaction went through. Almost everything they owned was in that house and the fire was gaining strength.

Dave ran back and forth to extract critical items like car keys in case they needed to go elsewhere for the night, which was looking more and more likely as the minutes passed with no sign of a fire engine.

'Call them again, Dave!' shouted Amanda. 'Maybe they didn't realise the urgency.'

As Dave's finger's dialled, they heard the sound of a fire engine in the distance and in minutes flashing lights and sirens filled the courtyard. It was fifteen minutes since the first call but it felt like hours. Amanda, Sophia, Ellie, Martha and Florence huddled into the background while Dave fielded questions from the burly fire chief.

The firefighters surrounded the house to hose from both sides. A half-hour later it was still blazing. The chief fireman left his men to continue the fight while he interrogated Dave further about the circumstances.

His staccato administrative style and serious demeanour, and the arrival of the police and the mayor, didn't help Dave's limited grasp of French. When he asked the chief to repeat the same question for the fifth time the fireman's frustration reached fever pitch.

'Maybe we could get Sophia to translate?' Dave said.

Seven-year-old Sophia was brought forward from the shadows at the back of the courtyard, where the kids were sheltering well out of the way, to translate between the fireman and the Moores. She transferred the questions to Dave with an authoritative French look similar to the fire chief's and returned his replies. With the question and answer session over, she translated the commentary that followed in the same imperious tone, following the chief's stance to a T, almost adding a wagging finger.

'He says you should have swept your chimney. He also says this chimney is not *aux normes* and will have to be condemned.'

She paused and looked at the fire chief, then translated the next volley of indignation.

'He says the house could have burned down. He says the house could still burn down.'

It had been over an hour and there were still flames licking up the side of the chimney.

'Why isn't the fire out yet? Can't they stop it?' asked Amanda, panicked.

'They are trying to control the fire without wrecking your house and furniture,' translated Sophia.

'But it's more important to put the fire out. Tell them to forget about the furniture, Sophia!' yelled Amanda.

'He says don't worry, it is almost under control.'

As Sophia said that, the flames died back and the whole team seemed to breathe a sigh of relief.

'There, you see. He says it looks like it is out now but there is so much heat in the bricks and stones that it could reignite. Dave will have to watch the house for at least five hours to be sure it doesn't restart.'

Amanda bundled the girls into the back seat of her pick-up truck and took them to our house for the night. Lying in our double bed, her mind racing about what could be happening to her house or what was left of it, she didn't sleep much. Dave, in the meantime, signed all the official paperwork that was shoved in front of his nose despite having no idea what it was. When the firemen left, he had to stay up to keep watch, so he decided to get on with cleaning the living room, which was awash with water and soot. By 3 a.m. there was no sign of fire and the place was spotless.

'Cleaner than it's ever been,' said Amanda when she arrived home with the girls at around nine the following morning. The smell of the fire and the blackened chimney were still apparent, but otherwise it was hard to tell that the exciting events of the previous few hours had happened at all.

Blissfully unaware of the near-catastrophe unfolding in Aquitaine, we drove peacefully back to Los Angeles, taking the coastal route to see Santa Monica and other famous beach areas north of LA.

My sister Jacquie, nicknamed Foo, was joining us for a few days. She and I were close in spirit but lived thousands of miles apart. She had lived in North America for more than twenty years and I had lived in Europe for close to twenty years. She was beautiful, I was plain. I had children, she had a small terrier. She had several homes across the American continent; we had a small farm in France. What she spent on clothes in one shopping spree was more than I had spent on clothes for my entire family in ten years.

All the fancier hotels were fully booked, so Foo was obliged to book into the basic Holiday Inn with us. I was delighted, since this meant that we were in rooms right next to each other and could spend hours talking like we used to. I had missed her. Every day we ran together then chatted non-stop while we got ready to go out. My sister was in the process of extracting herself from a ten-year relationship with a bizillionaire. There was a load to talk about.

Naomi, now CEO of Reserveage, had come a long way since her first visit to our farmhouse kitchen two years before. Not only was she buying our grape skins and covering this trip, she also treated us to team-building dinners and extended the invitation to my sister when she heard she was in town. Stepping into a stretch limo Hummer the first night, Thierry, Isabelle, Seán and I felt like *ploucs* surrounded by the glamour of Los Angeles. The inside of the limo was cavernous and low, mirrors reflecting images back at me from every angle. Seeing Foo's feet stretched in front of me, I complimented her on her stunning platforms.

'Thank you. They're wirecell,' she said.

Isabelle and I exchanged a look; neither of us had heard of this new designer.

'Wirecell?' I asked.

'Yes, you know, Wirecell,' said Foo.

'I've never heard of them,' I said, not surprised since I didn't read *Vogue*. I read *La Vigne*.

'You know Wirecell,' said Foo, now really frustrated. 'Wirecell, as in Yves Saint Laurent.'

'Oh! You mean Yves Saint Laurent. YSL,' I said.

'Exactly. That's what I said,' said Foo.

We laughed like dingos; a North American accent and two decades separated by an ocean gaped between us. Despite the yawning gap, we were sisters, closer in spirit than our current circumstances told.

At a lush Italian restaurant on the coast about fifteen minutes' drive from Anaheim, Naomi feted us and a group of twenty employees, clients and partners. Thierry ordered the wine. Once it was poured, I took the table through how to blind taste; what to look for, how to find clues from the look, the smell and the taste to work out what the wine was.

By deduction and a bit of luck I guessed the appellation on the white, a Pouilly-Fuissé, and the appellation and vintage on the red, a 2005 Châteauneuf-du-Pape. Chins dropped onto the table. Seán was impressed. Even Thierry was impressed. The wine-tasting boot camp with Matthew was paying off. Everyone wanted to know how to do it and I promised to help start a Reserveage wine club.

The Natural Products Fair was the largest organic and natural products fair on the west coast of America. At the main door, a small crowd was picketing against a brand called 'x organics' that was using 'organics' in their brand name and marketing, although there was nothing organic about most of their products. In Europe, the company leaders would have been in jail, not presenting at a show.

Inside, the Reserveage stand was tastefully constructed with large photos of vineyards, wooden furniture printed with French words like *soleil* and *terroir* and lovely wrought-iron display shelves and tables and chairs. On a screen, the harvest video taken at our vineyard the previous year looped, showing the autumn vineyards in all their magnificence. It was inviting and the products looked fantastic. Naomi's range had grown from her first resveratrol capsule – an antioxidant proprietary blend including resveratrol and our grape skins – to include other products like a collagen booster with resveratrol that I found helped keep wrinkles at bay. We met her New York distributor, who said they were number one in the New York market for organic resveratrol food supplements. He was bubbling with enthusiasm for Naomi and the company.

From her visit almost two years before, when she had an idea but no company and not even a brand name, to this show,

Naomi had created a national brand. We wondered if the same was possible in France and were sure that it was not. Getting approval from A, B and C would have held up the creation for years, if not decades. This ability to proceed with speed for those who had talent and ideas was a contributor to the dynamism of the US economy, although it also left loopholes like the one the people outside were protesting about.

Saying a tearful goodbye to my sister, I wondered how long it would be before we would see each other again. She had some challenges to face that meant she wouldn't be visiting us for a while, and we wouldn't be doing an international trip for a long time unless another fairy godmother like Naomi flashed her wand.

Still unaware of the fire scare that nearly razed Chateau Bonté, we returned home late evening, having caught our connection in Paris thanks to Isabelle's stubborn desperation to see her children. At the flight-connection security point, she pushed aside a few able bodies, shouting 'I have to get home to see my sons'. As she prepared to do the same to a team of handicapped basketball players, Thierry restrained her. We still just made it.

We had missed Sophia and Ellie so much we went to fetch them from Dave and Amanda despite the late hour. They had missed us a little too. According to Amanda, about halfway through our trip Ellie had said, 'I am so pleased Mum and Dad are coming home tomorrow.' Amanda had had to break the news gently that it was a few more days than that. I felt my heart break as she told the story.

Amanda gave a quick synopsis of the fire and I realised what the strange sooty smell was. As she recounted the events I felt a jab of fear, despite the fact that our girls were safely sound asleep in the next room. I tried to stop my mind from running down the road of what might have happened.

We woke the girls from their slumber and embraced like koalas. A half-hour later, sitting on the couch back home, we chatted about our ten days apart. I was worried that the fire would have left an impact, perhaps generated nightmares, but they were totally relaxed about it and more interested in the gifts we had for them and in telling us what fun they had had with Martha and Florence. We finally got to bed in the early hours; everyone, including Dora, happy to be in their own beds.

Getting away from the farm had done wonders for Seán and me, easing the tension left in the wake of our fight before Christmas. We were inspired and invigorated from our trip, filled with motivation for our business and the burgeoning notion of the tasting room and lodge. Travel had broadened our horizons and brought new ideas. As Vince Lignac, a friend in Saint-Émilion often said, travel was that and more; it helped you get to know yourself. We were poised for our next big step. My head said 'No, it's too risky', but my instinct said 'It's the only choice to make'.

Part Three

Flower

In biodynamics we talk of a flower day when the air forces are powerful. It is a good time to plant a flowering plant like calendula or to pick grapes for wines that we want to express floral aromatics. Being Libran, an air sign, I always feel energised, light, ready to take on the world on a flower day.

Flower days occur when the moon is in the air constellations: Gemini, Libra and Aquarius.

In wine-tasting we find that floral elements – elderflower on sauvignon blanc, acacia on botrytis sémillon, or violets on red wines – are reinforced on flower days.

The value of doing something does not lie in the ease or difficulty, the probability or improbability of its achievement, but in the vision, the plan, the determination and the perseverance, the effort and the struggle which go into the project.
Helen and Scott Nearing

Living the Good Life: Being a Plain Practical Account of a Twenty Year Project in a Self-Subsistent Homestead in Vermont (Social Science Institute, Harborside, Maine, 1954) (courtesy of the Goodlife Center)

Chapter 16
The Gestation

The local tourist office representative, a young woman who had become supportive of what we were doing after an initial bout of scepticism, visited to collect brochures and leave us with the new version of the *Route des Vins* map. I casually mentioned our idea for a new tasting room and lodge.

'That sounds like something that would be supported by the EU programme for rural diversification,' she said. 'The aid programme can contribute up to a third of the project costs. It's an EU initiative to develop non-agricultural revenue on farms in rural areas. But be careful,' she added, seeing the excitement on my face. 'It's a minefield of bureaucracy and red tape. Many people have said to me it's more trouble than it's worth. You can end up doing so much more to be *aux normes* and to meet their requirements that you can spend more than you originally budgeted, even with the payment of the aid.'

Warned but not daunted, we attacked the plans with renewed energy. The aid could provide a financial lynchpin for the audacious project, as much as the trips to California and Alsace had provided inspiration.

Sébastian Bouché, a local builder specialising in traditional methods and deeply ecological, was recommended by a few people. Two of his five kids were at school with ours, the indomitable Judicaël in Ellie's class and Silouane in Sophia's.

When he arrived to meet us for the first time, Sébastian looked like a twenty-something Adonis with a hip blonde ponytail; he did not look like a harassed father of five. Sitting in the garden in the shade of the cherry trees, we discussed the project and I gave him my rough pencil drawings of how we wanted the buildings to look. After touring the site he had more of an idea of what was required. To continue the process he invited us to visit their family home, which he had constructed solo. I wanted Seán to accompany me but he was too busy already in the frenzy of early spring in the vineyard.

The Bouché house was a large and beautifully proportioned wood structure in a roughly A-frame style. Inside, natural light was pervasive, with two banks of windows meeting at a right angle in the corner of the kitchen. Sébastian introduced me to Véronique, his wife, whom I had met in passing through school. She was an imposing woman with a mass of red hair and a 'don't mess with me' look. With five kids, she needed to be tough. Véronique was the research, administration, purchasing and organisation behind the partnership, Sébastian the artist and builder.

We talked through what we were looking for, the budget, timeline and materials. Véronique offered me a hot drink and we sat down at the dining table in the large open-plan living space, the whole family including five kids and myself, for green tea and home-made cake. They were eco-warriors: the house had a composting toilet, no flushing loo, and they ate organic. They lived gently on the earth.

Between telling the kids off for one misdemeanour and another, Véronique questioned me on different aspects of the project, while Sébastian flicked through one of his eco-building books, showing me photos to see my reaction to different building styles and methods. I had spoken to many artisans and had numerous quotes on file, but as I looked around their stunning, original house and experienced their sensitive approach, I knew I had found my team.

They agreed to do the plans for a reasonable fee and Sébastian said he would introduce us to a stonemason, Thomas, who he worked with regularly for the stonework, and to another contact for the internal walls. Closing the solid handmade wooden gate from their garden, my project notebook and a building-design book lent by Sébastian gripped tightly in my hand, I felt excitement mounting. The project was taking form. It was a significant step for us and a significant risk. I was thrilled and scared.

Flush with ideas from the wine-and-food-pairing experience in Napa, we invited Dave and Amanda to join us to come up with pairings to offer as one of our wine experiences. This would be 'ready to wear' rather than haute couture, since we couldn't afford to hire a Brian Streeter-style professional chef for Terroir Feely. Maybe one day.

I lined up local organic specialities like smoked trout, a small, white goat cheese from down the road, smoked duck finely sliced, and black chocolate, along with the nine wines that typically make up the Feely range in a given year.

A few months earlier, as we tackled the challenge of planning the annual bottling, Seán and I had spent many evenings brainstorming about the brand and names for our wines. A loyal client of five years had called and asked 'is that Château...

um…?' It was the call to action we needed. If he couldn't say the name to us on the phone, he couldn't tell his friends about us. I read that one of the reasons Château Lafite, a *premier grand cru classé* in the Médoc, did so well in China was because it was easy for Chinese speakers to say. Our old name, Château Haut Garrigue, was a mouthful few could say and even fewer could remember. We took the leap to change the brand to Feely, our family name, something we had been discussing for years but had been too scared to do.

I was horrified that we hadn't grabbed the bull by the horns sooner; we had wasted five years of marketing, including the windfall television show, on a bad brand name. It was a wonder we were still in business. Barry O'Brien, our friend in Dublin and an astute businessman, had said call it Feely Wines right at the start. To maintain the ideas that we were a French vineyard and producing natural wine, we made it Terroir Feely, sending the message that 'it's not about the *chateau*, it's about the *terroir*'.

Since we were making a major change, we decided to brainstorm the names of the cuvées in order to give each wine an identity rather than a varietal. I wanted the wine names to reflect what they were about. Our everyday white blend of sémillon and sauvignon blanc, for example, was called 'Luminosité' to reflect not only the colour of the wine and a light but fulfilling flavour, but also the change of colour that we had noticed in the soil since going biodynamic. It was as if it had light reflecting in it, luminosity, a beauty that it didn't have before.

We started the pairing evening with our *méthode traditionelle*, or MT, a blend of sémillon and sauvignon blanc like the Luminosité, but fermented a second time in the bottle to create the bubbles, as with real champagne.

'That tastes great to me,' said Dave, tasting it with the salty chips I had set out on the table.

Amanda and Seán nodded in agreement. Each of us had a pencil and paper for our own notes but I was the master note-taker, jotting down my own observations but also capturing key points made by our official tasting team.

'It's the acidity in the champagne setting off the fat of the chips, and the salt of the chips setting off the fruitiness and acidity of the champagne,' I said, touting some of my new knowledge. 'It's a classic pairing.'

'Highlighted by Marilyn Monroe in *The Seven Year Itch*,' said Amanda.

'Wow, you are good!' I said, pouring the next wine, Sincérité, so-called because our pure sauvignon blanc grown on limestone was sincerity: straight-talking, linear, direct, sometimes a little difficult at first but with a depth of flavour and a truth to its *terroir* that made it one of my favourites.

'That is superb, Madame Feely,' said Dave after taking a sip.

'It's the master winemaker,' I said, then tasted, sensing the level of acidity in the back of my cheeks and on the sides of the back half of my tongue, a lip-smacking, cheek-drawing-in tartness that made my mouth water as it did with lemon juice. Slipping a tiny sliver of the fresh white goat cheese into my mouth, I experienced a burst of flavour. The fruitiness of the wine came forward and the flavours of the cheese were enhanced.

'That really brings out the gooseberry,' said Seán.

'I think Sincérité would be good with a light fish dish served with lemon, too, Caro,' said Amanda. I made a note. 'I wish we had some sauvignon blanc,' she went on. 'That's the first thing we'll be planting when we create a new vineyard. Oh, I almost forgot! I can eat cheese tonight! I have found this amazing little pill that protects me from the lactose for the odd splurge.' She reached for a sliver of the goat cheese.

'How are things going?' I said.

'Oh, all right,' said Amanda. 'You know how it is, Caro, don't you? Our first planning-permission request was rejected. We feel like we are scrambling to keep up in the vineyard.'

I knew exactly what they were going through.

'Don't worry! It gets better. But don't say I didn't warn ya!' I said as I poured Générosité, the barrel-aged blend from ancient sémillon vines.

They laughed. They had read the draft of my no-holds-barred account of our tough first three years.

'That is all roundness, vanilla and grilled peach with sweet spice,' said Amanda.

'With a touch of smoke in the finish,' said Seán.

'Wow. You are right, Seán. My gosh, that is *really* smoky in the finish,' said Amanda.

'Do you know why?' I asked.

'No, tell me,' said Amanda.

'Where this sémillon grows there is a seam of silex that runs from the plateau down the slope and the smell is a smoky note of flintstone.'

'Really?' said Dave looking sceptical. 'I thought all that guff about minerality was a load of bollocks.'

'Dave! It's totally for real!' I said. 'I heard Claude Bourguignon, one of the top soil scientists in France recently. He explained that at one and two metres below the earth's surface are critters that eat rocks for a living. They excrete the rocks as soluble minerals, thus making them available to plants.'

'No way!' said Amanda.

'Yes! And farming chemically kills those critters and other soil life. When he explained it, I felt like jumping up in the hall full of people and shouting "hallelujah!" I knew I tasted minerality in some wines but with all the naysayers… ' – I looked meaningfully at Dave – '… I had begun to question myself.'

'Incredible,' said Amanda.

'I'll get his book that has photos of the critters,' I said and ran off to find it.

The death of the critters is also one of the reasons our food has become poorer in fundamental minerals, despite being richer in calories. People were taking more vitamin supplements than ever before to compensate for the lack of good, vital food, but they didn't offer the same value as the real thing.

'Pretty scary-looking little devils, aren't they?' said Amanda as I showed them the photos on my return.

'But, oh so good; Bourguignon says doing what the critters do for free in a healthy soil would take several hundred man hours of work per acre per year. Hearing him I felt the same as I had after watching the bee documentary that showed orchards in China being hand-pollinated after their bee populations had been decimated by pesticides.'

Bourguignon didn't hold out much hope for the earth, but he was doing his best to turn the tide. I knew that, like him, I had to do more to communicate the real cost of industrial agriculture.

The Générosité wine was a total contrast to Sincérité. The age brought aromas that were more cooked fruit than fresh fruit, and the overlay of spice and vanilla from the oak was accompanied by a little trace of wood tannin.

'Whatever about the rocks bollocks, it tastes good to me,' said Dave, taking a piece of home-made bread with the smoky, smooth nuns' cheese Echourgnac and a taste of the wine, then slowly chanting 'yum yum'.

'I feel like we're taking part in a strange religious ritual,' I said.

'I am,' said Dave. 'Food is a religion for me.'

We laughed and I poured our La Source 'no sulphites added' red wine.

As with the sauvignon blanc, a sliver of goat cheese brought a heavenly burst of berry flavour that enhanced both the cheese and the wine. Amanda pointed at the dark chocolate on the table, then at the wine, and nodded vigorously. She had a fantastic nose and palate and was a great chef who could turn out lactose-, gluten- and meat-free wonders. I took note of everything she said that evening. She was right, the chocolate and La Source pairing was black magic, a dangerous discovery for me.

It was risky to make no-sulphite-added wines; without extreme care, one could produce wines that had oxidative notes, almost sherry-like. But there was a clear health benefit and, when well made, the no-sulphite wines offered fresher fruit. This one was like biting into a handful of fresh-picked blackberries. Sulphites are an inflammatory that can contribute to a headache the morning after. Not only that, they kill the natural vitamin B present in the wine, something that helps the human liver to process the alcohol more efficiently. So far we hadn't tried to make no-sulphite white wines. Reds had tannins that helped preserve them, making it slightly less risky. The tannins are antioxidants and protect the wine, thus increasing its ageing potential, but they can mask flavour.

The thing with tasting wine and food together is that it is difficult to spit. Tasting back and forth that night I was surprised we remembered anything. Luckily I was writing furiously as we tasted.

We ended the evening with our Saussignac Premier Or, a golden, unctuous dessert wine with waves of passion fruit, apricot, spices and acacia honey, and a lift of acidity in the finish to cut through the residual sugar. For perfect pairing, matching the characteristics of the food and the wine on three key principles seemed to be the secret: balancing the weight of the wine with the richness of the food; having at least as much acidity in the wine as in the food; and reinforcing, complementing or contrasting aromas or flavours. The naturally sweet Saussignac with Roquefort blue cheese was a classic contrast pairing. I said a quiet thanks to the monks who originally discovered the botrytis dessert wine magic and made our hills famous.

We tasted and laughed until we almost cried, exchanging stories from the ten days we were away and catching up generally. While we laughed again at Dave's description of Sophia translating the fire chief's words, I felt a stab of guilt and fear for our daughters, then quickly quashed it. We had to learn to let them fly on their own. We could not always be with them. They were both unfazed by the experience; in fact, Sophia was quite proud of her contribution.

As spring was due to arrive, Thierry Daulhiac and I pulled into a sodden parking lot and picked our way through mud to find our places among the trestle tables around the outer edge of a large event tent, set up on the lawn of a small organic *grand cru* estate in Saint-Émilion. I noted my table was on the corner where the tent edges met and an icy wind swept through. We hulked our boxes of samples and cooler boxes through the sludge.

En Primeurs Bio was a show held by our local organic winegrowers association, organised each year at the same time as the *grands crus classés* showed their new vintage to the wine professionals of the world. *Grand cru classé,* a Bordeaux construct that denoted highly rated vineyards, was most famous in Médoc to the north of Bordeaux city and Saint-Émilion to the east; but it was also in place in Graves, south of the city, and in Sauternes, the sweet-wine southern end of Graves. The *En*

Primeurs was an opportunity for the *grands crus classés* and the most well-known brands of the region to pre-sell their wines. Some of the chateaux sold 80 per cent of their wine this way, while it was still in the barrel and a long way from being bottled.

This fantastic way to finance the costs of barrel-ageing and bottling was unfortunately unavailable to those of us who needed it most. The *En Primeurs Bio* show was not to sell, but merely to *present* our wines while a large portion of the world's fine-wine buyers and journalists were in town.

As the day progressed, the weather worsened and the mud encroached despite wooden pallets set up as a makeshift walkway. Like the previous show I'd attended, this one brought little footfall. The few buyers that passed through wanted to taste Saint-Émilions and Pomerols, not Bergeracs. I shared more of my wine with other growers than with potential buyers. At the table opposite, Thierry was next to Laurent Lazare, an iconic winegrower in the Bergerac region. I had read about him, visited his vineyard and tasted his wines but never met the man himself. Thierry introduced us.

After the usual pleasant introductory exchanges he asked to taste our wines. Despite the major challenges Seán had faced, we were happy with the vintage. The whites were mineral and had the acidity to carry off the higher alcohol of the hot vintage, and the reds had finesse. He nodded to each of the whites, then held out his glass for the reds. I gave him the barrel-red and he nodded again and held it out for the merlot. I poured. He swished and spat.

'You'll never sell this. This isn't what the market wants today. There is something seriously wrong with this wine. There is something wrong with the winegrower. You'll never sell this. Where are you? I must come and visit you.'

I felt like I had been punched in the gut. Tears welled up but I fought them back, adamant that I would not cry. After a few more blows Laurent took off, leaving me to my devastation, a false smile fixed to my face to stop the true feeling from exploding out.

I offered tastes of the battered wine to Thierry and Franck Pascal, both winegrowers I respected, and asked for their opinion. They thought the wine had minerality and finesse. I knew them both well enough for them to be honest. Franck wasn't known for pulling his punches. Their feedback helped, but I was gutted, drained, whipped.

'Don't worry, Caro,' said Thierry. 'Laurent did the same to me in front of a large group of winegrowers many years ago. It was my first vintage, I was so proud of it and he assassinated it. He is known for this.'

In this tight-knit winegrower community things were not easily forgotten. Perhaps his feedback was honest and he felt it would help us, but right then I couldn't see anything but the tears on the edges of my eyes.

Thierry and I dissected the day while travelling home – what the visitors were like, who we saw, the other winegrowers, and my horrendous experience both with the glacial wind spattering rain onto me all day and the encounter with Laurent Lazare. En route, the cold overwhelmed me and I started to shiver, my throat sore and my muscles aching. The following day I was racked with fever. I would never forget Lazare's unprovoked attack on our wine. It affected me perhaps even more than when a wine buyer called our first white vintage 'thin, Italian style'.

A couple of days later I was over my flu and Sébastian brought a contact of his to quote for the internal walls. He seemed solid and personable. At the end of the meeting he gave me his card. It announced 'Lionel Lazare'.

As soon as he left, I asked Sébastian if he was one of *the* Lazares.

'Yes, he is a son of the famous winegrower, Laurent,' he said.

Horror flashed across my face. If Sébastian picked it up, he said nothing. I liked Lionel a lot less, but told myself to grow up.

In France, children are responsible for their parents and vice versa; if a son or daughter runs up gambling debts, the parents are responsible and, if the parents run up debts, the adult children are responsible. There were some hilarious films about this law and it did instil a sense of responsibility to family. Lionel *was,* in a strictly French sense, responsible. But I resolved not to hold it against him.

The same day, Sébastian brought his mason friend, Thomas de Conti, to meet us. He was dark with curly hair, a wiry body and thoughtful, like a poet. We talked through our ideas and Sébastian's initial drawings. Thomas had good ideas for bringing the old walls and the new structure together in an aesthetic manner. He listened to what we wanted and I instantly took to him. Having two friends used to working together on the project made a lot of sense.

The project plans were advancing, my ideas for complementary tourist activities like the wine and food pairing were taking shape, and Seán was well into his second year of conversion to biodynamic agriculture. The work in the vineyard and winery was becoming instinctive with the power of experience. It felt like our fight after the trip to Alsace and Burgundy was from another life. Working on the plans for the building project was bringing us back together.

Chapter 17
Saint-Émilion Stories

While Sébastian and Véronique drew up detailed plans and the planning application, I gathered quotes, calculated the overall budget and put together the aid application. We wanted the buildings to be ecological: large roof overhangs for shade in summer; expansive windows to capture the winter sun on tiles, allowing natural light to flood in and making the most of the vineyard views; and natural materials and colours while keeping the original stone walls.

With the plans in hand I measured out the space and set up tables and chairs in the empty area where the old lean-to was and visualised the new building. Seán thought I was mad but I needed to imagine how many people it would seat, to know that we were planning the right thing.

Thinking of all the work we had put into renovating the lean-to and surrounding terrace, I felt sad because we would now have to undo what had been done. When we arrived it had been an old, rotting wooden shed, the earth floor covered with rubbish, the ceiling and walls strung with massive cobwebs that made me think of the giant spiders in *Harry Potter*. At the back end there had been a pigsty and a hole-in-the-ground toilet; an area Seán had since transformed into a modern bathroom with the composting loo – same idea, different look. We had removed the rotting planks and created a tasting-room terrace with a white concrete floor, with a rockery area and diamond-shaped paving squares at the entrance. I'd spent days humping rocks and painting the exposed wood of the ceiling with whitewash. Now the space would become the new tasting room. We were entering a new era. The old had to make way for the new.

A new law in France meant that any public building had to be fully wheelchair-accessible, and even the furniture had to be carefully selected if we wanted the EU aid. This added complexity. With the aid application package was a detailed document outlining the technical aspects of compliance. My French had improved significantly but I still found legal and technical documents slow-going so I gave copies to the team, hoping they would ensure we were *aux normes*.

Spring brought more guests than ever. With Anna, a lovely, delicate-looking Swede, I visited Château Guadet, a beautiful little *grand cru classé* in Saint-Émilion, owned by the Lignacs. Anna's boss, a Russian oligarch, had several thousand bottles in his cellar on the Côte d'Azur and she needed to know more about the wines he had, and the wines he should consider having. She was on call 24–7 but was so well paid she said it was worth it. She lived in luxury in his palatial villa while he globe-trotted. He had three full-time personal secretaries, one in each time zone, but he still called her at all hours of the day and night. She never said his name or gave any more details. She always referred to him as 'Mister'. I was intrigued.

Our visit was hosted by Vince Lignac, a lithe and charming thirty-something with a mixed American–Australian twang to his English thanks to ten years working overseas. Dressed in working clothes, strong boots and a kangaroo-leather Stetson hat, his look matched his accent.

Vince's family had bought the vineyard from the Guadets in the 1840s after the Guadets' ancestors, members of the Girondins political faction, made the mistake of abstaining from voting for the death of the king during the revolution. As Vince said, 'It was, like, you know, bad for your head.' Marguerite-Élie Guadet hid in the tunnels under the chateau for months and was on his way to Spain when one member of his fleeing party, rattled by the sound of fireworks, shot himself, raising the alarm. Soon after, Marguerite-Élie had his head chopped off. Just one month later he would have been home free, as it became Robespierre's turn to get to know the guillotine. Much of the family followed Guadet to a similar bloody end, except his wife and children, who sold the property to the Lignacs two generations later.

The revolution was a gruesome chapter in France's history that I didn't like to dwell on. I preferred other parts of its history, like the troubadours and Eleanor of Aquitaine. She was heiress of our province, and she and Henry II, her second husband and king of England, gave Saint-Émilion their city rights in return for an annual share of *vin honorifique*, their equivalent of *grand cru* today. It sounded like a good deal to me. Eleanor was quite a lady. She married the French king at the age of fifteen; you can see the city gate commemorating it in Bordeaux. Some fifteen years later, despite having produced healthy children with him, she convinced the pope to annul the marriage on the basis of consanguinity and promptly married Henry Plantagenet, who soon after became king of England. She went on to outlive all her children. In her seventies she rode on horseback from Aquitaine to Spain to vet a suitor for a granddaughter. For that ride alone she was worthy of her legendary status.

Saint-Émilion is named after a hermit monk who settled there around AD 750. His healing miracles made the village a famous pilgrimage stop on several of the Santiago de Compostela routes through Europe. Émilion was most famous for his fertility miracles. 'Leave your wife in my cave for an hour and I will see what I can do,' was an irreverent quip from one of my American clients.

After years of visiting Saint-Émilion, I could identify which of the different soils a wine came from: the limestone plateau, the south-facing slopes, the gravel back-end near Pomerol, or the sandy soils at the bottom of the area. It fascinated me. Wine was a subject of never-ending depth and breadth. Each time I thought I understood I would see another dimension and taste a different nuance in a new vintage or a new slope.

Vince had a quiet sense of place, a wisdom and serenity that came from the combination of his deep family anchor in Saint-Émilion and a knowledge of himself from travelling the world before returning by choice. 'We taste the wine every day during the fermentation to decide how many pump-overs to do. It is a question of balance. Just like in life, after all, it is all about the balance,' he said.

Saint-Émilion was more famous than ever and had become a hot 'must visit' destination for wine lovers. We were lucky to be so close, a 45-minute drive through beautiful vineyards, a boon for our growing tourism business. While growers in appellations nearby struggled to give their wines away, that afternoon the lovely Laurent Benoit of Château Angelus, soon to become *premier grand cru classé A*, explained that they had released their latest vintage for *en primeur* sales at a consumer price of over 300 euros a bottle. All 100,000 bottles available were sold in under an hour. The wine crisis I felt when selling our wines to the trade was not something they were experiencing.

The Reserveage payment for the first batch of our dried certified organic grape skins hit our account *and* Naomi ordered four pallets of our red wine. It was the second-largest order in the history of our vineyard and another vital boost to our confidence to proceed with the building project. She was saving our skins in every way.

To close the sale we had to find a US importer to bring the wine into Florida. I contacted several and settled on one that appeared reliable and physically close to Naomi. Then, for the American market we needed to add a special label with the importer's name and the Surgeon-General's health warning, just as we had done for Jon. Before doing this, the front and back labels had to be submitted to the American authorities for verification. The initial submission was rejected because they wanted an English translation of the text on the main label added to the back label. Clearly the assessor of the label didn't understand French, since they didn't realise that the English text featured on the main label *was* a translation of the original French. I felt like screaming but instead resubmitted with this clarification and got another rejection, this time for an unacceptable font size on one of the headings on the back label. We corrected and resubmitted.

As we crept closer to Naomi's deadline I became more and more stressed. She needed the wine for a trade fair four months away. Where international shipping and wine-related red tape were concerned, this was not much time. The labelling pedantry seemed like a lot of administrative tussling about nothing, particularly for wine that was a private sale and not for resale to the public, but we had to adhere.

Following approval, third time lucky, Isabelle printed the precious labels for us. I set a production line up in the barn and steadily unpacked 200 twelve-bottle cases weighing around 18 kilograms each, carefully added the extra label to each bottle then repacked the box and stacked it onto a new pallet, a special kind required for exporting to the Americas. Over a couple of days I lifted three tons several metres vertically and horizontally. My exercise programme did not lack for new and entertaining ideas.

Sophia and Ellie were also getting their share of exercise by collecting the eggs of our free-range chickens from all over the farm. The chickens liked to test their stamina and cunning by regularly changing nest location. When the girls found Mother Blacky brooding on a nest of about twenty eggs, I recalled a trick from my grandmother about floating or sinking being an indicator of age; the Internet confirmed that if an egg floated, it was bad. Most of these did.

At lunch that day Seán and I were debating yet another aspect of the project, oak doors versus clapboard doors at a quarter of the price. We had been through everything: longevity, look, budget.

'They *are* French oak,' said Seán.

'What's that got to do with the price of eggs?' I said, thinking he had lost it; French oak for wine barrels, sure, but for doors surely French oak versus other oak made no difference.

'Why are you asking about the price of eggs when you are talking about the price of doors?' said Sophia.

We all laughed and I explained what we meant when we used this saying in English. The girls were becoming more French by the day.

Seán was right, though. The doors were not only French oak but also FSC-approved: buying locally and responsibly was important. With each day we were becoming more aware of what our purchases meant; rather no doors than doors that would pollute the environment and end up in landfill. These doors would last many lifetimes.

After a few false starts the wine for Naomi was collected with all the necessary paperwork. The truck was taking it to a port in Holland, where it would be containerised for its onward trip to Florida. I confirmed the successful collection to the US importer, feeling a wave of relief. The wine would be in Florida by the first week of September, just in time for Naomi's deadline of mid September, so that it could be served at a show in late September in another state.

Continuing with logistical work, I emailed a UK chain of delis that had ordered two pallets of our white wine, putting pressure on them to collect. Digging work for the project was due to start and would hamper access to our warehouse. We had signed for the initial terracing work but were not yet fully committed to the main project; like a rabbit in car headlights, we were frozen with fear at the risk.

It was a full week since the deli's requested pick-up date and I was getting worried. Wine sold to trade was only paid two months after collection. If the wine was not collected on the collection date stated on the order, we could not invoice the client. On the other hand, we had to hold the wine for them since it was contracted. It was a catch-22 that could destroy a wine estate if a large order got stuck in this no-man's-land.

This order and Naomi's were key sales to funding the initial stages of the project, but thereafter the path was not clear. I had many sleepless nights asking myself if we were completely insane but I knew we had to do it to progress. I prayed we wouldn't lose our balance in the process. Doubts dragged us into inaction until a postcard from our biodynamic association arrived with a quote from Goethe:

As long as we do not engage, doubt reigns; the possibility of withdrawal remains, and inefficiency prevails. This is an elementary truth, the ignorance of which has numerous implications and has aborted splendid projects. From the moment we engage fully providence starts to move in the same direction.

Everything you can do or dream of doing you can undertake. Audacity confirms in us genius, power and magic. Start now.

We took it as a sign and committed ourselves fully to the tasting room. The decision began a new era of 'feeling the g-force'. The growing season had Seán engrossed in the vineyard and better weather meant non-stop tour guests for me. We hardly had time to wave at each other as we passed morning and evening: Seán going to bed long after me and me getting up way earlier than him. Sophia and Ellie were growing at speed. I felt like I was missing it. Pulled this way and that by the project and by marketing trips, and working weekends, I was barely there.

Chapter 18
The Imperfect Day

Seán's birthday, the last day of August, was the anniversary of our move to France five years before. It also signified the end of the summer holiday and of the builders' holidays, so it was the official kick-off date for the project.

Mr Jegu, a gentle giant who had helped us through earth-moving experiences in the past, started the project with a flourish, opening up a trench across the courtyard to lay the electricity and water for the tasting room and lodge. The hammering of the *brise-roche* (rock-breaker) was accompanied by extremely high-pitched squealing from the rusty tracks of his old digger. My head was throbbing.

The trench blocked access to the winery and the warehouse and forced our gîte guests to park elsewhere. They were unhappy about the noise, guaranteed to destroy a holiday even for the most easy-going – and they had just finished a long and nightmarish building project on their own house. This vacation was to get away from it all, and instead they found themselves on yet another building site.

My wine-school guests were compromised too. The class that morning had to decamp to Château Les Tours de Lenvège next door, where the guests were staying, as the noise was so intense we could not hear ourselves think or drink. In the darkness of the chateau I did my best to run the class in a professional manner without my usual supports, like the correct light, maps, fridge and a spittoon.

Now, after an afternoon back at my desk accompanied by the high-pitched screaming and hammering of the digger, I was close to pulling my hair out. It was only day one of the building site and I could not wait to get away. For his birthday I had planned a romantic dinner with Seán. It would be our *first* night out together in Bergerac, our nearest town, *ever*; a sign of how little spare time and money we had had in the previous five years and how much we had neglected our relationship.

The girls were going to our friends Pierre and Laurence for a sleepover. I felt sure there would be no problem getting a reservation since it was a week-night. But when I called the restaurant I wanted they were fully booked. After a few more calls I realised that going out on the town was not so easy, even on a Tuesday night. Some places were on holiday, others were renovating and more were fully booked. Despite mixed reviews from gîte guests, many of whom had tried more local restaurants in a week than we had in five years, I called L'Imparfait, a gourmet restaurant guaranteed to cost far more than we could afford. After the day I had had I needed a blowout night. It was my lucky day: they could squeeze us in.

Feeling better, I took note of the address then dialled into my messages, opening my email at the same time. It was nearly five in the evening. A phone message and an email from the UK deli's transporter said they would collect the two pallets of wine the following morning. It was ten days since their requested pick-up date and I had been asking for confirmation of the day for weeks. They had to choose the moment the courtyard was inaccessible to collect. I felt like screaming. Angst rising, I ran outside to find Mr Jegu. He promised to have the wine warehouse accessible the following afternoon after 4 p.m.

I called the transporter to delay the pick-up to the afternoon and they informed me they did not have a tailgate on the articulated truck and that we, therefore, had to supply a forklift. We didn't have one. I made a mental note to ask Pierre if we could borrow his when we dropped the girls off.

Seán came in from the vineyard bearing his toolbox.

'I'm going to fix the toilet before I get ready,' he said.

The toilet had been dripping for a few days and I hated wasting water, but we had several years of experience to prove that plumbing jobs could not be squeezed into a few minutes after-hours. For us, plumbing jobs needed days, several trips to the local hardware store and a visit from our professional plumber at the end for good measure. I mumbled a warning.

'What? It's a simple matter of tightening the joint,' Seán riposted.

I shut up. It was his birthday after all.

A few minutes later I heard frantic cursing and water-gushing. In the process of tightening the connection, the old tap that fed the toilet had snapped off and water was pouring out of the broken copper pipe.

'Feck!' I added to the volley of expletives already flowing from Seán, and grabbed the towel he had wrapped around it in a futile attempt to stem the leak. He sprinted outside to switch off the mains. I could see my planned bathing and beautifying before our big night out disappearing like a mirage on the horizon. Seán and plumbing spelt disaster. Knowing this, it was hard to fathom why he had decided to start this delicate job in the evening but I reminded myself again that it was his birthday and bit my tongue.

It was 5.45 p.m. and the chances of getting a plumber were slim. The only way to stop the gushing inside our house was to leave the mains for the whole property off. Now our unhappy gîte guests would have noise, no parking and *no water*. No flushing toilet, no water to cook with, no water for tea, no water to drink. 'Feck' was not enough.

Before I could say 'buy water', Seán leapt into the car and raced down to the *quincaillerie*, our local hardware store in Gardonne, one of his favourite haunts, to buy a closure and some plumbing tape.

I called Monsieur Lambert's office, miraculously catching him as he closed up for the night. He promised Jean-Marc would come round immediately to see what he could do. Monsieur Lambert had become very responsive since we began the grand project of the tasting room and Wine Lodge.

Maria, our gîte guest, walked onto the Wine Cottage terrace and announced that they were about to fill the kettle for a cup of tea and did I want to join them. I broke the news that there was no water for tea and promised to buy water as soon as Seán returned from the *quincaillerie*.

I felt like jumping off a cliff but instead leapt into the car Seán had just returned in, raced down to the Utile and stocked up on 20 litres of water.

Thinking the day from hell could only get better, I opened my email to check for the confirmation of the afternoon pick-up by the deli's transporter and found a note from the Florida wine importer: 'Due to engine trouble the ship carrying the Reserveage order had to return to port and the wine is now delayed and will only leave Europe on 3 September.'

Suddenly no water and a broken toilet seemed like no trouble at all. Jeopardy for our second-largest order ever meant I saw red and our bank account soon would too. We would have to fast-track the order to prevent Naomi cancelling because, if she did, we would have to pay return shipping costs and would have four pallets of wine labelled for her that were not sold. I felt sick. I left a message for the importer stressing the urgency and demanding action.

By the time Jean-Marc, my knight in shining armour for all things plumbing, arrived, Seán had closed the pipe sufficiently to turn the mains back on. He wasn't so bad at plumbing after all.

As I told Jean-Marc about my day, he kept repeating, '*Oh, la misère!*'

I couldn't have said it better myself.

Jean-Marc checked Seán's seal, added some professional tape and said he would return to repair the toilet properly the following day. I rushed out to announce the victory to our gîte guests and almost ran into Mr Jegu at the door. The channel was taking longer than expected and the work would take at least one more day. The access to the warehouse could be in place for the wine collection but the noise would have to continue.

I didn't know how to tell our guests they had another forty-eight hours of hell instead of twenty-four. I felt like leaping off the gîte terrace but instead gritted my teeth and delivered the message, offering half the week free to sweeten the bitter pill.

If this was what the building was going to be like, I would not make it to the end of the week, let alone the end of the project. At least the water was back on and I could look forward to a fast shower before drowning my sorrows in fine wine at L'Imparfait. 'The Imperfect' was a fitting name for the day so far.

In Bergerac the last rays of sunlight caught the tops of the medieval houses leaning in over the streets of the old town, their facades a mix of cream stones, weathered wood and peach-tone tiles. The night air was warm and velvety. Young, happy couples strolled with insouciance, and the afternoon from hell seemed a lifetime away. Down a tiny lane packed with tables we found L'Imparfait. Waiting to be seated I was unexpectedly embraced by Pascale. Pascale and François had run the Lion d'Or in Saussignac for years until François was struck with a fast-acting cancer and passed away almost before anyone realised what was happening. Pascale had moved on, unable to continue the restaurant alone. We missed them. It was great to see her and we caught up quickly as she led us outside. She had sold the hotel-restaurant François had bought for her before he died and now she was helping at L'Imparfait temporarily. I felt sad. She was bouncing back but loss was still etched on her face.

We squeezed into a tiny table on the narrow terrace, flanked by tables filled with diners on either side. It was so tight that, as pedestrians passed along the lane behind Seán, their legs touched the back of his jacket. Despite the tight seating, the ambiance was relaxed, languid, like a peaceful late-summer afternoon totally unlike the one I had just experienced. I felt luxurious. The old walls facing me danced in the candlelight as if the stones were alive.

Dressed in a clingy, chic yellow dress, a hand-me-down from my glamorous sister Jacquie, possibly wirecell but what did I know, and some lovely strappy silver flats by Prada, also courtesy of my benevolent sister, I felt on top of the moon, stylish, almost pretty... Not like someone that had just humped three tons of wine across a barn and wrestled the day from hell into submission.

We perused the menu and the wine list, feeling thoroughly opulent. It was a delight to be a wine buyer for a change, hesitating between this and that, revelling in the wonderful moment of anticipation. We settled on a Pouilly-Fumé to start, a superb sauvignon blanc with mineral flinty notes and good body, magic with Seán's starter portion of langoustines and my red mullet fillets served on a fennel salad. The imperfect day slowly dissolved as the meal progressed.

My main course, melt-in-the-mouth sea bass with creamy ginger sauce on a perfectly dressed plate, was so heavenly Seán told me to quieten down – what would people think? I was Meg Ryan in *When Harry Met Sally*.

A Saint-Nicolas-de-Bourgueil red wine sent us down memory lane to the day we discovered France and her wine and our lives were never going to be quite the same again. That day, at the Pierre-Jacques Druet estate in the Loire Valley, the chalky cliffs outside the cellar hewn out of the rock had glowed cream-gold in the afternoon sun. His descriptions of the harvest and the wines as we tasted from his barrels transported us to a new place.

'The wines are grown, not made; I am the shepherd of the harvest, not the winemaker,' Pierre-Jacques had said. Between his poetic descriptions and his passionate explanations we were smitten. From then on our lives were consumed with the dream of becoming winegrowers in France.

From the reverie of Bourgueil we talked on dreamily of holidays, of appreciating our fast-growing daughters, the future and the project. Returning home replete, we found the house bizarrely quiet. Not having our daughters at home felt strange. We felt out of place and at a loss. Some candles strategically placed in the bedroom helped us find something to do.

Chapter 19
Volunteers and Red Tape

We were expecting a hundred people for our harvest weekend. Niall's television show the year before had generated a bumper turnout. The event needed James Bond precision and our 007 team had just landed.

Spring Webb was a powerful 'can do' Kiwi with fabulous dreadlocks. She more than matched our Kiwi expectations set by Helen and Derek, the titans who cleared the forest around the site for the new tasting room and lodge. With Simon Golding, her partner, a Brit with dark curly hair and a philosopher's perspective, they were a formidable team, having worked multiple vintages on estates in New Zealand.

We were hesitant about using volunteers because of a few bad experiences. Brian had been a young, fat engineer with little appetite for work and a great appetite for Internet and hot chocolate, though with a good sense of humour that was his saving grace. He was followed by Brad, a young, overweight graduate with even less appetite for work and a large one for cigarettes despite 'no smoking' being clearly spelt out in the guidelines provided when he first contacted us. They added little and took up unnecessary time to manage and extract from the farm. After experiences like these, Seán was emotionally drained and our work reversed rather than advanced.

Now we only accepted volunteers who were super keen to learn about organic farming, the main reason for us offering the volunteer places; and for short periods with a non-negotiable maximum of two weeks. Under these new rules Simon and Spring had visited in early summer. Over those two weeks they were a Bond-worthy team. Simon set up our Internet networks – he had been a skilled network engineer before giving in to his passion for wine and vineyards. Spring tore into outdoor work without hesitation and organised everything she touched. My half-day for a group of journalists invited by the regional tourism body was planned with military precision. The tables were beautifully laid in the shade in the garden. Spring and Simon positioned them to the millimetre for views of the vineyards and the Château de Saussignac in one direction and the Dordogne valley's orchards, vineyards and villages below us in the other. The food was perfect, the service impeccable, and I was able to focus on explaining our wines and organic and biodynamic farming. For most of the journalists it was their first time hearing about biodynamics and they were entranced.

After lunch we had sweated around our newly marked guest-walking route as the thermometer climbed to 36 °C. When we returned hot and parched, we found tables and chairs positioned in the shade of the lean-to terrace alongside the old tasting room with great jugs of iced water decorated with slices of lemon and home-grown mint. Spring was always a step ahead. I would think of something that needed to be done and as I was about to say it she was already there, like a mind-reader. They were a mean team. We loved them and so had invited them back for as long as they liked at harvest time.

One of the guests that journalist day was Stephan Thierry, the marketing manager of our provincial tourist board in Bordeaux, a mover and shaker in the world of wine tourism. He emailed to thank me and suggested we apply for the 'Best of Wine Tourism' awards the following year.

The Internet revealed the awards were part of the global awards run by the Great Wine Capitals network that brought together the top wine destinations of the world: Bilbao for Rioja, Bordeaux for Aquitaine, Cape Town for the Cape Winelands, Christchurch for South Island in New Zealand, Florence for Tuscany, Mainz for the Rheinhessen, Mendoza in Argentina, Porto in Portugal, San Francisco for Napa Valley and Valparaíso for Chile's Casablanca Valley. It read like a roll call for a WSET wine tasting. The pitch looked way too grand for us given the heavyweights involved, but there was no harm in finding out. I sent an email to the organisers asking for an application form.

By the time Spring and Simon returned for harvest, the lean-to against the old tasting room was gone. Mr Jegu, our digger man, had finished the trench and was making inroads into the foundations for the new buildings.

Simon and Spring settled into the caravan in the limestone amphitheatre surrounded by panoramic vineyard views. The bathroom Seán built, that served as their washroom, now floated above a large white moat of solid limestone, the foundation for the new tasting room. To reach the facility they had to traverse it, as would all my tour guests. Spring and Simon constructed a handy bridge of wooden pallets to make the passage easier.

The weekend of their return an apricot sunset over the vineyard announced perfect conditions for a barbecue. Simon and Spring produced bottles of the wines they had made in New Zealand, I raided my supplies of tasting samples and bottles from our trip to California and we blind-tasted New World vs

Old World. Sniffing and swilling, I experimented with my blind tasting skills, needing to practise. The 'Certified Wine Educator' course at the WSET school in London was set to test my abilities in a few weeks. With the qualification and the new tasting room we would be a certified wine school.

Spring found the old world wines had a clear signal that she called 'dusty' and she picked them out correctly. We laughed and tasted, sharing experiences and getting to know each other, creating the bonds necessary for the intense teamwork of harvest. The late night didn't put Spring off helping me clean the Wine Cottage for guests the following day. She was a cleaning machine and when she declared that she loved cleaning, I said she could stay forever.

Harvest brought cleaning and sterilisation of vats, stressed planning of dates and worry that we might be served the bad driver again. I called Serge to put my foot down and he said the person had ceased to drive for the co-operative. I could barely contain my delight as I marked this little stress off the most intense time in our annual cycle.

Seán, Simon and Spring walked the vineyards every day, tasting the grapes to determine the ideal picking date for the sauvignon blanc. Now, in our fifth year, Seán was confident about his decisions, aware of the small differences from one side of the vineyard to another, of the top of the slope compared to the bottom, of the slight change in vigour of the vines depending on their location, and in the resulting taste of the grapes in the barely perceptible dip in the middle. He could visualise the wine based on the fruit on the vine.

The sauvignon was ready. The weather was perfect. I booked the harvest machine.

Waking up before dawn was a privileged moment of feeling I had the earth to myself, of silence, of sensing the magnificence of nature with the hoot of an owl and the flicker of a hare disappearing down a vine row. Waiting for the harvest machine I marvelled at the star-studded dome above us, as filled with wonder as I had been the first year.

Benoit, the new driver, arrived right on time. An introductory chat revealed he was a farmer, which gave us confidence. He knew how important harvest was to us, as only another farmer could.

I ran down pointing the sauvignon vineyard markers, beautiful big bows made from pink Lycra strips at the start of each row that Spring had attached the day before. Turning to head back up I exchanged a wave with Benoit and saw a wide smile. He had never seen a vineyard marked with baby-pink ribbon before.

The first load went smoothly from harvest machine to trailer, then Seán backed up the tractor and we pumped the juice from trailer to vat. Simon was positioned as a stabilising point under the main harvest pipe, I was on duty dosing carbon dioxide gas and a tiny shot of sulphur dioxide to protect the juice from oxidation, and Spring was reading Seán's mind.

Before he said a word she grabbed the big white food-grade spade and pushed the grapes left along the sides of the trailer down so they would be pumped through and not left to oxidise. Seán looked astonished and gave her the thumbs up.

Minutes later, with the load safely transferred, he turned off the tractor and climbed up onto the vat to check how it looked. She handed him the first bucket of grapes drained from the auger pipe of the trailer and I got ready to pass the next. There was almost no need to talk – it was telepathy and instinct. Before my words formed, Spring had taken it from me.

That night, with all the sauvignon blanc safely in the vats, we celebrated the successful start of vintage with a recipe from the Cakebread book bought on the trip to California: duck and home-grown dried cherries and walnuts matched with a medley of roast potatoes and courgettes and a bottle of La Source from our first year. It was perfect for the cold that announced the start of autumn and a chance to reminisce about our trip. We toasted the safe passage of the sauvignon blanc grapes destined to be our Sincérité pure sauvignon. It was the first vintage of white grapes that would be pressed with the 'new' basket press. Seán had decided to leave the juice on the skins for one day of maceration. We didn't keep the skins with the juice for the fermentation of white wine as that could create bitter tannins. However, limited skin maceration could be interesting, particularly for sauvignon blanc, as it helped to draw the polyphenols, all-important aroma compounds, into the juice.

Wine is made with grapes, and not other fruit, because of the concentration of these magical properties within them. In oranges and apples there are hundreds of such properties, whereas in grapes there are thousands. When man first made wine around ten thousand years ago, he already realised that wine made with grapes was better than anything else. What ancient man knew, modern man had proved with science. In Australia, the Wine Research Institute measured the pepper polyphenol aroma in shiraz, which we call syrah in France, and found, incredibly, that it was several thousand times the power of actual pepper.

We left the sauvignon blanc for a day and the effect was just right. In previous years we had pumped the fresh harvest straight into our old Vaslin presses, skipping the maceration, so this was an important new step for us.

Seán ran off the 'free run', the juice that had liberated itself naturally as a result of the weight of the grapes effectively pressing themselves overnight. But after draining the tank of the free run we found the grapes were still full of juice. Seán hosed himself down then jumped in and stomped the grapes in the tank in an effort to extract more free run. A little more juice was released but after draining that, what was left was still very liquid. We couldn't transfer with the 'vendange pump' and neither could we dig it out. It was too wet. The only way to transfer the juicy grapes from vat to press was by hand, bucket by bucket. I returned home after a day in Saint-Émilion to find them still working. Seán was frustrated. Digging out the red grapes that had only a little juice left in them and using the basket press the previous year had been simple but tough work. Pressing fresh white harvest with our basket press seemed impossible. As the pressure built with the pressing, the juicy grapes and skins regularly exploded out of the sides of the oak cage.

'Caro, it's like standing behind a cow with diarrhoea!' said Spring. It explained why all three were encrusted with grapes. I laughed but felt a twist of anxiety. Even after hours of pressing, the grapes left were still juicy *and* it was slow and laborious. For all the benefits and gentleness of the press, if it was not efficient and did not extract sufficient juice for the whites we would have to change it, but a new press was a significant investment, one we were not in a position to make with the commitments on the project.

But their hard work paid off in taste: the juice was extraordinary, a step change in quality compared to previous vintages. It was our second year fully certified organic and our second on the path to biodynamic certification, so the health and quality of the grapes themselves was also responsible, but, for all the difficulty, frustration and lower volume, the basket press delivered exceptional taste.

A couple of days later we harvested the sémillon under a perfect full moon. The wine I had originally nicknamed 'wild moon white' was living up to its name. Some of it would go to our Luminosité white blend and some would be barrel-aged for Générosité. Seán, Spring and Simon worked through the following day carrying out the same difficult pressing process, while I welcomed a group of guests for a day wine adventure in the tasting room.

Dave, Mr Greedy, arrived to help, part of an ongoing exchange programme, our home team helping the Moores on their harvest mornings and vice versa. It was their first harvest on their new farm and they were experiencing similar joys and challenges to us in our first year. Seán was their volunteer advisor, providing an alternative view to the Chamber of Agriculture, their official advisor's version of the truth.

The difference in the chamber's service since we arrived was astonishing. In five years the organic vineyards had grown from around 1 per cent to 4 per cent of the vineyard surface area in France. With that, we had seen a distinct shift from us being considered wacky, hippy types to being taken seriously as a form of agriculture. Advisors, suppliers and other support bodies were organising themselves to better serve this fast-growing market.

France had a long way to go. They had fallen from the top of the European tables in organic in 1980 to the bottom in 1990. In that decade, EU agricultural funds that most other EU member states used for encouraging organic conversion had been used as aid for conventional dairy farmers in France, increasing the milk lake and ensuring that through the 1990s and later France had to import a large part of its organic needs instead of providing for itself, despite being the agricultural powerhouse of Europe. With organic produce now a key and fast-growing part of the food market, that had been truly short-sighted folly.

As harvest progressed we saw the shape and size of our new tasting room forming, as Thomas, our stonemason, worked the foundations. The official start date, three months after submission of the planning request, had passed and we had heard nothing, so officially we were home free and could start. Then, about two weeks later, as Thomas started wall construction, we were notified that the Security Commission and the Handicap Commission had given an *'avis défavorable'*, meaning that we did not have our planning permission.

Seeing the letter's headline, panic overwhelmed my brain and adrenalin pulsed through my body. I felt like running away. I told myself to calm down, then carefully read through the page of feedback. There were simple things like making sure all the doors were at least 90 cm wide – most already were – but there were also seemingly insurmountable ones. The principal one was wheelchair accessibility for the tasting-room toilet. There was no way Seán's stone building could meet the strict wheelchair-turning-circle requirements and the budget had not included a new facility.

Sébastian then called to say he would come back from Brittany two weeks later than planned at the end of September as his work there was taking longer than expected. I almost spun out of control.

'What will we do?' I lamented to Seán. 'The plans have to be redone for the wheelchair accessibility. Sébastian needs to get on with the work. Our deadlines are tight. We can't afford a delay.'

We both knew that it only took one skipped beat for us to be in trouble with our delicate financing. The tasting room had to be ready for guests by April when the season began, and the Wine Lodge by June when the renting season gained pace.

'You have to keep your calm, Carolinus. You need to keep the team motivated, and going off the deep end won't do that,' said Seán.

But that was easier said than done. I took the shopping list off the cork board in the kitchen and added five slabs of dark chocolate to it. My consumption increased with stress and it was clear over the next few months it would be substantial.

I was short with Sophia, Ellie and Seán and slept badly, locked in a state of panic about these loose ends that could be our undoing.

We had gone so far; we had to have the aid so we had to have the toilet. The tasting-room project was signed and committed. We hadn't signed the final quotes on the lodge, but the two went hand in hand, both using the same access ramp. The Wine Lodge gîte, while it was a bigger expense, was also a more certain revenue stream. If we put it off and finished only the tasting room, work at a later date would be almost impossible since access was via what would be the tasting-room deck. Putting it on hold was not an option.

'Don't worry, Caro,' said Thomas, our stonemason, always the calm voice of reason. 'This is no problem. We will put a wall over here, connect to the wall of the dry toilet there; put a door in here and *basta*! No problem.'

Thomas put together an estimate. It was an honest quote but any addition to the budget made me stress. After reading his quote I reached for the shopping list to double the number of chocolate bars.

'Isn't ten slabs a little excessive?' said Seán.

I bit into another square, trying to control the nervous tic in my eye and making it clear it wasn't. I was not sure if my heart would withstand this pressure for another nine months, but the project was now well underway and there was no turning back.

Seán and I discussed budgets, pros and cons and next steps deep into the night. There was the budget issue, but now we didn't have official planning permission either. All the work done so far, and what would be done in the coming weeks, was going ahead illegally and could be rejected.

On the other hand, we could not send Thomas and Sébastian away while we sorted out the planning permission since we risked losing them to other projects; plus, months lost would mean missing key summer revenue the following year, which would destroy the fragile financing.

There were red 'beware' signs flashing in all directions. Every route was risky. We decided to continue the work. We had to get on and do it and deal with the consequences.

Sébastian returned. We reworked the plans and resubmitted.

As well as the chocolate-overdose-inducing accessible-toilet facility, we now needed security glass for the windows and doors that doubled the cost of the glass areas. These were required for a public building, which a tasting room was classified as, no matter the size. There was, however, a silver lining: the new plans were so beautiful that I was more excited than ever. The project was like a flower blossoming.

Each day brought more decisions. Going into the project I had no idea that a custom build would generate so many: the exact toilet location in the new accessible facility, the height of the small stone wall that would hold the massive panorama windows in the tasting room, colours, materials...

Incorporating the original stone walls of the nineteenth-century barn and *chai* added complexity. The exact levels and hence the length of the ramp could only be calculated once the foundations had been dug and the final levels relative to the old buildings had been fixed. Now the foundations had been dug, and the solid stone level had been fixed, so we *knew*.

We *knew* the lodge was a few extra centimetres below the level of the tasting room, thus the ramp needed to be even longer to meet the strict accessibility law, generating more cost.

We also *knew* that we needed to raise the walls a little higher than expected to ensure that there was no change in ground level between the living area and the bedrooms of the Wine Lodge. When I thought I would go completely mad with the stress of it all, news that our reworked plans had passed the two commissions arrived.

The work had official sanction. But our fine-tuned budget needed constant feeding from wine sales and wine tourism. One missed beat and we were in deep, deep water. I paddled harder and faster, pushing all the buttons I could to get good PR for the wine and fighting to get a TripAdvisor listing for our wine tours, which were gaining momentum.

Chapter 20
One Hundred Guests

We swung into high gear for the harvest weekend with the aid of our dream team, Spring and Simon. A hundred people were confirmed and we needed an ace caterer. Fabrice was recommended by Laura, a lovely Englishwoman who managed the two magnificent chateaux on our doorstep, Fayolle and Les Tours de Lenvège.

He arrived for an initial meeting, a handsome, finely dressed young man in a black suit and pointy patent leather shoes. Pointy men's shoes were a 'no-no' for Seán, a sure sign of a salesman and an instant reason for him to distrust the unlucky person wearing them.

On the contrary, I was convinced. This was not due to his handsome visage or toned body as Seán hinted, but to the photos on his website – of his food. I explained that we had booked the Château de Saussignac, which had very basic kitchen facilities. Fabrice said he would stop in to see it but he had catered there before so he had an idea. In the end he was so busy he didn't come back to see the facilities. We agreed the menus on the phone and by email.

Anne McManus, a beautiful blonde artist of around fifty with the body of a twenty-year-old, her adult daughter Nadine and a friend settled into the Wine Cottage. They were the perfect antidote to pre-harvest-weekend panic. Anne was into chakras, biodynamics, divining rods and alternative medicine. She drew a map of how she felt the farm. The most powerful positive forces were the old sémillon vines, planted in 1945 and now surrounding the Wine Cottage, winery and building site. These old vines were sculptures, each one a beautiful set of curves, twists and gnarls; individuals rather than the clones that became the norm in 1982.

Vines are like people. When farmed naturally they follow a similar life-cycle. From zero to five years they can do little for themselves, requiring significant labour and investment as we had found with our baby cabernet sauvignon. Then they offer a small harvest: like a kid that can unpack the dishwasher or dress themselves. From five to fifteen they produce fruit but it is more about energy than finesse, the phase we called 'education'. They need guidance and the chance to get their roots deep into the earth to refine their energetic output into something with depth. It is for this reason that the fruit from vines younger than fifteen years is seldom used for an estate's top wine; they go into the second wine.

If farmed naturally, vines offer good yield with complexity from fifteen to sixty-five, when they begin to wind down, the volume decreasing with complexity as compensation, hence the pride with which 'old vines' is displayed on a label – not a legislated term but generally only used on wine made from vineyards over forty years old. With great age, vines can offer wines of depth that improve further with ageing in the bottle.

Chemically farmed vines are lucky to live beyond forty years, exhausted and worn out from overproduction before they reach this sweet spot. Our old vines had withstood thirty years of conventional farming by previous owners because, before that, they had had thirty years of old-style farming with animal traction, cow dung and hand work – how most owners farmed until the seventies brought mass industrialisation of farming. They had a fundamental strength and disease resistance from their thirty-year good start. Some of our other vines were middle-aged and had had thirty years of conventional farming in their formative years. Despite being half the age of the 'grandmammies', they were finished. They couldn't recover. Like a malnourished child fed good food in later life, even with nurturing they were not returning to full health.

Two days before the harvest weekend we walked the vineyards to taste the grapes. They were magnificent; it was a confluence of nature that the biggest hand-picking team ever, the bumper turnout resulting from the television show, fell on such perfection. We set the harvest weekend date a year in advance so guests could plan and book their travel, hence we never knew exactly what we would pick. Some years the reds were ready, other years it was the first pick for the dessert wine. With a hundred people we expected to pick half our red grapes in one morning.

The other half, merlot grapes planned for machine-harvest, the wine we called Résonance, was also ready. In the pre-dawn darkness I greeted Benoit then ran ahead indicating the rows, hardly taking the time that I usually did to breathe in the special moment. Seán, Spring and Simon were ready. When the dawn broke through the vineyard we were halfway. As we finished pumping the last trailer of grapes into the vat, the first set of harvest weekend guests arrived. We were on fast forward.

Spring and I turned the Château de Saussignac into a stunning banquet hall with white tablecloths of recycled paper, brown linen runners, tea lights and crystal glass, while Seán and Simon signposted the roped-off parking area and prepared the winery.

Each of us attacked our respective list of responsibilities with focus. It was the big league.

The following day dawned bright and I said a thank you to the sky. We split into two groups, me on one side of the farm and Spring on the other. Dave Moore picked up the buckets of harvested grapes with the tractor, rushing back and forth between Spring's group and mine, aided by Simon. They barely had time to drop the grapes before we required our buckets and bins to be emptied again. Seán and Ian Wilson, like tireless wind-up toys, processed the harvest at the winery.

By midday, the spring had unwound and Seán demanded we stop, there was so much harvest; he couldn't cope with any more. In the garden under the trees near the new tasting-room foundation, tables and chairs, picnic blankets and benches, anything that could hold a bottom, were set alongside tables groaning with pâté, cheeses, breads, crudités and different dips.

For the first time, the covers were totally compostable: paper plates and wooden knives, even paper cups. Ian opened bottles of wine, the pile of empties at his feet growing as fast as he could open new ones, while the serving plates were emptied and refilled by Brigit. By the time Seán and Dave realised how hungry they were, all 5 kilograms of pâté were gone. I was so on the hop dealing with questions, orders and organisation that I didn't even think of food. We were pulling off a 100-person event without any hitches. Despite the lack of second helpings of pâté, guests were thoroughly enjoying themselves; roars of laughter regularly broke the happy hum of conversation.

The previous year, Dave and Amanda had been with us for harvest night; but this year, installed in their new vineyard, they offered to have Sophia and Ellie for a sleepover. As the girls enjoyed Amanda's superb vegetarian cooking, we arrived at the chateau ready for a gourmet sensation delivered by a hot Frenchman.

Fabrice drove in with a refrigerated truck and a team of smartly dressed youngsters right on time. With his good looks came fast-flowing speech that I sometimes struggled to keep up with, but the horror on his face at seeing the kitchen facilities in the chateau didn't need words.

'My team will give this place a thorough swabbing so we can use it for washing up, but for cooking absolutely *non*.'

I felt dizzy. With under an hour until guests were due to arrive, my mind raced to potential solutions.

'Not to worry,' said Fabrice, 'in the back of the second truck I have two restaurant-grade gas-fired ovens just in case. I'll set them up in the vaulted hall and use that as the kitchen.'

Within minutes Fabrice had the ovens installed, tables erected to handle the dressing of one hundred plates by his expert team, and protective screens delineating this new 'kitchen' area. Delighted by his professionalism and confident that everything would be perfect, I dashed home for a shower. Seán was knee-deep in grapes. I told him about Fabrice's reaction to the facilities.

'What did I tell you?' he yelled, his voice echoing eerily round the vat he was working in. 'Fancy pointy shoes!'

It was so unseasonably warm that Fabrice's waiting staff were serving Feely *méthode traditionelle* sparkling wine to the lavishly dressed crowd outside on the rough stone patio. Tea lights twinkled on the tables, their soft light playing on the stone walls of the massive hall. Seán arrived and we called for guests to take their seats, beginning the evening with awards for best pickers, noisiest guests and latecomers as per tradition.

The starter was dressed to perfection: *Fondant d'aubergine et de poivrons rouges au cumin aux queues de langoustines, vinaigrette vierge de fines herbes et copeaux de vieux Parmesan* – in short, langoustine tails with aubergine fondant, a sensation of flavours, accompanied by Luminosité. I was in heaven and so were our guests, the crowd carried along by the good humour that comes from a fulfilling day of relaxed exercise in the sun.

Fabrice's main course, *Tournedos de canard aux cromesquis de foie gras frits, rissolée de girolles fraîches et petites rattes, jus de morilles aux sucs de vin de Terroir Feely* – duck tournedos with mushrooms and potatoes – was matched with La Source red. The duck tournedos, despite being cooked for a hundred people, were perfectly medium rare. Even Seán grudgingly admitted to being impressed by Fabrice's cooking skills. The timing of the presentation and clearing of courses was perfection. He was a real pro.

With the main course served, I felt a great sense of relief. The heavy lifting of the event was done; we could relax and enjoy coasting through the next courses. Seán and I clinked glasses and I walked across to do the same with Simon and Spring; then Seán rose and read out a piece he had adapted from a Seamus Heaney poem to toast our harvesters. Tears of emotion welled up in my eyes as the hall exploded with applause.

An impressive cheese sculpture paired with the Générosité barrel-aged white set off an impromptu tin whistle concert by Larry, a guest from Dublin, and the crowd clamoured for more. Then Liz, Larry's partner, broke into a beautiful Irish ballad as the finale was served: *Gourmandise chocolatée aux fruits rouges, sorbet cru de fraises à la fleur de thym et tranché à l'huile vierge* – chocolate mousse and strawberry sorbet with red fruit and thyme, and Saussignac dessert wine. The song was haunting and beautiful; I didn't want it to end. I didn't want the dessert to end either; the plate was an artwork, a chocolate sculpture, with spun sugar and beautiful red berries; it was a travesty to eat it. But it had to end. *Café et mignardises,* sweet delights served with freshly brewed coffee, signalled the moment and groups began to drift off in taxis or on foot.

Simon, Spring and I smacked high fives before taking the mountains of bottles to the bottle bank. Fabrice and his team cleaned up and left as Seán swept the last dust off the floor. We were exhausted but deeply satisfied, thankful for the quality of the harvest, the gorgeous dinner and the wonderful people that had been part of it.

The following day I had a stiff cup of tea, so strong you could trot a mouse on it, to knock myself into shape for the guided walk of our farm. I could see the end at last and the fast-forward feeling I had had all weekend began to slow down.

By mid October the tasting-room walls were up, the project was flying ahead and we were keeping to our tight deadlines. Spring and I marvelled at Thomas. Watching him working was like watching a dancer. He was at one with his work, a true artist. We saw it in his precision with traditional stone, but also in simple tasks like filling his concrete mixer with sand and cement. His movements with the spade were fluid strokes, each following the other in perfect rhythm, like music.

Spring and Simon had been a positive force provided at a critical moment in our development. Towards the end of their stay, though, their relationship was weakening. Simon wanted to return to the UK and Spring to New Zealand. We saw rifts; where Spring was accommodating before, now she let Simon know she was exasperated. Before they had cooked together, turning out wonderful vegetarian food and sushi and working as a fluid team, but now they disagreed. As the time to say farewell approached it seemed they would be saying farewell to each other too. I felt sad. It was the end of an era.

But it was also the beginning of another. The successful event and follow-on orders gave us the confidence to sign on the dotted line for the Wine Lodge. Now we were fully committed to the beautiful design Sébastian had created.

Staying with my sister-in-law Glynis in London for the wine-educator course a few weeks later, I found several books on her shelf I thought I would enjoy. Between studying and attending the course I read all three: *Serge Bastarde Ate My Baguette*, *Tout Sweet* and *A Chateau of One's Own*. They were wonderful – hilarious, uplifting and full of the richness of life in France. Incredibly, they were all published by the same publisher. I took note of the address and got back to studying. The days flew by; going to wine school every day was fun.

Like the WSET 3 with Matthew, the course was a stretch and at times I felt out of my depth. Many of my classmates were already holders of the WSET Level 4 two-year wine diploma. They included the wine buyer of a smart chain of wine hotels, a dynamic and talented wine specialist with a wine school in India, a winemaking consultant for one of the major drinks groups, the head sommelier of a top Michelin-starred restaurant and an Eastern European wine journalist. The group was as diverse as the wines we tasted.

While most were far more experienced wine tasters than me, I was able to give the facts on organic and biodynamic wine and a winemaker's perspective that most of the others didn't have. The

European regulations for organic viticulture and winemaking and the certification of those were evolving, leaving wine buyers and end-consumers confused. As producers, we were directly involved in the setting of the standards. I was surprised at how little knowledge the group had about what organic meant in winegrowing or why it was so important. It made me even more determined to find ways to share my awakening with others.

At the end of the course the practical exam included presenting a chunk of theory then going through the WSET systematic approach to tasting a wine in front of a panel of judges. My days as a consultant presenting and running workshops paid off. When Seán collected me from Bordeaux airport he congratulated me on my newly minted 'certified wine educator' status as he hugged me. On the way home he recounted problems and delays on the building project. I already had a large group booking for April and I needed the tasting room finished. I felt stress coursing through my body.

In the meantime, running the classes in the tiny old tasting room was a nightmare. A few days before I had left for England, two New Zealanders attending the wine-and-food-pairing lunch were subjected to swarms of flies and a nasty smell. Only when they left did I realise Thomas had connected the composting loo's urine pipe to the new all-water septic tank system and the smell had travelled up the waste pipe recently positioned in the old tasting room. It was the ultimate horror for a wine-tasting zone, not the kind of pee smell we wanted, even on our sauvignon blanc. Simply filling the offending pipe with water stopped the stench – unfortunately too late for them.

But the consequences of serious delays were way, way worse than a whiffy waft on the air. I grilled Seán on the details as we turned onto the last stretch home – then I saw the roof of the tasting room in the distance. The structure had been raised while I was away, a beautifully carved *ferme* of oak and Douglas fir beams. With Thomas's rounded wall it made a striking impression. Seán had been teasing me. The wine school tasting room was a reality. Sébastian and Thomas were right on target.

That evening I looked up the publisher and found that they took submissions from authors so I packaged up a letter and the first three chapters of my manuscript as outlined on their website and crossed my fingers.

Chapter 21
Noël aux Chandelles

After more than a year, the *Last of the Summer Wine* television show was still delivering a bounty of vine-share orders, thanks to word of mouth from the people that attended our bumper harvest weekend. Wanting to maximise sales from last-minute shoppers, I set the deadline for vine-share orders as midday on 24 December.

On the morning of the 23rd six orders had already come in when a heavy snowfall cut our electricity. The power-out continued through the night. By midday on Christmas Eve, my cut-off time, I was in a panic. I needed to know how many orders there were and I needed to process them. Usually power cuts were short – an hour, a day maximum. We were into the second day. No electricity meant no PC and no vine shares. I felt like I had the year before, trapped in the snow in Burgundy.

The outage also meant no heating and a chance that the pipes would freeze and burst. It was not good. I called a few friends, hoping to find electricity and an Internet connection. Thierry and Isabelle in Razac had none; Pierre and Laurence had already left for the Pays basque for Christmas with family. Then I saw lights in Saussignac and called Olivier, our immediate neighbour closest to the village. He had power and, not only that, he offered to lend us a fuel-powered generator until ours came back. I felt like kissing him.

Seán plugged the PC and Internet box into an extension cord running from the generator set up outside the kitchen door. With its erratic chugging diesel engine it was not recommended for PCs but it was an emergency. I emailed the vine shares in record time, fear for the PC creating super speed.

Breathing easy for the first time in twenty-four hours, I went upstairs to put a basket of washing away. Noticing a smell of urine in the WC upstairs I absent-mindedly flushed it, realising in horror as I did that without power, my old friend the *broyeur* – the macerator that turned our upstairs loo waste into a fine liquid that could pass through a small pipe – would not work. The original house structure built in the 1700s didn't have sewage pipes in the metre-thick solid stone walls and so the macerator was a necessary evil that had brought many unhappy surprises over the years. I watched, frozen, as the contents of the toilet rose, splashed over the edge, flowed around the bathroom out of the door and down the stairs – then screamed for Seán. He offered me a bucket and mop and disappeared from the noxious scene.

Rather than leaving all the Christmas cooking to him, our master chef, as I usually did, a few days before I had shopped and planned the perfect Christmas Eve dinner. Seán's dream of a wife who baked bread, had a hot lunch ready each day and cooked fabulous Christmas feasts was going to be foiled *again*, though. After cleaning the floor it was late afternoon and the chance of having electricity in time for dinner was not looking strong.

But a way out was at hand, thanks to a four-plate gas stove-top that worked during a power cut. The original induction stove-top had been fried in a storm that summer. I was delighted then, and even more so now. I had hated the induction; the noise it made and the strange magnetic field I felt near it were horrible.

Using the gas stove-top I cooked pan-fried fillet steak topped with a nugget of organic butter, wild spinach, red beans in onions and red wine, and a sprinkle of our home-grown walnuts lightly pan-toasted. It was one of the best Christmas Eve dinners we had ever had. Afterwards we discovered the peace of candlelight, time together in front of the fire, no TV, no PCs, no tablets. It was so good we considered making it a tradition to unplug the power for *Noël aux chandelles* every year.

My 'certified wine educator' certificate arrived, another building block on the road to the wine school, like each brick in the new tasting-room wall. As the work on the Wine Lodge gathered pace, each day brought a mass of decisions. The number of people on the site had increased, with plumbers, electricians and Sébastian working alongside Thomas.

It meant progress and another unexpected result: the need to empty the composting loo. It was almost two years since we had bought it and infrequent use meant it hadn't needed emptying until now. The new all-water tank for the tasting room and gîte would only be connected to the toilets at the tail end of the project when all the piping was complete. I couldn't put it off. My duel with the dark matter was nigh. The waste had to go.

Sébastian opened the apparatus, removed the industrial bucket that held a super-thick compostable membrane and tied it around the dark matter. All I had to do was take the bucket to a hole we had made for composting, empty the dark matter into it, cover it with soil then wash the bucket and the apparatus. I did it.

In a moment of madness I had considered putting composting loos in for the new tasting room and Wine Lodge. The experience of emptying that bucket convinced me that my decision to put real loos with low-flush systems in was dead on. With an all-water tank that clarified and returned the matter to our farm anyway, the solution was ecological and far better for my stomach.

Sophia and Ellie were in the grips of a children's toy phenomenon that could teach me reams about marketing. 'Monster Highs' were Barbie-style dolls created in the image of famous monsters from fairy tales – werewolves, witches, ghouls – all part of a make-believe high school in a kingdom of monsters. Along with films, books and a website about Monster High, they could collect each of the monsters in their normal size and in their mini version with many, many accessories. It was a never-ending moneymaking dream with new versions coming out all the time, totally original characters but also remakes of old monsters, a tweak here, a new outfit there.

Monster Highs had been top of their Christmas list so we had succumbed and given them each one. Now they were desperate to get more. The dolls cost as much as a pair of shoes, so you can imagine how likely that was going to be.

'Why don't you start the egg business we have been talking about so you can buy them yourselves?' I said. Our chickens were getting old and their laying was slowing down. There were barely enough eggs for our own needs. That summer we had discussed getting more so the girls could run a small egg business.

'What's that got to do with the price of eggs?' said Sophia, applying the English phrase she had learnt a few months before.

Seán and I cracked up and the girls looked puzzled. There started the first 'Business 101' lesson for our five- and seven-year-old daughters.

'If you use the money you have saved to buy some new chickens then you can sell the eggs to people in our neighbourhood and, depending on the price you get and how many you sell, you can make enough money to buy a Monster High or many Monster Highs. In this case, it really has got something to do with the price of eggs,' I explained.

The girls giggled. We toasted the garden-fresh quiche made from home-grown eggs and vegetables and tucked in.

We still had a mountain to climb on the project, and the financing of it was far from being a fait accompli, but I felt a hint of serenity, a sense that our frantic paddling, if we could just keep our balance, was going to pay off. Despite my worries about planning permissions, budgets and wheelchair accessibility, I felt a fulfilment, a sense of achievement that we had even got this far.

Part Four

Fruit

In biodynamics we talk of a fruit day when the heat or fire forces are powerful. It is a good time to plant a fruiting plant like tomato, to harvest fruit or seeds of plants like wheat. As humans, we can relate fruit to the removal of the old and the recreation of a stronger self, like a forest fire making way for new growth or a fruit offering up its seed to create the next generation.

Fruit days occur when the moon is in the fire constellations Aries, Leo and Sagittarius.

In wines we find that fruit aromas and flavours, what we typically want to dominate in wines, are reinforced on fruit days so this is the ideal day to harvest grapes and to taste most wines... or to plan a tasting for wine journalists.

Better than any argument is to rise at dawn and pick dew-wet red berries in a cup.
Wendell Berry

Chapter 22
Rose Hips and Risk

Bright rose hips decorated the spiky brown bush like drops of blood on the frosty background. I picked one and gently squeezed the orange-red paste into my mouth, taking care not to get any of the hairy pips. Once the first frost of winter hits, the rose hip's interior becomes soft and transforms into perfect pockets of vitamin C donated free by the hedgerows. In the late spring and early summer the dog roses offer a mass of pinkish-white flowers that later turn into these bountiful rose hips.

Hedgerows are a key part of farming, offering biodiversity that helps to keep nature's balance. As I squeezed another pocket into my mouth, I wondered if we could keep our own balance. We were facing our latest crisis on the project. We had planned for Lionel Lazare to do the interior walls of the Wine Lodge, but he had fallen behind on other projects and couldn't keep to our deadlines.

Deep down I was secretly delighted that we wouldn't be able to use him after all. His father's tirade, though now almost a year past, still provided a fresh sting of anguish each time I thought of it. But we couldn't miss a super-critical milestone: laying the liquid concrete over the underfloor heating. The concrete company had been booked months before and walls, windows and doors on all the buildings had to be finished by the booked date. The floor then needed several weeks to dry before tiling could begin, so there was absolutely no chance of pushing it out.

We couldn't change that date. The walls had to be up. I made my way back up the hill to the house, energised by the vitamin C and called A2S, a company that Thomas had recommended. Eric, the manager, arrived within hours. He was medium height, fortyish with light brown hair. He seemed professional.

Standing in the Wine Lodge building site I looked out of the cut for one of the bedroom windows and was taken aback by the beauty. Winter sun caught the brown canes of the vines, creating a sharp contrast with the bright-green grass underneath.

'We want to use ecological products and solutions as much as possible,' I explained, handing him a copy of the inner layout I had created on Open Office Impress.

'We can use Fermacell,' said Eric. 'It's ecological plasterboard for the inner walls. It's more expensive but it lasts longer and is more robust.'

'How much more?' I asked, wary of budget creep.

'I'll put the difference into the quote so you can decide,' he said.

'Great. We also need to meet these rules,' I said, passing him a copy of the accessibility guidelines.

He whistled the kind of teeth whistle that signified trouble as he looked at my layout plan and pointed to the guidelines.

'I don't see how you will fit a double bed into this room and still have a ninety-centimetre passage.'

I felt a moment of panic but explained that I had measured it and was sure it would work out.

He whistled again.

'Your plan hasn't taken into account the insulation of the outer wall. That's ten centimetres lost.'

I felt a blow like I had with the *avis défavorable*.

'We have to have the ninety-centimetre passage or our financing is toast,' I said.

Eric remeasured everything and promised to try his best to come up with a solution. We were up against the wall, in fact quite a few. The exterior walls of the old *chai* could not be moved. Eric sent his plan, including the all-important wall insulation that mine was missing, via email that evening. By making the bathroom smaller, while still keeping to the accessibility rules, the passage just made the required 90 centimetres. I went to bed hyperventilating after a solid dose of chocolate. Seán murmured calming refrains then went outside to double-check the measurements himself. It was as fine as a hair's breadth.

A few days later the *ferme* structure of the Wine Lodge living area went up. I filmed every nail-biting second of the installation of the beautifully carved structure, a wonder of accuracy and skill. Sébastian and his apprentice finished in the dark and I gave them each a bottle of wine to celebrate. After they left I went out into the cold night to take more photos and was filled with wonder at the transformation of the old ruin.

With the full skeleton in place there was a sense of completion, a noticeable 'phew' from everyone on the team. Still, worries about the budget and timing, intimately connected as they were, combined to give me eczema and sleepless nights. Sébastian, too, was showing signs of strain, and he called a friend in to help. Usually he was upbeat with a great sense of humour and a spring in his step. Now his movements were slow and his eyes had lost their sparkle; a friend of his had recently committed suicide, which aggravated the feeling of descending into a deep gloom. Thomas, usually energy personified, no longer arrived like clockwork at eight, but closer to nine. The project had entered a dark phase in keeping with winter.

A couple of days later I ran a half-day wine tour in the old tasting room. I made sure to fill the smelly pipe with water before we started, then took the group round the vineyards, explaining winegrowing and organic farming. We returned for the wine-tasting education and lunch. As we reached the crème brûlée ice cream, passion fruit sorbet and Saussignac dessert wine course, a guest received a call from their architect.

'You won't believe it,' said John to Karen, his wife. 'Our builder just went bust.'

'What? They've been in business more than fifty years. How can they?' she said with a little urgency but no major panic in her voice.

'Yep... and they had the best reputation of all the builders we considered,' he said. 'If you'll excuse me I need to step outside to make a few calls.'

'You seem very relaxed,' I said to Karen. 'If our builder went bust I'd be jumping off the cliff out there.'

'It sounds bad and it's bad for the company, but we're protected,' she said. 'We'll be mildly delayed but we won't lose money since we only pay weekly tranches as they finish parts of the build, rather than in big chunks upfront. It's frightening how many small businesses are going under with the crisis. Luckily we had thought through this scenario and prepared for it.'

John came back in and we moved on to coffee. It seemed they were sailing through the crisis with barely a care. But that night I tossed and turned imagining all the horrible repercussions if it happened to us. I had never considered this angle. Paying a third up front, a third midway and a third at the end was standard practice in France.

Sébastian had moved on to working on the lodge. Getting it ready for the liquid concrete was the priority, rather than finishing the tasting room that only had about 10 per cent left to do. He gave me the outstanding balance invoice and asked me to pay it.

Awakened to a lack in my education by Karen and John, I had given myself a crash course on managing a building project the night before. As part of my cramming session I read that you should never pay the final amount until all the work is finished, since builders are notoriously slow to do the final bit. I was super-anxious. I said I preferred to pay when the wood panelling was finished.

A few hours later Véronique banged on the door. With her red hair flaming she demanded payment of the final sum. I said I would talk to Seán – my standard fallback for any difficult situation.

Seán clumped in for lunch, his back aching. Getting back into pruning after almost a year off was always a tough transition. Our lunch conversation that year almost always revolved around the project: design, finance, people, the list was never-ending. As I served up pumpkin soup I explained my showdown with Véronique in the courtyard that morning.

'What happens if they go bust?' I said.

'I don't think they will go bust,' said Seán. 'It's more about making sure the final bits are completed and don't hang around for months or years.'

'Exactly. We have to have it finished to provide proof for the aid. We have to meet the deadline for that, come hell or high water,' I said. 'So what will we do?'

'We know Sébastian and Véronique,' said Seán. 'They will respect the deadlines and the work. Look at how they have managed the project so far. For the sake of goodwill on the project, I think we have to pay it now. After all, we know where they live.'

I was torn but when Sébastian came back after lunch I gave him the cheque.

A few days later Sébastian and Véronique arrived together with dark rings under their eyes and I expected the worst; that they had gone bust. I joined them in the courtyard, angst exploding in my stomach.

'Caro, we had a horrible sleepless night,' said Véronique.

I could see that.

'The company providing the windows and doors telephoned yesterday to say there is a six-week delay on the ones for the Wine Lodge.'

I felt a moment of deep relief sweep through me. They hadn't gone bust. Then the panic returned as I realised we wouldn't be ready for summer rentals, some already sold.

'Don't worry, don't worry!' she said. 'We have found a solution. A2S can supply the windows and doors in time. They are more expensive but we will absorb that extra cost. They will also fit them, so that will give Sébastian breathing space.' What had seemed like a disaster had turned into an opportunity.

Sébastian needed a break and Véronique had booked a Mediterranean cruise for them. I, for my part, said a prayer to the God of Construction asking that no one – including ourselves – would go bust in the meantime.

Chapter 23

Killer Chemicals

The blossom buds forming on the trees announced spring – and with it the respective *bulletins d'alerte* issued by the local chemical supplier and Chamber of Agriculture started up. The newsletters alerted us to the weeds, bugs and climatic conditions about to strike our farm and what killer chemicals we could use to foil them. They read like chronicles from a war zone.

At a viticulture conference I learned that the products used were exactly that, the products of war. The creation of nitrates for cannonballs began in the late 1800s. As demand from World War One dropped, these nitrates were then recycled to become agriculture's first chemical fertiliser. The next step was the creation of pesticides, including fungicides, by recycling killer chemicals 'innovated' during World War Two. The third wave was the creation of herbicides like Agent Orange, used during the Vietnam War to destroy food and cover of anti-government forces.

Such chemicals are routinely used on our food, unless it is certified organic. They create massive profits for agricultural chemical companies. One of the largest agro-chemical companies even call themselves 'a sustainable agriculture company' – their new tag line when I looked up their website. It shows what a mockery has been made of the word 'sustainable' by industrial agriculture.

Each *bulletin d'alerte* announced in big red letters the arrival of the latest insect or disease that would spread doom and devastation through our vineyards. At the start of our adventure, each one brought a racing heartbeat and a sick feeling in the pit of my stomach. Now I knew these insects and diseases were a direct result of intensive chemical farming. We had learned to take the alerts with a pinch of salt. Bad farming created opportunities for disease and pest outbreaks. On our farm, with the strong health of naturally farmed vines and the balance of the biodiversity, they were no longer scary.

We were constantly observing our vines and practising good husbandry. The vines did not look after themselves, contrary to the belief of some guests – quickly changed after a few days of watching Seán labouring through the windows of the Wine Cottage.

My new understanding of the struggle between conventional and organic farming, namely the huge profits made by chemical companies and their resultant power over politicians, horrified me. Seán said I was arriving at a kernel of political and social awareness at last. He had always read more widely than I had, a habit started as a young journalist. I felt like I had my eyes wide open for the first time. It was a horrible realisation.

At least it meant I could take action. I bought books on ecology and on the facts behind chemical farming and read them from cover to cover, then placed copies in the tasting room and Wine Cottage. I shared information via our Facebook page. I realised every single thing I did, no matter how small – and especially every purchase we made – was supporting one method or another. Buying organic was not just for me and my family's health; it was for the land, the grower and the producer. It was choosing natural means rather than chemicals of war as the method of farming I wanted, and the future that went with it.

Spreading a gossamer-thin sheet onto our bed – one we had bought twenty years before in Johannesburg – I reflected on the irony that, while we used ancient, threadbare towels filled with holes, and the children's beds had sheets that hailed from my childhood, the Wine Lodge was about to be furnished with luxury, super-soft organic sheets and towels. We were just surviving in our rundown farmhouse next door, stretched to our limits to support this bold new step. I hoped the new lodge and tasting room would move us from holey to whole. So far it had added significantly to our workload and overheads, but soon it would be open for business.

After making the bed I pulled on running shorts, grabbed my Walkman earphones and went downstairs to take Dora for a run. As we dropped down into the valley of Saussignac I felt nature's embrace and turned off the earphones. The birds that had been singing started an urgent warning call. It was their notification that Dora had entered the forest. A little squirrel, hearing the warning, barrelled up the hill towards us with an apple in his mouth, thinking the danger was below him where the birds were calling. A few metres from Dora he looked up, saw her, dropped the apple and sprinted up the nearest tree, his face the image of Scrat in *Ice Age* when he loses his nut. I stood for a moment taking in the wonder of nature, laughing out loud. Dora looked up at me and seemed to be smiling too.

The commune track dropped down from the village towards Gageac, passing through a wilderness with a stream running through it. It was home to other animals, like marmots and wild boar, and to wild plants like feathery, delicate horsetail and tall, bold stinging nettle. As I ran I was overwhelmed by earthy aromas, dense and fungal but delicious, like the smell of a fine black truffle mixed with the forest floor.

When I arrived home I looked up the day on our Maria Thun biodynamic calendar. It was a root day. Even the aromas in the valley reflected it. There was something truly powerful at work. The root sign meant earth forces were strongest, making it the ideal time to plant root crops and to do work related to root systems.

It didn't seem possible but a few days later in the same place I was overcome with floral aromas, as if I'd stuck my head into a bouquet of wild flowers. Again, I had no idea of the day but when I returned and checked the calendar I found it was a flower day, the perfect day to transplant flowers and do activities related to flowering or flowers; for example, picking camomile flowers for camomile tea. It sounded crazy, but it was like clockwork. Seán thought I was mad. I knew it was real.

On our farm I found these smells were reinforced close to our well; perhaps water had a heightening effect. Some days I felt I was growing into the earth, like I had roots and had attached myself to our small piece of paradise. I read detailed books on biodynamics and signed up for a course, keen to understand more about how and why these phenomena worked as they did.

The apple farmer near Gardonne about 5 kilometres downstream from us sprayed chemicals on his orchard about forty times a year. He wouldn't eat his own apples. When a farmer won't eat his own produce it makes me worried. The Gardonne well was one of 500 polluted wells in France, given 'special project' status to try to decrease the level of pollution. It was crazy to think that it was being legally poisoned by the farmers around it.

In a feeble attempt, the local Chamber of Agriculture contacted all the farmers in the catchment area to meet with them and help to change their ways. They organised a group meeting to show the alternatives. The only people who turned up were the bureaucrats themselves and those, like us, who were demonstrating our mechanical weeding equipment as a non-polluting alternative to herbicide. The soft 'phone and meet' method would not create change.

I learned that in the nineties, the city of Munich had encouraged farmers in their water catchment area to go organic – via money, not phone calls – after seeing a significant rise in agricultural pollution in their water. It had been a mega-success. They converted most of the farmers to organic and did not need to undertake costly cleaning of the water. The cost of the organic incentives was a third of the cost of cleaning the polluted water of nitrates alone. I was amazed by the clear logic of it and shocked we weren't doing more in France.

The unseen costs of chemical warfare on farms came back to us in taxes and higher charges for water, when they should have been levied on the agricultural product that used the chemical in the first place. The number of beekeepers in France had halved in the previous decade and so, to encourage more to enter the profession, France allocated a 40-million-euro programme to encourage beekeeping. On the other hand, they did not ban the pesticides that had killed the bees, the main reason for fewer beekeepers. It was farcical.

We could change the world one gesture and one cent at a time. Each person who demands organic engages the change. With organic farming we have clean water and healthy bees. Organic seems more expensive comparing prices on a supermarket shelf, but considering the consequences of a world without bees and without clean water – hence no human life – it is not so expensive after all.

As I came to first blush of social and political awareness, spring was in full flourish and the old Sébastian we knew was back. He had a young, upbeat apprentice who brought new energy. The project rushed like a runaway train towards our deadline for pouring the liquid cement. The tiles could only be laid after the heating had run under the concrete for a full month. The kitchen could only be installed after the tiles were laid. My project management skills from my previous city life were forced back into action.

We were meeting our deadlines; Sébastian's woodwork was truly magnificent and Thomas's stonework an art.

I had all but given up hope of publishing my book *Grape Expectations*, the story of our first three years in France, when an email from the publisher announced they were somewhat interested if I was willing to rework the parts that needed editing. I spun into seventh heaven. Getting a publisher was the silver bullet for a wannabe author like me, something I had barely allowed myself to dream of. After all the years of work and of thinking of this moment it seemed too good to be true. I kept rereading the email. Of course I would be willing to rework the manuscript. I would rewrite the whole thing if they liked.

That night Seán toasted my success.

'To Carolinus, soon-to-be-published author!'

He was excited for me.

'Thanks SF! Here's to you, too! I wouldn't have got on and done it if I hadn't read Maeve Binchy's advice in the book you gave me last year. But we mustn't count our chickens before they've hatched, either.'

Over the following weeks, I ping-ponged the manuscript back and forth with my editor, Jen Barclay. The publisher wasn't ready to commit yet but the improvements made thanks to her guidance were marked. The work we were doing meant it would be in better shape for self-publishing or another publisher if this one did fall through. I desperately hoped it wouldn't.

As we entered the last phase of the project a second wind, a new energy, filled the team. Thomas's wife, a dark-haired beauty, visited to see the buildings for the first time.

'What great fortune! Fine artisans, handsome and half-nude too!' she exclaimed, pointing to her husband and Sébastian working bare-chested on the roof in the late spring sun. Seán didn't know that I had chosen them for their looks; luckily they had turned out to be great artisans as well.

Aideen and Barry O'Brien, our friends from Dublin, arrived with their son, Cillian, and daughter, Juliette, perfectly timed for painting the Wine Lodge and bottling the new vintage. It was Sophia's birthday and Easter. With the fast-forward project that year, I felt like I had missed part of my children's growing up. Seán had been like a single parent at times while I disappeared for long days touring, away to Ireland or the UK for marketing, wine shows or WSET. We laughed heartily with Aideen and Barry about how each day Seán was disappointed when he came in from work at lunchtime, especially in winter when he was pruning, expecting a hot meal, only to find me deep in my work and unconscious of the time. But for Seán it wasn't a laughing matter.

'You forget how hard it is to do physically exhausting work all day. I need a good lunch to refuel. It is impossible to think, my brain is as exhausted as my body just with the process of physical survival out there.'

The way to a man's heart is through his stomach, I recalled. I promised to do better.

That year, I had everything planned for the bottling well in advance. It required military precision and infinite patience. We had nine different labels every year, and each had to be carefully created with details from laboratory analysis (like the alcohol content) to organic certification, then sent to three different parties for sign-off. Seán said that when he came to bed at 2 a.m. I writhed and said 'Bottles, capsules, labels' in a panicked voice then turned over. I woke at six still dreaming – or having nightmares – about bottling.

Despite my angst, the bottles, labels, capsules, corks and wine were perfectly aligned. I did have everything right and Pierre de St Viance, our friend and bottler, did not have to bring out his Marseille expletives that had been de rigueur in the past.

Cillian was a bottling master and also, we discovered, a painting genius. For the Wine Lodge we had selected natural chalk, an ecological paint but a challenge to the painter, no easy one-coat wonder. Cillian had skill and patience, creating walls that begged to be stroked.

On the last night of the bottling we held a celebratory barbecue with the de St Viances, the O'Briens, and the Wilsons, our friends that regularly helped with harvest time. We raised a glass to Seán's skill. The beautiful, balanced, deep wines showed the progress made in the health of the vineyard but also in Seán's winemaking confidence. I felt very proud.

Surrounded by great friends who had been part of our journey, with the smell of tomatoes roasting on rosemary branches on the barbecue and the new tasting room in the background, I felt like we were turning a corner. But to do it we had taken a great risk. On the finance front we were far from serene.

Chapter 24
Wine Adventure

For all our careful planning, we were slipping into the red. Our extras here and there had added significantly to our outgoings and we still hadn't been paid a cent of the promised aid. Seán and I pored over spreadsheets and pulled in every outstanding payment from clients. We were still short. Over a few days the pressure mounted to the point where we were snapping at each other and at Sophia and Ellie.

'Just go away!' I shouted at Seán as he slammed the door. Hearing the words and the tone, I wondered who had said it. It wasn't *me*! But it was; it was *me* that had lost control, like a scene from a nightmare. This time the girls didn't cry. They stared stony-faced, too shocked for tears.

The bottling costs hit, along with the repayment on the tractor. We had planned for them but, as with most small businesses, nothing was certain and some of the planned income we needed had not materialised. We also expected to have half the aid for the building work by then, but had yet to receive anything.

I took bookings for tours using the first Wine Lodge room that was ready, while the work continued alongside in the living section and the second room. Guests sailed through water cutoffs, noise and cursing workmen on the opposite side of the door and kept their cool despite a heatwave. The views from the lodge appeared to have a calming effect.

The full-day visit we offered wasn't called the 'Wine Adventure' for nothing. With the tiles installed I began to use the new tasting room, complete with large gaps where woodwork needed finishing around the tops of the doors – the dreaded 10 per cent. With no surrounding deck our clients had to venture across the open foundation to reach the toilet, balancing on carefully placed wood like they were playing some bizarre game of 'walk the plank'. After tasting a few wines, the game was even more fun.

Using the new tasting room for a large group for the first time that spring, though, I had an inkling of what a difference it would make to our lives. Setting the tables with white cloths, stylish cutlery and crystal tasting glasses, I felt at home. It fit like a glove.

The large room had huge panoramic windows that looked onto the vineyard and filled it with light. The high ceilings panelled with creamy poplar were lined with the structural copper-coloured Douglas fir beams, creating a wonderful colour contrast. Nested in the highest section above the main glass doors was a porthole window, panelled with strips of wood that made it look like the inside of an oak barrel. The wood and stone, combined with the chalk and hemp insulation on the walls, made for a living, breathing environment. In this new place, explaining our methods and passion for wine and organic, biodynamic farming felt even more natural and instinctive.

After walking the farm as part of the morning tour, my large group settled into the tasting room. I laid out the wine-and-food-pairing lunch and explained the different pairings. The birds were singing; the vines were waving in the breeze in the idyllic vineyard setting below. It was a haven of peace.

Just then Poc Poc, the head chicken, leaped onto the table squawking and bounced up and down the full length of it, knocking glasses flying, stomping onto plates of food and creating total havoc. There were shards of glass, cheeses with great chicken footprints in them; one guest was soaked by a flying wine glass. Chaos reigned. For a moment I was frozen, stunned, then I jumped into action, chased Poc Poc out, closed the doors, asked if everyone was alright and ran to our kitchen to call Seán. He was about to sit down to lunch with our daughters.

I slammed the door to make sure none of the other marauding fowl matrons were behind me, gave a fast explanation and finished with, 'That chicken is going in the pot!'

Sophia and Ellie burst into tears. They thought I was really going to kill the chicken.

I calmed them, assuring them I would not kill the chicken, much as I felt like it. Seán and I swung into damage control. We moved all the guests into the garden, charged fresh glasses and quickly reset the table and redid the lunches. Diane, a guest staying in the Wine Cottage, lent clothes to Carolyn, the unlucky guest who was doused. They and their partners arranged to meet up later that week to visit a night market. Connections were made; guests found the whole thing rather funny; the ambiance was heightened by the hilarity of the crazy experience.

I had learned my lesson, though, and the doors were kept firmly closed at lunch thereafter; our free-ranging chickens would not have an opportunity to create Chicken Chaos II.

With good TripAdvisor reviews and our growing reputation, we received more and more visitors. My day for these full-day wine adventures began with room-preparation before the girls left for school. Each person would receive two pocket guides, one on French wine and the other on wine and food pairing, placed with a pencil and a feedback form at each table setting, along with three crystal glasses for easy wine comparison.

After dropping Sophia, Ellie and our neighbours' kids at school, I collected visitors who needed a lift from the station. With guests on site, the vineyard tour would start at 10 a.m. Back up in the tasting room an hour later we became detectives as I took them through how to wine-taste, how to pick up the nuances of a wine and then use those clues to define what the wine was and what it would pair with. A brief introduction to the principles of wine and food pairing was followed by the preparation and serving of the wine-and-food-pairing lunch so they could try it for themselves. Tasting how the more acidic Sincérité white paired better with a more acidic white goat cheese than a creamy Camembert explained the principles better than words ever could.

At that point I would race inside, down a glass of water, grab a bite to eat, share a few high-speed words with Seán then race back out to clear up and serve dessert and coffee before the afternoon tour of the winery and explanation of the winemaking. The day officially finished at 4 p.m., at which point I would return guests to the station if required and start cleaning the debris left from the day. On top of this I shoehorned the orders for wine and vine shares that arrived via the Internet, as well as the general administration and email follow-ups.

My parents visited and my dad said, 'You have to slow down, Toots. You can't keep up this pace or you'll be old before your time. Dead before you reach retirement.'

I didn't tell him our Social Services Agency required us to work until we were eighty-three to get our full French pension of a few hundred euros a month, despite taking most of our income since we had arrived. I probably would be dead by then, or at least more than ready to say *au revoir*. At least he didn't say anything about the 'corridor of crisis', the term he had coined for our house in the early years. Now the girls were a little older, the corridor was less of a crisis.

My mum helped me serve the lunches, do the laundry and clean the gîtes. I wished they lived a little closer than Qualicum Beach, Canada: an ocean and the North American continent away.

Even with the growing success of the business we were not able to meet the project's growing demands without the aid payments. Some of the bills had been due a long time, but we strung them out some more. Monsieur Lambert, our plumbing merchant, was slow to react and for once I was delighted. Eating slabs and slabs of organic black chocolate wasn't easing the stress as much as it used to.

My life was on the edge and I felt like I was going to fall into the abyss. I was going too fast, working all hours and barely keeping it together, and all this at the price of my family life. Seán and I had another fight. I left him making soup for supper and fled to the barn to prepare orders that needed to ship. On my return I found Seán and the girls sitting at the table, Sophia and Ellie with tears rolling down their cheeks.

'What's wrong?' I asked.

'Tell Mum what you told me. Tell Mum what it feels like, Ellie,' said Seán.

'It feels like you aren't with us anymore. We don't see you. It feels like you don't care about us anymore,' said Ellie, crying harder.

'Oh my poppet, I am so sorry,' I said leaning over to comfort her in an embrace, the tears starting to roll down my cheeks too. 'I do care, oh so much, but I feel like I am racing and still not keeping up.'

'You used to bring us hot chocolate in the morning and now you don't,' said Ellie.

'I know, my darling. I have been too busy trying to juggle all the balls for the new buildings, the gîtes, the wine tours, the wine sales,' I said.

'But we miss you, Mummy,' said Ellie, crying all the more.

'I am so sorry,' I said, my tears flowing freely. 'I miss you too.' I hugged her tight and felt like my heart would break.

In the past I would wake them with hot chocolate every morning, along with tea for Seán. I was up a couple of hours before the rest of the household to respond to emails, orders and booking requests, and to work on my book. Usually I would reach a natural break at the time they woke up. This season, with the hectic days of touring and non-stop guests, I'd never caught up, and there had been no natural break. The email was constantly full; there were not enough hours in the day. Under the intense pressure I had forgotten the small things. 'You used to read to us in bed at night,' said Sophia, who loved reading and she started to cry too.

'I know, my poppet, I am so sorry,' I said wiping more tears away and leaning over Ellie to hand Sophia a tissue.

I went round to the other side of the table to give her a tight hug and saw water welling up in Seán's eyes as he watched the scene. Until then I hadn't realised the serious impact my long hours had had on my family. We were all quiet for a moment, taking in all that had been said and trying to get control of ourselves. I gave Sophia another squeeze and returned to my seat next to Ellie and put my arms around her.

'I promise I will do better. I will bring the hot chocolate like I used to,' I said, more sobs rising up. Ellie had inherited my tendency to lose breath when crying took hold, and now we were both hiccuping and gasping for air.

'It's time for some deep breathing,' said Seán. 'Breathe in, be calm, breathe out.' We followed his routine. A few breaths in, Ellie and I exchanged a glance and burst out laughing, both finding the scene totally ridiculous at the same moment. It felt like a strange prenatal class but it did the trick. With control over my airway, I could at last say what I wanted to say next: 'Why don't we go and read a chapter of *The Faraway Tree* together now?'

Hugging them both like bushbabies, we climbed the stairs and read together. It felt so good. I had forgotten how much fun it was to be with my daughters. I felt deeply sad, a longing as if I had lost something. In a way I had; they would never be the same age again and that time would never be recovered. I felt the tears welling up again as I put the light out. I pushed them back, not wanting to create more distress.

Descending the stairs I felt guilty too. Ellie wasn't nearly as keen a reader as Sophia. It was probably my fault for not reading with them as often as I used to.

I sat back down at the old pine table in the kitchen with Seán. 'I don't know what to do,' I said. 'I feel the weight of the financing of the project, the extra responsibility of our burgeoning tourism business, and the new Wine Lodge on my shoulders, but I have to keep doing all the other things like the admin, the wine sales and marketing, then order preparation.'

'I know. But we have to remember family is the priority.'

'But what can I do? I am working all possible hours and not coping,' I said. 'Maybe we need to hire someone part-time.'

'We aren't in a financial position for that and you seem to be forgetting the horror stories we have heard.'

Seán was right. We had close friends who had lost more money on one bad hiring than we had made in six years. Employment law in France was heavily weighted in favour of the employee.

We had also heard that the bureaucracy alone could drive you mad; that the employer had to fill out nine different forms every month for each employee. We were too frightened of the bureaucracy and the risk to seriously consider it.

'You have to start saying no to tour requests,' said Seán. 'You have to prioritise.'

'But it brings in good revenue and I really enjoy it,' I said.

'I know you do. You can still do it. You just have to choose the right ones to do. Maybe you should say no to working on Sunday,' said Seán. I was about to reply when Seán put his hand up to stop me. 'All I know is that those two little girls need you. I can only do so much for them. They need their mother.'

With those words he started off a fresh flood of tears. I felt like I was pulled in every direction, but I had to put the priority on my family. Seemingly small things like hot chocolate in the morning and *goûter*, the afternoon snack when they got home, and reading together at night were necessary. I needed to call a halt before I drowned and took them with me. The following night I had a nightmare: Dora was attacked by a fox. I saw her thrown into the air. Her spine appeared to be broken but, in the weird dream conditions, I wasn't sure if she was OK or not. I had to get to Saint-Émilion to meet clients. I didn't have contact numbers so I couldn't call to tell them I was delayed and had to go. Not knowing exactly what was happening to Dora I left, taking our only car, so Seán had no vehicle to take Dora to the vet. When I got home Seán and the two girls just shook their heads at me. Dora had died.

I woke up feeling horrible. In the 5.30 a.m. darkness I made my way downstairs, feeling intensely responsible for what happened. It was so real I almost couldn't believe Dora was lying safely in her bed. She looked up at me with her beautiful trusting eyes, brown honeycombed with gold, snuggled down and went back to sleep. It was a message. Family was more important than work.

I was about to push myself into working another full weekend for clients that would provide a large chunk of money towards the never-ending drain of the new buildings, when Seán told me to stop. I had not had a day off or a Sunday with my family in months. I was so focused on keeping the bank balance out of the red I was not taking into account the effect it was having. I had lost my sense of balance. I took Seán's advice and when the clients asked to change a key part of the programme I had proposed I took it as an opportunity to bow out of the booking before it went any further. Fortunately they hadn't confirmed with a deposit yet. I withdrew as delicately as possible and resolved to start saying no to Sunday bookings.

A new kind of tourism was becoming fashionable – using a GPS (Global Positioning System) to find a place where a box of 'treasure' was hidden. Once they found the box, the finder would exchange that 'treasure' for another 'treasure'. This could be as simple as a key ring or a corkscrew. The most famous website for it was called 'Geocaching'.

Spring and Simon had seen it working well in New Zealand. It was a good way to bring tourists to our farm and could generate sales at the chateau door. They had set up a GPS 'treasure box' on the farm and we had sold two six-packs to happy hunters the autumn they were with us. This summer the visitors to the GPS box had changed, though: they came, found and left. They did not take the time to look at the farm or to taste the wines.

Our beloved chickens were entering their fifth season, very old for chickens. The matriarch Poc Poc had aged significantly in the previous two months and her days of sowing chaos in the tasting room were over. She would settle in a sunny spot on cool days or in a shady spot on hot days and have a little nap, like an old lady on a bench in the village. One day a group of GPS treasure-hunters parked their minibus in our car park as I served the Saussignac dessert wine with some Roquefort. They went off to search, returned having found the box and exchanged the treasure, got into their car and took off. Unbeknown to everyone, our pet and egg-layer Poc Poc was by then napping in the shade of a wheel. It hit her and she took off clucking. After a few paces she fell in a heap, mortally wounded and Blanchette, her friend, rushed up and jumped on her in a final embrace. I saw the catastrophe unfold from the window of the tasting-room kitchen, screamed and ran outside crying. I hadn't realised quite how much I cared for her until that moment.

The bus stopped and heads looked back. They were aware of what they had done but did not return to apologise. I was more horrified by their irresponsibility in driving away than by the act itself. I knew it had been a mistake, horrible as it was.

Drawn outside by the commotion, Sophia and Ellie saw the pile of rumpled feathers splattered with blood and burst into tears. I herded them inside, yelling for Seán. He sprinted from the hangar.

With a group of guests, my show had to go on so I tried to get a grip. I had just witnessed our pet go from living out her last days pecking happily to lifeless in one swift press of an accelerator. I felt like going inside and howling with Sophia and Ellie but I cleaned off my tears to serve dessert and coffee and give a controlled explanation of what made Saussignac dessert wines unique. After saying farewell to my guests I walked purposefully down to the tree where the 'treasure' was hidden, removed the box then removed the entry from the GPS treasure website.

Alongside prioritising my family, we had to limit what we did to bring clients to the chateau door. After that experience I decided this was one to strike off the list.

Through the project I learnt that aid payments, even once officially granted, are not guaranteed. Each step requires mountains of paperwork. Even once the Is were dotted and the Ts were crossed in triplicate (and sometimes several times more than that), and each version had been signed in original by our accountant, the actual payments were not certain. They were dependent on full compliance with the accessibility and security requirements. I spent hours searching for the correct furniture and measuring 90-centimetre passages, doing everything I could to be sure we were *aux normes*, but I knew despite the preparation that an unexpected hitch could block us at the last hurdle.

The second half of the aid, if we ever received the first, would also depend on several thousand euros' more expense to ensure we were *aux normes* with our spraying machine and treatment of effluent. The EU used aid programmes like the one we had applied for as a carrot to make sure that farmers receiving the aid for projects like a tasting room or accommodation met new environmental standards for seemingly unrelated things like the sprayer and the effluent treatment. The standards for these farming norms were set for large-scale farming and often made no sense when applied to a small farm, especially an organic one. The sprays we used were natural and would cause mild skin irritation at worst, but we still had to meet the norms for the spraying machine required for spraying highly toxic and dangerous chemicals on a large conventional farm.

One of the rules was adding a second vat to provide clean water for the spraying machine. This was required so that the machine could be rinsed with clean water, and that the water used for the rinsing – now a dilute version of the toxic spray – could be used out in the field where the operator was, rather than bringing the toxic rinse waste back to the farm courtyard. On our small farm, with no toxic sprays and with water butts metres from where Seán finished spraying, it was a joke. But we had to do it and it cost well over a thousand euros.

The second part, treating the effluent, or waste, from the winery, was even more of a joke. The only 'effluent' we produced was small quantities of dilute grape juice or wine in water, so good and healthy we used it on our fields as a natural fertiliser. Knowing that the farmer in Gardonne who would not eat his own apples could be *aux normes* while poisoning the water made it all the more crazy, but we had to do it. I resolved to programme these two necessities as soon as we got the first payment of the aid money.

Jen Barclay emailed from the publishers to say that the manuscript had been read by several colleagues and appreciated. It was looking hopeful. I dared to believe and felt a rush of excitement in my belly. The advance they would pay me on signing would help the finances. Then, just when I thought we would never see a cent of it, a lump of aid money arrived in our account. There was no notice, no explanation. We were over the moon and so was Monsieur Lambert. He and our other patient suppliers could at last be paid. I felt deeply relieved. We were seeing light at the end of the tunnel. Now I could take Seán's advice to stop working on Sundays and spend some time with my daughters without causing myself a racing heartbeat and insomnia. When I heard Sonia's tyres on the gravel that afternoon around 5 p.m. I went to hug Sophia and Ellie at the door and pointed to their special *goûter* of banana bread surrounded by fruit cut into shapes to make a face on each of their plates. Their broad smiles filled my heart with joy. I sat down with a cup of tea and we chatted about the day. As we talked I experienced a deep sense of happiness, a profound sense of fulfilment.

'I'm not working this Sunday,' I announced gleefully. 'What would you like to do?'

Their eyes went wide with delight.

'Let's do a picnic outside!' said Ellie.

'Let's go shopping for books!' said Sophia.

I laughed. 'You forget the shops are closed on Sunday in France. But we can go picnicking and take some books with us to read. Imagine: a lovely walk, a delicious picnic, lying down on the picnic blanket looking up at the blue sky, reading… How about it?'

'Yes!' said Ellie pulling her fist down through the air like she had just scored a goal.

'If you buy me a new book to read,' said Sophia. At a mere eight years old she was a skilled negotiator and debater; all the reading was paying off.

'I'll get you one when I go shopping tomorrow,' I said.

'Really, Mommy? Can you get me *Ma vie selon moi*?' said Sophia, almost unable to believe it possible, we had been living so lean for so long. It was usually the library or nothing.

'Yes, I'll get it,' I said, knowing it was something she had been hankering after for a while. 'I'll get a new book for Ellie too.'

'I can't wait,' said Sophia.

'Me too,' said Ellie.

'It's a date!' I said happily as I cleared away the plates and my teacup and stacked them into the dishwasher.

Chapter 25
A Shocking Death

Yannick Chenet's face, deformed by poison, stared out of the photo at me. He was communicating from the grave; dead at 43 years of age, officially recognised by the French government as killed by the pesticide he sprayed on his vineyard. One of the jets of his spray machine broke and he was doused in the poison he usually reserved for his grapes. In a few months it was all over.

One of his last comments was: 'In hospital I discovered that the same company that made the pesticides that were killing me was making the pills they were giving me to fight the cancer. I said, "It can't be true."' But it was.

For my newborn social and political awakening it was almost too much to take.

Reading on, I discovered that more than a quarter of the roughly 220,000 tons of agricultural pesticide used in Europe per year was sprayed on French soil – and 20 per cent of that amount went onto French vineyards, though vineyards accounted for less than 4 per cent of the country's crop surface.

I was stunned. We never sprayed pesticide on our vines and had experienced no crop loss at all from pest outbreaks. On our farm, natural habitats encouraged good bugs like ladybirds that kept the unwanted bugs, like aphids, in check. Even the Achilles' heel of competition from fellow members of our commune had a silver lining: less than a fifth of our border areas were on chemically farmed vineyards.

Soon after we moved in I recall seeing the skull and crossbones sign on the cans left by the previous owner. I looked closer and read, 'Do not enter the vineyard for 48 hours after spraying.' Then I hadn't known that much about it, but common sense alone told me that putting something so toxic on food, or in the vicinity of homes and children, made no sense. Grapes are not washed before they are made into wine.

On conventional farms these pesticides are complemented by a range of herbicides to remove all growth that can be competition to the crop. Two types of herbicide are applied: one to kill the plants that are already growing, usually a glyphosate like Roundup, and then another called a pre-emergent herbicide to stop the seeds from germinating. In this way the only living things left in the vineyards are the vines themselves, ensuring they are the only target for plant-eating pests living or arriving in the area. To fight those pests, the farmer then sprays the highly carcinogenic pesticides, including those so toxic they can kill a grown man like Yannick.

The ironic twist in the tail is the third part of the chemical cocktail used by conventional winegrowers: systemic fungicides, applied to kill downy mildew. They are sprayed on and are absorbed by the leaves then go to work on the inside to kill all fungi, including good ones. They are like antibiotics: if you use them non-stop, as some conventional farmers use systemic fungicides, you would weaken your system because the beneficial bacteria that you need to keep your stomach working properly would be dead. They are critical to your health, including the combatting of seemingly unrelated ailments like heart disease.

Not only do the systemic fungicides stop beautiful wild orchids and delicious truffles from growing, but they also stop the vine's natural access to nutrients offered by their symbiotic relationship with mycorrhiza, essential soil fungi. This weakened access to natural food in the soil means more chemical fertilisers are required to achieve an economic yield. These have mineral salts that make the vine thirsty so it takes up more water and holds more water in its cells – as we do when we eat too many salty snacks – and this extra water makes them more susceptible to fungal disease, meaning more systemic fungicide is required, and so on in a never-ending vicious circle that ends with a desert instead of a farm.

Each time I explained this on our vineyard tour, people were dumbstruck. It seemed so illogical to be caught in this cycle – why would anyone be farming with chemicals?

Bulk farmers are trapped in a low-margin business. Converting to organic takes three years of hardship, what I now call the 'Valley of Despair', the phase I described in my first book. Vines need to go through cold turkey, like someone coming off drugs, and struggle to cope; their immunity is low. They need more care and attention than they will in a few years when their resistance has improved. You have to invest in new equipment and new methods, but can't charge more for your product since you can't mention organic until you are certified. It's a dangerous traverse that many conventional farmers are not in a position to make financially, even if they wanted to.

I tore myself away from the horror story about Yannick, pulled on my hiking boots and my backpack, slicked on a quick stroke of lipstick and a spray of sunscreen, and grabbed my hiking pole.

Andrew, a solid, blonde Dorset farmer and his tall, dark-haired, elegant wife Elizabeth had arrived the night before for a vineyard walking tour. This, my favourite activity on our tour menu, offered a challenge as I never knew exactly what level of fitness the group would have. Each of my circuits had a shortcut and an extra loop. For the fit, like this Dorset farmer who did a warm-up of 4 kilometres every morning before I appeared with breakfast, I added extra loops.

We set off at a good pace and I pointed out dandelion, stinging nettle, horsetail, willow and other plants we use for our biodynamic concoctions as they appeared on the track or in the hedgerows. I started to talk about the benefits of hedgerows and organic farming.

'You're speaking to the converted,' said Andrew laughing at his pun. 'We converted our dairy farm to organic ten years ago. We actually only went organic because there were cash incentives for conversion – I did it for the money. But now I'm a total convert. I will never go back to conventional farming.'

'Wow,' I said. 'You sound like Saul on the road to Damascus.'

'I'm a hard-nosed farmer. It's about the benefits versus the costs. All the products we were buying, the chemical fertilisers and chemical herbicides, and the vet bills, they were totally unnecessary. We were lining the pockets of big agro-chemical companies at the cost of the health of our farm. After a couple of years, when the aid was finished, we made about the same amount of money as before, but looking at the whole farm, the cows, the employees and me, we are happier in the organic system. But seeing all this,' he pointed across the valley back to the Wine Lodge and our vineyards, 'I'm thinking of going into vineyards.' He laughed heartily.

He ran a big, successful farm with 2,000 cows and twelve full-time employees; I didn't get the feeling he was going to give that up anytime soon.

'How come you don't have the vet bills now?' I asked.

'Our cows are a hardy local breed rather than a super-productive special breed. They're outside all year round and rarely get sick. The cows calve naturally. The super-breeds that produce enormous quantities of milk – a must for a conventional dairy – usually need intervention to calve. Looking back on it, it was a never-ending cycle of intervention. With the drop in organic prices resulting from the financial crisis, considering only litres produced and money made, we're not doing as well as the conventional producers. But there is still no way I would go back to that.'

With biodiversity and natural farming more labour was required, but it was compensated for by not buying expensive chemicals – and by *being alive*. I knew what sort of farming Yannick would be practising now if he were still with us.

Since Poc Poc's sudden demise, the other chickens had been quietly dying of old age; one had settled in the woodshed and gone into the long sleep from which we do not return; another did the same snuggled up against the kitchen door. We felt sad but OK; they were ready.

An invitation to attend the Best of Wine Tourism awards ceremony at a grand chateau in the Médoc arrived at lunch to lift me out of my gloom about another death in our chicken clan. It was accompanied by a letter asking us to supply bottles of wine for the tasting on the evening of the awards. I felt a flutter of excitement. If we were being asked for wine, perhaps we had won something.

That same week Jen emailed to say the publisher wanted to go ahead with publication of my book. She sent a draft contract via email and asked me to read it over. Taking a moment to lie in the hammock under the trees, I read through the legalese. Feeling a real publishing contract in my hands and realising I would soon be a published author, I was overwhelmed with joy. The money would be handy but the deal meant so much more to me than that.

Sébastian and Thomas had pulled out all the stops and kept to our deadlines. With the arrival of summer, the Wine Lodge was officially open for business. The void left by the departure of the team was rapidly filled by guests, but I still felt a gap. After nearly a year of working together it was strange not to have Thomas's stable presence and Sébastian's effervescence constantly on site.

That Friday the gîte guests left a day early to make their ferry booking so we took the opportunity to test out our new Wine Lodge terrace. Watching the sun set over the vineyards, we ate a delicious barbecue made by Seán. The view up the valley towards Saussignac and across to Gageac was breathtaking: rolling vineyards and forest dotted with stone homesteads, all perfectly touched with the evening's palette of pinks. The girls ran around the deck of the lodge and up onto the terrace of the tasting room, playing hide-and-seek. I opened the tasting-room doors and put on a CD and we danced like sprites.

Seán had drawn a man-sized triskell onto the rounded wall of the tasting room and Thomas had skilfully traced it with a mosaic made from shards of terracotta tiles. The triskell, a three-way spiral, is an ancient Celtic symbol and spirals are often used as symbols for biodynamics, so we had chosen the triskell as our logo to go with the new name Terroir Feely on our bottles. Seeing it on the tasting-room wall that night as we danced, I felt a deep satisfaction. After all the effort and stress, the new tasting room and lodge were a beautiful reality. Our place and our wines were transforming into what we wanted.

Chapter 26

Chasse au Trésor
Périgord-style

Isobel, Lucy and Lucy were high-flying twenty-something lawyers from London. Lucy One was training for a walk up Kilimanjaro to take place ten days after the tour with me. It was sure to be another case of adding circuits to my walking routes.

That autumn I woke up a little earlier than usual so I could go down to the bramble hedge and pick fresh blackberries for breakfast each morning. It was magical, almost meditative, a moment of calm to collect the best berries I had ever tasted.

A couple of hours after picking blackberries one morning, I started my three days of walking with the three gals from London, passing below the Château de Saussignac where a giant sculpture about 12 foot tall of a hiker striding with a walking cane appeared in the morning mist. Behind him, leaning demurely against a tree, was a stone nude, her pretty face and perfect small breasts pointing in the direction of our path that descended into the valley where I often found the aromas that gave me a clue about the biodynamic day and which elements had the upper hand. When it smelt earthy, it was a root day;

when it smelt leafy, the water element was strong; floral aromas meant the air element had the upper hand; and fruity smells meant the fire element was strong.

Our village of Saussignac was transforming into an artists' haven. Mike Snow, a painter, and Tim White, a photographer, were two Americans that started the trend soon after we arrived. Since then more artists, including Renépaul, the sculptor responsible for these unexpected sculptures, had arrived.

As we walked through the valley of the aromas I warned the three women to beware of the stinging nettle on the side of the path and held out my hand to feel the delicate tickle of the mare's tail fronds that crowded the path's edge, jostling with the nettle for space. I caught a strong smell of leaves and herbs as we crossed the stream and climbed up towards Gageac, then passed into a forested track filled with birdsong. From the shaded woodland we moved back into vineyards on our left and peaceful cream cows on our right. The Charolais cattle watched us walking by, their heads moving in unison like a dance troupe in slow motion. At the top of the hill we stopped for a short break to take in the views. The sky was cloudy with pinky tints where the sun was trying to break through. Looking back towards Saussignac we could see the perfect front face of her chateau; and to our right, the Château de Gageac-Rouillac, older than Saussignac even. Dating back to the 900s, its left tower was the oldest *donjon*, keep, in the entire Dordogne department. The crenellated chateau surrounded by a moat could have modelled for a fairy tale. Between the two chateaux, and directly in front of where we sat drinking in elderflower cordial and the view itself, plunged the Dordogne valley. It was a mix of picturesque vineyards, forests, stone hamlets with church spires, and the river. This was one of my favourite spots, a place I often brought Dora running.

A couple of hours later at our lunch destination, the nearby Relais de Monestier, a hearty welcome and an offer to put our socks in the drier warmed our souls, while salad with hot mushrooms, poached egg and bits of bacon warmed our stomachs. It wasn't raining, but there was so much dew that our feet were soaked. Like the smell of the leaves and herbs in the valley of aromas, the heavy dew meant the water forces were strong. With toasty socks came a beef and autumn vegetable stew. We melted into our chairs, succumbing to the joys of Dordogne autumn food. Philippe, *chef extraordinaire*, crowned the lunch extravaganza with a *moelleux au chocolat*, crusty on the outside and oozing rich dark chocolate from the inside. We sat for a while soaking in the satisfaction of a hard morning walk and magnificent lunch, contemplating life. Satisfied physically and spiritually we took off at a brisk pace in the bracing air and soon felt light as a feather and ready to do it all again. When we returned home that evening I checked the calendar. It was a leaf day: the water forces had the upper hand, just as I had suspected from the clues on the walk.

On the third and last day we crossed the valley ridge from Saussignac to Razac to visit Thierry at Château le Payral. It was a gorgeous autumn morning; cold and sunny with a hint of smoke in the air. We strode through orange, gold and green-flecked vineyards past Château de Fayolle, down the valley towards Patrick and Chantal at La Maurigne, where we had experienced our first ever Saussignac-growers evening just a few days before we started our very first harvest; I had been charmed that night as much by the rustic army tent filled with golden samples and candlelight as I had been by charismatic growers like Thierry.

From La Maurigne, we took the forest path that linked us with the small road to Razac. Below us was Le Chabrier where

I had hand-picked Saussignac grapes and met winegrowers like Joel at a marketing event organised by our commune the year we arrived. Back then, everything seemed foreign. The names made no sense. I couldn't remember anyone or anything, having no familiar hooks to hang them on.

Now everything was familiar. We knew most of the people living on the road. When it had snowed heavily the previous winter, Seán took the children to school when the bus wasn't running. He said he wasn't worried because, if he got stuck between us and the next village, he would know the nearest farmer and they would pull him out with their tractor. There was a sense of security in knowing our community that was true luxury.

Leaving behind the views of the Dordogne valley, a stunning patchwork of vineyards and plum orchards, we entered the forest and fecund, earthy aromas flooded our lungs. With each footfall more rich perfume puffed up and filled the air. As we turned out of the forest the village of Razac-de-Saussignac appeared in the distance, its Romanesque church bright in the morning sun.

'Someone's rubbish has been dropped on the side of the road,' said Isobel pointing to a small mound of plastic up ahead.

'It's strange to see a pile of trash in the middle of pristine countryside,' said Lucy One.

'It looks like packages of something,' said Lucy Two, who was closest.

We gathered round. I gingerly picked up one of the packages. Silver backing on one side and vacuum-sealed meat on the other: it was not just any meat, but a top-end brand of whole foie gras, six entire packs, unopened, packaged that morning and still cold. We packed three into my backpack and Isobel, Lucy and Lucy carried one each as we continued the last stretch to Château le Payral, laughing about our strange treasure.

Isobel proffered hers to Thierry as I told the story.

'Someone must have dropped it,' said Thierry.

'Not it. Them.'

I pointed into my bag.

'*Wiouw*. That is a *sacré* mountain of foie gras. It must be worth at least 300 euros,' he said.

'Who would order that quantity of foie gras?' I said.

'Château des Vigiers. No one else near here would order that much,' said Thierry.

Château des Vigiers was a four-star chateau hotel with spa, golf and two restaurants a few kilometres away. Thierry's good friend, Léonie, was a manager there. Thierry called her and she laughed and said it was our lucky day. We should keep it. The traceability was lost so they couldn't use it and neither could the supplier. Thierry, chuckling, put our Périgord treasure in his fridge and took us into his winery and barrel room to explain their process of winemaking to the women. I later offered Isobel and the Lucys a pack of foie gras each but they were travelling back that evening and didn't want to wrangle sniffer dogs at Gatwick.

I enjoyed the taste of *foie gras entier* sliced and pan-fried, but since visiting a foie gras farm a few years before I wouldn't buy it, so we hadn't eaten or served it in years. Now, with a mountain of the stuff having fallen free at my feet, I was faced with an ethical dilemma that I tried to argue away. The ducks were long dead. Not eating what they had died for would make their death meaningless. I didn't want to buy foie gras and contribute to the industry, but I didn't want to throw away the windfall. That evening, after saying farewell and dropping the three women at Gardonne station, I collected the ethically-thorny-but-free bounty from Thierry and gave him one pack as a thank you.

The first official Wine Spirit Education Trust course and exam was about to take place at Terroir Feely. With three participants signed up we would only use a tiny section of each of the forty-plus samples of wine I had purchased or swapped. To make the most of them we would have our friends join us to taste through the samples the evening the course finished. Thierry's Isabelle took two packs of bounty foie gras to turn into *foie gras mi-cuit*, semi-cooked foie gras, for the occasion.

That month our guests were coincidentally arriving in sets of three women and I was enjoying it. I missed time with girlfriends like I had missed my daughters. These three women had booked the course separately and came from different corners of the world. They were lively, asking great questions, some that had me scrambling for Jancis Robinson's *Oxford Companion to Wine*, a comprehensive dictionary that almost always came up with an answer. I loved having to look things up; each question I couldn't answer was another opportunity to learn. When the course results arrived a few weeks later, all three women had passed with distinction, leaving me glowing with pride.

Within hours of the end of the course our friends' tasting marathon started. Pierre was first to arrive so we took the opportunity to draw on his mechanical skills. The ancient forklift we had bought from Thierry that year, a museum piece that cost less than a tenth of a new one, was as unreliable as memorabilia could be expected to be. It had stopped working a few days before, as was its wont.

Pierre tried everything to no effect. Finally he leant his head onto the forklift frame and I expected him to start banging it methodically onto the metal bar – what I felt like doing – but instead he paused Zen-like and began to stroke it. Having done nothing but stroke calmly, he turned the key again and it leapt to life. My eyes wide, my eyebrows halfway up my forehead and my mouth open, I watched in awe as he quickly moved the pallet we needed transported into place. He was 'Zen and the art of machine maintenance' personified.

While the Feely, Moore, Daulhiac and de St Viance younger generations took over the main house, playing music and games, eating dinner and then settling exhausted in front of a DVD, we pitted our wits against rounds of wines, blind tasting from one end of the globe to the other while I tracked results on a flipchart. Pierre was the most gifted blind taster, picking up the nuances of what the wine was, where it was from, the farming and the winemaking methods, all with a quick swish and a swirl. No need for WSET for him. Years of bottling wines across the region and beyond had left his receptors extremely fine. He was master, closely followed by Isabelle. Palates exhausted, we sunk our teeth into little toasts covered in treasure-hunt foie gras.

Laurence and I caught up standing next to the windows of the tasting room and enjoying an aperitif of *méthode traditionelle*.

'*Comment ça va, mon amie?*' How are things going, my friend? asked Laurence. She was slim and dark-haired, always neatly dressed, and thriving since passing her *concours* to become a full-time primary teacher. As part of passing the teaching exam in France, candidates had to run the 800 metres within a specified time. It had been part of Laurence's motivation to run with me, and now she was a full-time teacher she also hadn't as much spare time as before. We hadn't had a chance to talk in ages.

'Really good, at last!' I said. 'This tasting room and the lodge were a good decision.' Laurence had been a bouncing board for me to talk through the idea of the renovation years before.

'Is it all finished?'

'Yes, we were lucky to have the O'Briens here for a holiday. *Nous avons peinté ensemble.* We painted together.'

She cracked up and lifted her hand over her mouth in amused embarrassment.

'Sorry, Caro! But *peinté* is slang for inebriated... whereas the past of to paint is just *peint*,' explained Laurence, trying to control herself.

I joined her laughter and we giggled together like two schoolgirls. After all that tasting, perhaps *I* was a little *peintée*.

Chapter 27
Gold for Green

The smell of sauvignon blanc hit me like a tsunami as I opened the insulation curtain to the winery. Seán was in shorts spotted with grapes, sterilised garden clogs and a smile. We had harvested our whites and Seán was preparing to do the last bit of pressing. He had improved the system since the previous year but it was still slow-going. We had also moved one of the large vats out and our winery was inching closer to what we wanted it to be, although it was still far from being there. Like the rest of the property, it would be part of our life's work. I waved at him to join me to say farewell to the van Sorgens.

Ad and Lijda had been with us for a few weeks to help with harvest, as they did every year. I was drowning in work again, every waking hour consumed and barely coping. Harvest meant 5 a.m. starts, full days of wine-tour guests and then finishing, if I was lucky, with replying to emails and calls by 10 p.m. Lijda quietly collected and folded laundry for me, picked figs, weeded the potager and made dinner. It was like having an angel to stay. Ad fixed tools for Seán, welded machinery, replaced bulbs that we had missed and helped with harvest. They were surrogate grandparents to Sophia and Ellie with both our parents living far, far away.

I kissed them goodbye and tears pricked my eyes. As they drove out, their familiar campervan with bikes attached to the back bouncing along the road, I was sobbing. It was with sadness but also with gratitude for what they meant to us. The people that had come into our lives through the vineyard were powerful and beautiful.

That evening the smell of a basil and lime candle, a gift for us from the marketing manager of my publisher, perfumed the air as we sat on our terrace planning the following year's summer holiday; our first summer holiday as a family ever. Hilary, an old friend from university, and her partner David had offered us their holiday house in Provence for a week. We had been down to see their beautiful *mas* for two nights a few years before. We were dreaming of lavender fields, Provençal olives and an infinity pool.

'Where is it again?' asked Sophia.

'The one in Provence. Remember? The house of Hilary, my friend. The place you fell in the pool.'

I had started to use French grammar like 'the house of Hilary' instead of 'Hilary's house'. Sometimes when writing an emotive sentence I would find the French words, not the English ones, in my head and be forced to click over to Google Translate.

'Oh yes, the place I nearly died,' said Sophia, who on our first trip had toddled into the pool and sunk like a stone, swiftly followed by Seán who scooped her up spluttering. Now they could swim.

'Hilary gave me the Richard Scary book, *What Do People Do All Day?*'

I laughed. 'Richard Scarry, not Richard Scary. There is no winegrower in there but if there was it would be Scary.'

Seán smiled.

'Can we swim every day?' said Ellie.

'Of course,' I replied. It would be a real treat for them since we did not have a pool of our own.

Sophia pushed her fork into the orange square on her plate, delivered it to her mouth and chewed thoughtfully. 'Now I understand why it's called butternut! That is the first time I tasted the butter and the nut,' she exclaimed.

Ellie grimaced; even if it tasted like butter and nut, it was an orange vegetable other than carrot and she didn't like it. That winter was going to be tough for her since Seán had produced about 40 kilograms of these and other evil Halloween-horror orange vegetables.

Seán's gardening was a triumph. Not only was he producing serious quantities of food, enough to feed us most of the year, but the food was delicious, offering a depth of flavour true to itself, as Sophia had highlighted.

Printing documents for wine-tour guests that evening, the printer stopped working. I felt like hitting it but instead took a Zen-like stance and stroked, then pressed the print button and stood, mouth open, as the perfectly printed pages fell into the receiving tray.

Hand-picking with Saussignac primary school was something I had wanted to do for years, a way to connect with our community. Not many winegrowers hand-picked their grapes, and with total mechanisation vineyards lost some of their life and joy. Saussignac, the dessert wine we made, had to be hand-picked but picking the noble rot was too complicated for children. Hand-harvesting our red merlot with six- and seven-year-olds would be better. There could still be some bloody fingers so we loaded the cart attached to the tractor with the first aid kit alongside buckets, secateurs and patience.

A tiny triangle, one of our vineyards closest to the school, was our target. It was just enough to keep them engaged for an hour while they ate their way through it – one bunch for the bucket, one bunch for me. We laughed at the red mouths and explained about how important farming without chemicals was. Sophia and Ellie ran back and forth, helping to organise and acting as nurses with the plasters and antiseptic. The morning sun filtered through the vines and the unique energy and excitement of harvest filled the group. When we returned to the winery, each child emptied their bucket directly into the vat so they could envisage the full process. Sitting in the courtyard to let them ask questions afterwards, I was impressed by the level of interest and the quality of some of their questions.

We sent three bottles of juice up to school the following day for them to taste with their lunch. Now as I arrived at Saussignac primary school each day I was greeted like an old friend. Running with Dora a few weeks later, a car passed me on the St Germain road, close to the ridge where once I had cried thinking we were going to have to sell the farm. The kids in the back seat turned with great smiles of glee spanning their faces as they recognised me and waved madly, almost leaping out of the car in excitement. I felt a glow of community warmth.

From picking with the school we flew into our fourth vine-share weekend. Back to a more manageable fifty, it went perfectly with help from John and Judy Burford, Australian winegrowers who farmed near Melbourne and who rented our Wine Cottage every two years. They brought a relaxed Aussie sense of humour. The harvest weekend was now starting to feel natural, like something we could do instinctively.

As the last harvest weekenders left, Nat, a specialist cardiologist from Florida, arrived for a wine tour. He was compact and neat, recently retired and fiercely patriotic, deeply grateful to the USA for the opportunities he had when he emigrated from India in his youth. He was also a wine connoisseur whose cellar contained greats like Cheval Blanc 1947, a hallowed estate and vintage from Saint-Émilion, and Château Margaux 1982, another mythic vintage, this one from the mega-vineyard in Margaux in the Médoc region; wines I had read about but never tasted.

We toured our vineyard and voyaged to Saint-Émilion and Pomerol. Our last day was to the Médoc, timed to coincide with the 'Night of the Stars', the official awards ceremony for the Best of Wine Tourism. I had an invitation for two and Nat agreed to chaperone me and act as official photographer. Seán was too busy with our own harvest to take a day off and with one car between us he couldn't make the trip later. He would walk the girls home from school and feed the family instead.

Château d'Agassac was lit up like a fairy castle, its Cinderella turrets and moat so perfect it seemed like a Disney creation rather than what it was, original Renaissance architecture from 1580. Renovation and modernisation of the stunning property had won them an international 'Best of Wine Tourism' award the previous year. The old *pigeonnier*, dovecote, on the front lawn was ancient stone on the outside but through the open door I could see the inside was wall-to-wall control panels with flashing lights and buttons; the technical centre from where the impressive 'son et lumière' shows they offered could be managed. Like some other wineries I had seen on my tours, the inside looked more like a setting for James Bond than a wine farm.

Perfectly manicured lawns were zigzagged with evocatively lit white paths that led visitors from the presentation hall to the main chateau and back to the car park. My feet crunched the gravel as I scampered back and forth ferrying wine samples and brochures.

With everything set for the wine tasting afterwards, my heart quickened with the activity and excitement. I changed into sleek stockings, a little black designer dress and a golden puff-sleeved jacket – all courtesy of my glamorous sister – in the washroom. Nat and I settled down in the front row as the room hushed and the awards, a who's who of the greats of Bordeaux, began.

There were six categories in the 'best of' awards and we had entered for two. The first one passed with nothing doing. When the final category for the night, Sustainable Wine Tourism Practices, was announced I felt excitement and butterflies in my stomach.

The third place was announced and it wasn't us; then second place. I was deeply disappointed, certain we couldn't be the winner. I had hoped to be a finalist, thinking this was why we had been asked for wine samples. There was a barrel roll but I was barely listening.

The red envelope was handed to the presenter; she opened it, looked out at the crowd and called our name.

Nat mouthed congratulations and I leapt to my feet, tears pricking my eyes, not expecting the emotion that the award unleashed. I climbed the steps onto the red-carpet podium, my heart hammering with excitement and adrenalin pumping through me. Keeping the tears at bay long enough to make a credible speech, I accepted the trophy. I hadn't realised just how much recognition of our work would mean to me.

Pitted against the top of the top estates, including certified organic *grands crus classés* with pockets so deep anything was possible, we had the gold. I called Seán, wishing he was with me. We were tiny, but our passion and conviction had won the judges over. They had evaluated the written submissions but had also booked a visit under cover to make their assessment. Looking back over the visitors we had had during the window in which the judges had made their assessments, we were sure that it was Seán who had taken the visit.

Seán didn't like doing visits; he was shy and reclusive, avoiding crowds at all costs. Seán's ultimate nightmare was a cocktail party or networking event, whereas I had been known as the 'queen of networking' by my old colleagues in Dublin. The award proved he could handle visits well, more than well. The cherry on the cake was that he had hosted it in French.

Sharing our wines with the glittering crowd at the reception afterwards, I wished I had a microphone to record the compliments for Seán. We had worked like crazy and taken risks but, as Goethe had predicted, the universe was working with us.

After six years of nagging, our local bakery produced their first organic baguette that October. It quickly became a staple of the range and represented a small triumph for me. Meanwhile, my stress-busting cherry dark-chocolate treat that had partnered me through the first years had gone missing. I looked in every supermarket but the 'touche de sérénité' had disappeared. It was a blessing, though, since it wasn't certified organic and my shopping ethic meant I would have had to stop buying it anyway.

And then, in my birthday presents, I found a delicately wrapped packet of handmade organic black chocolate encrusted with cherries. Seán had dried cherries from our garden back in May and then coated them in divine darkness. They were beyond delicious and touched my heart. The thought, planning, time and skill that went into it showed his love more powerfully than anything.

Two weeks later Luke, a down-to-earth Canadian, arrived to help for a few weeks. Strong and fit, with dark curly hair and beard and a happy smile that made you want to smile with him, he was just what we needed. He was a friend of a friend; a twenty-something with a sense of humour, no fear of hard work and a deeply ecological ethos. With him and Ian Wilson, our friend from Pécharmant, we prepared to press the reds. Now that we saved our grape skins for Naomi, the job had become significantly more labour-intensive and we needed extra hands.

After a morning of pressing we loaded the wagon with skins and made our way to Miaudoux, Gérard's farm where we dried the marc. With spades and muscles we dug the grape skins from the trailer and moved them to the drying trays. About three hours later, Thierry arrived to check how things were going. We introduced him to Luke and they struck an instant rapport.

'So how's it going, Luke?' said Thierry. 'Can't wait to see the back end of this trailer? Seen enough grapes to last you a lifetime in one afternoon?'

We all laughed.

'I'm loving it,' said Luke picking a skin out of his hair.

'You are special, then,' said Thierry. 'Looking for a job next year?'

'Hey, *ce sont nous les premiers*!' We get first dibs! said Seán.

Luke was such a keen worker and got on so well with Thierry that when Thierry arrived back with a load as we left, he stayed on to help.

Sitting on the wagon behind the tractor as Seán drove us back to Terroir Feely, I reflected on the previous three years. Thierry had been invaluable in advancing our opportunity with Naomi.

Her grape skin purchases had provided a new revenue stream that had saved our skins at a critical moment. We still didn't know if the aid money was certain. Although we had been paid half, if we didn't meet the final accessibility test, or if our effluent system did not meet the requirements, we would have to return it.

We still had to find a way to cope with the extra demands of our growing tourism business, the new Wine Lodge and the tasting room that was busier each year with the rising reputation of our wines. But it was a good problem to have and we had reached a level that meant we didn't have to worry about how we would pay the social charges each month or buy a pair of shoes when the girls outgrew the ones they were in.

Through a few lucky breaks and a lot of hard work we had turned our barely viable vineyard into a successful organic and biodynamic farm where we could share our ethos. We have decades of ideas for permaculture, biodynamics, beautification and eco-friendly living, and I feel compelled to tell people about the implications of chemical farming. Often I feel that the world is in a deep sleep, unaware or unwilling to face the dangers of pesticides, herbicides and systemic fungicides until the level of cancer or one of the other diseases they cause becomes like the plague of the Middle Ages; or until the impact of air pollution becomes so bad that we can't breathe. Each time someone walks away from our farm changed, with a new perspective on these important issues, it fills me with hope. Like the renaissance of our farm, it gives me renewed energy.

We clattered into the courtyard of Terroir Feely and Ian and I jumped off the wagon to wash the tools. As we worked we chatted about this and that. I found that when I talked to Ian even about mundane things I discovered things about myself. He was like a guru.

With the tools cleaned, we found Seán starting a vine-wood fire for our barbecue planned for that evening. His new barbecue apparatus was an old oil barrel welded onto steel legs complete with shelves where he needed them and enough space to burn entire vine trunks and cook for large groups of friends and family. Ad's welding training was coming in handy in all sorts of ways. We had discovered the joys of barbecuing on vines years before, on that fateful visit to France when the seed of our dream was sown; it brought a delicious fruity touch. Seán had placed the barbecue barrel far from the new tasting room and lodge, because, beautiful as they were, they were now a work zone for us.

The two new buildings were working out even better than we had planned. We had more visitors than ever and, with the additional footfall from the publication of *Grape Expectations*, direct sales were flying. It was great, but now, at the end of the season, we felt relieved that peace lay ahead; I was looking forward to the calm of winter.

Seán left Ian to watch over the fire in the company of a large glass of wine and took a shower while I set off to collect the girls from school on foot. When the weather was good we avoided the car, turning to walking or cycling instead. After the day of digging grapes I needed to stretch out. As we walked back along the road from Saussignac to our farm I felt wonder at the beauty around me and at my lovely daughters. No matter how many times I walked that serpentine road it filled me with joy; it was the same but different, colours changing with the seasons, with the weather. Now that I regularly walked it with Sophia and Ellie it meant even more to me. We would share stories about the day, pick a dandelion from the roadside, run with Dora, laugh at a wisecrack from Ellie or her friend Alane. It was bliss. Instead of a harassed rush up in the car to jostle with the other parents for a parking space, I could enjoy the fresh air and the company of my daughters.

With the girls home, I showered then went to join Ian. The seating area around the barbecue was a mishmash of chairs, a beer crate turned over, a broken bench waiting to be fixed and two old plastic sunloungers from the Wine Cottage that had broken in a storm and been replaced with smarter FSC-approved wooden loungers. Seán cracked a bottle of Feely *méthode traditionelle* and poured for us. We clinked glasses and toasted the day's work.

Now that the red vats were drained and the skins were dried, the work in the winery would drop off. Seán would move on to vineyard maintenance, spraying the biodynamic 500 preparation on the vineyard before it got too cold, and preparing for pruning. Nature's cycle, with its comforting rhythm that governed our lives, would start again.

Ian's wife Brigit and daughter Chiara arrived as Thierry dropped Luke back to us. I ran inside for more glasses and home-made elderflower cordial with sparkling water for the girls. With the sparkle added it became their special treat in tall plastic wine glasses, as good as our real champagne. Seán poured some more *méthode traditionelle* and Thierry took the smallest, saying he needed to get home. We toasted the vintage, taking in the gorgeous autumn evening and company of friends.

After chatting for a while Thierry knocked back what was left in his glass, said his goodbyes, looked meaningfully at Seán and said 'Luke, remember to call me about that job offer for next year!' He cracked up and took off, leaving us laughing in his wake.

The duck breast was nearing perfection on the barbecue so Seán threw two great handfuls of rosemary into the fire. The herb's essential oils rose up in flames, searing the meat; Seán was our master chef and duck was his speciality. After piling our plates with home-grown courgettes, potatoes, tomatoes and the succulent duck, we tucked in. Murmurs of appreciation echoed around the new barbecue nook set on the white limestone laid by Mr Jegu outside the new hangar that Seán and Ad had completed a few weeks before, another phase of the ongoing renovations. Seán was becoming sustainability personified, growing most of our food and *all* of our drink. Our neglected relationship had weathered the stresses of a frosted vintage and a significant building project, boding well for the future. With nurturing, I knew we would get it back to full health, bring back the zing.

While I cleared up, Seán finished off the construction of a bonfire he had made between the hangar and his new potager. Brigit and Ian moved the makeshift chairs closer and Seán set the bonfire alight as the cool night closed in. Luke fetched my guitar from inside and struck up a Neil Young tune. He was good. We all listened, soaking in the sound and the starry night, warmed by the fire. Sophia and Ellie were transfixed.

But not for long: they hadn't forgotten that there were marshmallows to be cooked. Luke took a break from the guitar to partake in the soft pink treats and I sat down gingerly on the broken bench next to Ian.

'So how's it going, Caro?' he asked as Sophia passed him a toasted marshmallow. 'Have you found Zen?'

I roared with laughter. I was hyper; Seán was Zen. It was going to take me a while longer to find it but I was getting closer. I didn't wake up with a racing heart panicking about our future like I had done in the early years. I had found that picking berries at dawn was definitely better than any argument. Moments like that, and this one around the bonfire, brought me a deep sense of peace. I looked over at Seán and we exchanged a conspiratorial glance. I had an inkling that, like sharing what we had learnt about agriculture, finding Zen would be part of our next adventure.

What Can You Do to Ensure a Healthy Future?

Every ecological gesture makes a difference: not using the car and taking the bike instead; choosing organic (ideally black) chocolate over the big-brand bar.

Give yourself a big pat on the back each time you:

- Buy certified organic produce, from food to cotton, or grow something organic. Even in an apartment an organic window box of herbs can offer joy. Demand organic everything everywhere, from your coffee shop and restaurant to your supermarket. This is the most important step to save our water, the bees and ourselves. I feel so good when I buy organic. I know deep in my heart that it is really doing good; not just for me and my body but for the producer, the land and our water supply.

- Bike or walk instead of driving a short distance, or use public transport instead of your car for the longer ones. Find a way to work exercise into your commute: good for you, your pocket and the planet. Since we started walking or riding bikes to school together, Sophia, Ellie and I are not only fitter but we have fun doing it.

- Say no to packaging that is unnecessary. Choose glass and paper over plastic. By not buying overpackaged products we stop them being produced.

- Make a plan to change your environment in every possible way, from reducing the heat control a few degrees in winter to improving your insulation and installing solar or other energy-efficient solutions.

- Try cooking from scratch. Simple food made from good ingredients tastes better and is healthier than complicated food from bad ingredients, and can be just as quick. 'More chopping, less shopping.' It seems like work but when you get into the groove of making it part of your day, a chance to unwind and enjoy listening to music or chatting and working together, it becomes a precious moment rather than a chore.

- Stay in touch with nature. A walk or run in a park or forest, taking a moment to look around at the incredible beauty of plants, trees and sky, even in the rain, is like a tonic. It reminds us that the world is worth protecting. A moment outside in the fresh air brings perspective like nothing else.

To feel the urge to take action we need to understand why it is imperative to do so. A few books and films I recommend on this quest are:

- *Organic Manifesto: How Organic Food Can Heal Our Planet, Feed the World, and Keep Us Safe* by Maria Rodale

- *Food, Inc.*, the documentary film and the book

- *Fast Food Nation*, the book by Eric Schlosser

- The documentary films *Food Matters* and *Hungry for Change*

- *Vanishing of the Bees*, another documentary film (a French documentary equivalent if you can understand French is *Le mystère de la disparition des abeilles*)

Join me on Facebook (Terroir Feely) and Twitter (@carofeely) for updated recommendations.

Each of us can make change happen. Together we become an ever more powerful force. We don't have to wait for government to legislate change. The death of farmers like Yannick Chenet and the rampant increase in cancer, especially among children, must not go unheeded; they must instead serve to raise the alarm.

I invite you to join our mailing list at www.feelywines.com; like us on Facebook (Terroir Feely); email me at caro@feelywines.com; visit us for a tour (www.frenchwineadventures.com); or come and stay with us (www.luxurydordognegites.com).

We look forward to connecting online and to seeing you in the Dordogne. Thanks for joining us on our journey!

À bientôt et merci, Caro

Acknowledgements

Writing a memoir is a wonderful journey, a way to relive the original voyage. I am deeply grateful to clients, friends and supporters that have been part of our vineyard adventure, both on these pages and beyond. Thank you also to the readers of *Grape Expectations*, especially those who took the time to write to me and to put reviews on their favourite book website. Their compliments offered enormous motivation to write the sequel.

Thanks to inspirational winegrower friends like Clément and Francine Klur and Thierry and Isabelle Daulhiac, and to the winegrowers we visited in France and internationally, for sharing their wisdom so freely.

Special thanks to our wonderful friends Ad and Lijda van Sorgen, Pierre and Laurence de St Viance, Ian and Brigit Wilson, Dave and Amanda Moore, aka Mr Greedy and Mrs Picky, the Naked Vignerons, all of whom were part of the adventure and have encouraged and helped us so much along the way.

Thank you to helping hands and lucky breaks offered by Helen and Derek Melser, Spring Webb, Simon Golding, Chandra Clarke, Jordan Forsyth, Luke Moyer, Ulrika, Laura Bolt and Niall Martin.

To Thomas de Conti and Sébastian Bouché for their beautiful buildings and contribution to this book, *merci!* My deep gratitude also goes to Naomi Whittel for her part in the story and in our adventure.

A big thank you to the team at Summersdale and especially to Jen Barclay; those pressured last-minute suggestions by a skilled editor make all the difference. Thank you to Ray Hamilton for the thorough final edit with a few good laughs included. Thanks to Anna Martin, my in-house Summersdale editor, and to Lucy Davey for the beautiful cover design. Thanks to Nicky Douglas and Dean Chant for their marketing work.

Thanks to Greg Joly, chairman of the Goodlife Center Publishing Committee and chairman of the board of the Goodlife Center, to Warren and the Goodlife Center for the use of the Nearings' quote. The Nearings' books provided great inspiration to us when we first thought of leaving the city to create a more self-sufficient life.

Thanks to Counterpoint and Wendell Berry, a favourite poet and wise commentator on agriculture, for the use of the Wendell Berry quotes.

A special thanks to Guy Bass, celebrated children's author, for his suggestion of the title of this book, so aptly made after hearing about our adventure with Naomi on a visit to our wine school.

Thank you to my parents Lyn and Cliff Wardle and Seán's parents John and Peta-Lynne Feely for their support both here and from afar. Thank you to Seán's sister Glynis Bristow for having those Summersdale books on her shelf and to my sister Jacquie Somerville for her great motivational emails (www. jacquiesomerville.com). Thank you to my brother Garth Wardle for his prayers and his comment on reading *Grape Expectations* 'I finished it the day I got it – it made me laugh and cry and inspired me to follow dreams.' I dream of welcoming him and his family to see the farm first-hand. We miss our far-flung family.

But, most of all, thank you to Seán, the love of my life, for his support, and to Sophia and Ellie for their wisecracks and input.

GRAPE EXPECTATIONS

A Family's Vineyard Adventure in France

Caro Feely

£8.99
Paperback
ISBN: 978-1-84953-257-0

I took a deep draught and swirled it around feeling the warming sensation of alcohol on the back of my throat. The wine filled my mouth with plum and blackberry. The finish had a hint of spice and an attractive saline minerality.

'Delicious.' I licked my lips. The wine filled me with joy. A picture of a vineyard drenched in sunlight formed in my mind. Sean drew me rudely back to the lounge of our semi-d.

'How can they be in liquidation if they make wine this good?'

When Caro and Sean find the perfect ten-hectare vineyard in Saussignac, it seems their dreams of becoming winemakers in the south of France are about to come true. But, rather than making a smooth transition from city slickers to *connaisseurs du vin*, they arrive in France with their young family (a toddler and a newborn) to be faced with a dilapidated eighteenth-century farmhouse and 'beyond eccentric' winery. Undeterred by a series of setbacks, including mouse infestations and a nasty accident with an agricultural trimmer, they embark on the biggest adventure of their lives – learning to make wine from the roots up.

Have you enjoyed this book?

If so, why not write a review on your favourite website?
If you're interested in finding out more about our books,
find us on Facebook at **Summersdale Publishers** and
follow us on Twitter at **@Summersdale**.

Thanks very much for buying this Summersdale book.

www.summersdale.com